OTHER VOICES IN
OLD TESTAMENT INTERPRETATION

Other Voices in Old Testament Interpretation

Untraditional Explanations of Selected Popular Old Testament Texts and Topics

W. Creighton Marlowe

foreword by Edward M. Curtis

WIPF & STOCK · Eugene, Oregon

OTHER VOICES IN OLD TESTAMENT INTERPRETATION
Untraditional Explanations of Selected Popular Old Testament Texts and Topics

Copyright © 2019 W. Creighton Marlowe. All rights reserved. Except for brief quotations in critical publications or reviews, no part of this book may be reproduced in any manner without prior written permission from the publisher. Write: Permissions, Wipf and Stock Publishers, 199 W. 8th Ave., Suite 3, Eugene, OR 97401.

Wipf & Stock
An Imprint of Wipf and Stock Publishers
199 W. 8th Ave., Suite 3
Eugene, OR 97401

www.wipfandstock.com

PAPERBACK ISBN: 978-1-5326-6860-9
HARDCOVER ISBN: 978-1-5326-6861-6
EBOOK ISBN: 978-1-5326-6862-3

Manufactured in the U.S.A.   SEPTEMBER 9, 2019

This book is dedicated to:

*First, my devoted wife Sherry without whose support, encouragement, and time allowance this project would not have come to fruition so quickly;

*Second, my doctoral and Semitic language mentor, Larry L. Walker, who exhorted his students as well as exemplified the challenge of translating and interpreting the OT in its historical and literary contexts;

*Last but not least, my first Hebrew and Akkadian teacher, Jack M. Sasson, who ignited my interest in Classical Hebrew and the importance of ANE texts and traditions for OT understanding, and in whose class I was affectionately known as Nimrod (the only name by which, I think, he remembers me).

Contents

Permissions / ix
Foreword by Edward M. Curtis / xv
Acknowledgements / xix
Abbreviations / xxi
Introduction / xxv

Part I—Exegetical and Contextual Insights in Genesis / 1
    1   The Poetics of Genesis 1:1—2:4 / 3
    2   The Form and Function of Genesis 6:1–4 / 23
    3   The Sin of Shinar in Genesis 11:4 / 41

Part II—Exegetical and Contextual Insights in Psalms / 59
    4   The Form of Psalm 23 / 61
    5   The Function of Psalm 23 / 80
    6   The Spirit in Psalm 51:10–12 / 95

Part III—Exegetical & Contextual Insights in Isaiah / 117
    7   The Spirit in Isaiah 11:1–3 / 119
    8   The "Messianic" Prophecy of Isaiah 53:9 / 134

Part IV—Lexical and Contextual Insights in the Old Testament about *Sheol* and Hell / 149
    9   "Hell" as a Translation of *Sheol* / 151
    10 "Hell" in English Bible Versions Since the 1611 KJB / 175

Bibliography / 195
Subject Index / 207
Selected Author Index / 211
Scripture Index / 213

Permissions

Previously Published Articles

"Patterns, Parallels, and Poetics in Genesis 1." *The Journal of Inductive Biblical Studies* 3:1 (2016) 6–27. https://place.asburyseminary.edu/jibs/; https://www.bepress.com/copyright/. © January 2016. Used by permission.

"Gen 6:1-4 as a Chiasm." *Scandinavian Journal of the Old Testament* 30:1 (2016) 129–44. © 2016. Used by permission.

"The Sin of Shinar *(Gen 11:4)*." *The European Journal of Theology XX:1* (2011) 29–39. © retained by the author. Used by permission.

"No Fear! Psalm 23 as a Careful, Conceptual Chiasm." *Asbury Theological Journal* 58:1 (Spring 2003) 65–80. https://books.google.nl/books?id=fy8hAQAAIAAJ&pg= PA37 4&lpg=PA374&dq=asbury+theological+journal+copyright&source=bl&ots=jsLkPpJ CbB&sig=ACfU3U0UAB5CT4I-yF3t_-3dXNzgLxQxpg&hl=en&sa=X&ved=2ahUK EwiBk6 WH05LgAhULZlAKHcxKDqUQ6AEwBnoECAIQAQ#v=onepage&q=asbu ry%20theological%20journal%20copyright&f=false. No copyright statement in the journal. Used by permission.

"David's I-Thou Discourse: Verbal Chiastic Patterns in Psalm 23." *Scandinavian Journal of the Old Testament* 25:1 (2011) 105–15. © 2011. Used by permission.

"The Wicked Wealthy in Isa 53:9." *The Asbury Journal* 64:2 (Fall 2009) 68–81. https://www. bepress.com/copyright/. Used by permission.

"'Spirit of Your Holiness' in Psalm 51:13." *Trinity Journal* 19:1 (Spring 1998) 29–49. © 1998.

"A Spirit Chiasm in Isa 11:2–3a." *Scandinavian Journal of the Old Testament* 28:1 (2014) 44–57. © 2014. Used by permission.

PERMISSIONS

"'Hell' as a Translation of שאול in the Hebrew Bible: Dehellenizing the KJV and NKJV." *Asbury Theological Journal* 57 (Fall 2002) 5–24. https://books.google.nl/books?id=fy8hAQAAIAAJ&pg=PA374&lpg=PA374&dq=asbury+theological+journal+copyright&source=bl&ots=jsLkPpJCbB&sig=ACfU3UoUAB5CT4I-yF3t_3dXNzgLxQxpg&hl=en&sa=X&ved=2ahUKEwiBk6WHo5LgAhULZlAKHcxKDqUQ6AEwBnoECAIQAQ#v=onepage&q=asbury%20theological%20journal%20copyright&f=false. No copyright statement in the journal. Used by permission.

"Hell in English Bible Translations since the 1611 King James Bible." In *The King James Bible (1611–2011) Prehistory and Afterlife,* edited by Tibor Fabiny and Sara Toth, 171–92. Karoli Gaspar Reformatus Egyetem. Budapest: L'Harmattan Kiado, 2016. © Editions l'Harmattan, 2016. Used by permission.

Bible Versions/Translations

American Standard Version

Scripture quotations marked (ASV) are taken from *The Holy Bible, American Standard Version*®. Electronic Edition STEP Files Copyright © 2005, QuickVerse. Use in this book is in accordance with public domain.

Authorized Version (= KJV[S])

Scripture quotations marked (AV) are taken from *King James Version with Strong's Numbers*® (KJVS). Formatted and corrected by OakTree Software, Inc. Version 3.5. Scripture quotations from The Authorized (King James) Version. Rights in the Authorized Version in the United Kingdom are vested in the Crown. Reproduced by permission of the Crown's patentee, Cambridge University Press. Total use or words or verses in this commentary does not exceed the limit requiring permission.

Contemporary English Version

Scripture quotations marked (CEV) are taken from the *Holy Bible, Contemporary English Version*®. Electronic Edition STEP Files Copyright © 2005, QuickVerse. Copyright © 1991, 1992, 1995 by American Bible Society. All rights reserved. Total use or words or verses in this commentary does not exceed the limit requiring permission.

Douay-Rheims Bible (Vulgate translation 1844)

Scripture quotations marked (DR or Douay) are taken from the *Douay-Rheims Bible*®. Copyright © 2003 OakTree Software, Inc. Version 1.7. All rights reserved. Total use or words or verses in this commentary does not exceed the limit requiring permission.

English Standard Version

Scripture quotations marked (ESV) are taken from *The Holy Bible, English Standard Version*®. Copyright© 2001 by Crossway Bibles, a division of Good News Publishers. All rights reserved. Total use or words or verses in this commentary does not exceed the limit requiring permission.

Good News Translation/Bible

Scripture quotations marked (GNT) are taken from the *Good News Translation*® (2nd ed.). Electronic Edition STEP Files, Copyright © 2005, QuickVerse; Old Testament: © 1976, 1992, American Bible Society; New Testament: © 1966, 1971, 1976, 1992, American Bible Society. All rights reserved. Total use or words or verses in this commentary does not exceed the limit requiring permission.

Holy Bible: from the Ancient Eastern Text, The (Peshitta)

Scripture quotations marked (Lamsa) are taken from the *Holy Bible: from the Ancient Eastern Text*®. Copyright © 1940 by A. J. Holman, Co., renewed 1968. Out of print. Total use is three words; Holman/Lifeway has no statement on permitted words or verses, other than fair use, which is not violated by the aforementioned usage.

Holy Bible, New King James Version, The

Scripture quotations marked (NKJB or NKJV) are taken from the *Holy Bible, New King James Version*®. Copyright © 1979, 1980, 1982 by Thomas Nelson, Inc. Electronic Edition STEP Files. Copyright © 2005, QuickVerse, Inc., all rights reserved. Total use or words or verses in this commentary does not exceed the limit requiring permission.

Jerusalem Bible, The

Scripture quotations marked (JB) are taken from *the Jerusalem Bible*®. Copyright © 1966 by Darton Longman & Todd Ltd and Doubleday and Company Ltd. All rights reserved. Total use or words or verses in this commentary does not exceed the limit requiring permission.

PERMISSIONS

King James Version Apocrypha

Scripture quotations marked (KJVA) are taken from the *KJV Apocrypha* or *King James Version Apocrypha*®. Formatted and corrected by OakTree Software, Inc. Version 1.4. Scripture quotations from The Authorized (King James) Version. Rights in the Authorized Version in the United Kingdom are vested in the Crown. Reproduced by permission of the Crown's patentee, Cambridge University Press. Total use or words or verses in this commentary does not exceed the limit requiring permission.

King James Version/Bible

Scripture quotations marked (KJV or KJB or KJVS) are taken from the *King James Version with Strong's Numbers*® (KJVS). Formatted and corrected by OakTree Software, Inc. Version 3.5. All rights reserved. Scripture quotations from The Authorized (King James) Version. Rights in the Authorized Version in the United Kingdom are vested in the Crown. Reproduced by permission of the Crown's patentee, Cambridge University Press. Total use or words or verses in this commentary does not exceed the limit requiring permission.

Living Bible, The

Scripture quotations marked (LB) are taken from *The Living Bible* Paraphrased®. Copyright © 1971 by Tyndale House Foundation. All rights reserved. Total use or words or verses in this commentary does not exceed the limit requiring permission.

Message, The (the Bible in Contemporary Language)

Scripture quotations marked (TM or *The Message* or Peterson) are taken from *The Message: the Bible in Contemporary Language*® by Eugene H. Peterson. Copyright © 2002 by Eugene H. Peterson. Copyright ©1993, 1994, 1995, 1996, 2000, 2001, 2002 by NavPress Publishing Group. All rights reserved. Or Electronic Edition STEP Files. Copyright © 2005. QuickVerse. All rights reserved. Total use or words or verses in this commentary does not exceed the limit requiring permission.

New American Bible

Scripture quotations marked (NAB) are taken from the *New American Bible*®. Copyright © 2010, 1991, 1986, 1970 Confraternity of Christian Doctrine, Washington, D.C. All rights reserved. Total use or words or verses in this commentary does not exceed the limit requiring permission.

New American Standard Bible

Scripture quotations marked (NASB or NAS) are taken from the *New American Standard Bible*® (1977). Copyright © 1960, 1962, 1963, 1968, 1971, 1972, 1973, 1975, 1977, 1988 by The Lockman Foundation. www.Lockman.org. All rights reserved. OakTree Version 2.4. Total use or words or verses in this commentary does not exceed the limit requiring permission.

New English Bible

Scripture quotations marked (NEB) are taken from the *New English Bible*®, copyright © Cambridge University Press and Oxford University Press 1961, 1970. All rights reserved. Total use or words or verses in this commentary does not exceed the limit requiring permission.

New English Translation of the Septuagint

Scripture quotations marked (NETS) are taken from the *New English Translation of the Septuagint*®, Albert Pietersma and Benjamin G. Wright, Editors. NETS Text Edition: 2014.

Copyright ©2007 by the International Organization for Septuagint and Cognate Studies, Inc. All rights reserved. Used by permission of Oxford University Press. OakTree Version 3.7. Total use or words or verses in this commentary does not exceed the limit requiring permission.

New International Version

Quotations designated (NIV) are taken from the *Holy Bible: New International Version*®. Copyright © 1973, 1978, 1984 by International Bible Society. NIV (1984) with Goodrick/Kohlenberger numbers (NIV-G/K). Scripture quoted by permission. OakTree Version 1.1. Used by permission of Zondervan Publishing House. All rights reserved. Total use or words or verses in this commentary does not exceed the limit requiring permission.

New Living Translation

Scripture quotations marked (NLT) are taken from the *Holy Bible, New Living Translation*®. Copyright ©1996, 2004, 2007, 2015 by Tyndale House Foundation. All rights reserved. Total use or words or verses in this commentary does not exceed the limit requiring permission.

PERMISSIONS

New Revised Standard Version, The

Scripture quotations marked (NRSV) are taken from the *New Revised Standard Version*®. New Revised Standard Version of the Bible. The Scripture quotations contained herein (Accordance module) are from the *New Revised Standard Version of the Bible*. Copyrighted, 1989 by the Division of Christian Education of the National Council of the Churches of Christ in the United States of America, and are used by permission. All rights reserved. OakTree Version 4.0. Total use or words or verses in this commentary does not exceed the limit requiring permission.

New Revised Standard Version Apocrypha, The

Scripture quotations marked (NRSVA or NRSV-A) are taken from the *New Revised Standard Version*®. The Scripture quotations contained herein (Accordance module) are from the *New Revised Standard Version of the Bible*. Copyrighted, 1989 by the Division of Christian Education of the National Council of the Churches of Christ in the United States of America, and are used by permission. All rights reserved. OakTree Version 4.0. Total use or words or verses in this commentary does not exceed the limit requiring permission.

Revised Standard Version

Scripture quotations marked (RSV) are taken from rom the *Revised Standard Version of the Bible*®. Copyright © 1946, 1952, and 1971 the Division of Christian Education of the National Council of the Churches of Christ in the United States of America. All rights reserved. Total use or words or verses in this commentary does not exceed the limit requiring permission.

William Tyndale's Translation (1525)

Scripture quotations marked (TNT or Tyndale) are taken from *William Tyndale's Translation*. OakTree Software with permission of the Wesley Center Online. Source document located at https://www.biblestudytools.com/tyn/ and https://wiki.logos.com/Tyndale_Bible. Use in this book is in accordance with public domain.

Wycliffe Bible (1384)

Scripture quotations marked (WB or Wycliffe) are taken from the electronic version, analyzed and corrected by OakTree Software. Accordance version 9.2. Also http://wesley.nnu.edu/biblical_studies/tyndale/index.htm. Use in this book is in accordance with public domain.

Foreword

I FIRST met Dr. Creig Marlowe some twenty-five years ago while teaching in Europe during a sabbatical from Biola University and Talbot School of Theology where I taught Hebrew and Old Testament for 40 years. Our relationship continued to develop as I regularly taught modular and full semester classes in Europe whenever the opportunity presented itself. I also saw Dr. Marlowe at professional meetings and heard him present papers at many of these conferences. I was always amazed by his ability to do excellent research in a context where resources were limited and where his time was spread among teaching and administrative duties as well as the various tasks that are part of being a career missionary. Beyond that he was a husband and father and still managed to pursue his musical interests.

The essays in this volume are academic papers prepared primarily for a scholarly audience. They reflect the research and careful thinking that characterize Creig's work. He writes with a broad awareness of the opinions of scholars who have preceded him and seeks to advance our understanding of the texts he addresses. His exegesis is thorough and he carefully analyzes each passage in the light of Hebrew grammar and relevant linguistic material, literary structure, metrical considerations, masoretic accents, and the like. He is attentive to the context, both literary and social, and he is aware of the development of ideas in Israel and considers relevant material from the ancient Near East where that is relevant. Dr. Marlowe is a capable exegete and is dedicated to careful exegesis. Those qualities are evident in these examples of his work.

The ten essays included in this volume address difficult texts from the Hebrew Bible that have been long debated. While significant theological structures should never be built on the foundation of passages of uncertain interpretation, such things have occurred in the long history of doctrine and theology. In some instances the ambiguity of the text has given rise to ideas that have become so solidly set into the tradition that they are promoted rather dogmatically by some. It is sometimes the case that uncertain conclusions based on traditional understandings of the text become marks of fellowship and orthodoxy, and that is never healthy for the believing community. Good exegesis helps us differentiate between those interpretive conclusions that constitute the central teaching of the text and those that do not.

In addition, proper exegesis helps us recognize which questions are answered by the text (for our edification) and which questions are either not answered or are entirely tangential to the teaching of the text. Professor Marlowe's exegesis helps us identify with greater clarity the central teaching of each passage and also highlights issues that still remain uncertain and unclear. Careful exegesis is a great benefit even when it reduces the certainty with which we hold certain long-held interpretive points. The goal is to listen to the sacred text and stand under its authority. Faithful teaching of the text should always differentiate between those conclusions about which we can be highly confident and those we should hold more loosely.

In these very difficult Old Testament texts that Dr. Marlowe has chosen to discuss, there are many issues that cannot be resolved on the basis of exegesis, and any answers must be tentative and speculative. Creig does sometimes address questions where conclusions must rest more on speculation and conjecture than on objective exegesis. This comes with the territory when dealing with problematic texts such as Genesis 6 and Genesis 11. Consequently, there are often points (usually, though, peripheral to the major thrust of the paper) about which people can and will disagree.

I do not agree with every proposal that Dr. Marlowe makes in these papers, but I commend him for his careful exegetical work. I found the papers enjoyable, stimulating, and beneficial. I am deeply committed to careful exegesis, but I often read the biblical psalms in ways that are more devotional than analytical. The two papers on Psalm 23 provided insight about structure and patterns in verb use that set my observations about the teaching of the psalm on a more solid exegetical base. I resonate with his words, "The emphasis is on YHWH's current and continuing provision and protection based on past experience. The future is in view, mainly in the second section, indicating what the psalmist believes he can expect YHWH to do in terms of protection and provision based on his present realities." Seeing the psalm in this way connects it thematically with Salvation History psalms 105, 106, 107 and similar psalms.

Marlowe's discussion of the tower of Babel passage stimulated my thinking in different ways. First of all, he presents the issues raised by the passage (confusion of languages, a historical context, chronology, etc.) in a way that came across more powerfully than has previously been the case as I have considered these matters individually. It has not really changed my mind about the passage, but thinking about the alternatives that Dr. Marlowe has proposed has stimulated my thinking in ways that may over time modify my thinking about certain details of this text.

Every Old Testament scholar that I know will welcome the warnings about assuming a fully developed Trinitarian theology in the Old Testament or supposing that the Old Testament understanding of Sheol reflects a post Intertestamental view of the afterlife and final judgment. At the same time, many of my seminary students and undergrads came into my classes unclear on those points, and they will be the pastors and teachers of the next generations. There are many other things in these articles that I found refreshing such as footnotes 6 and 7 in the article on the function of Psalm 23 regarding the meaning of "righteous" and "evil." I cannot imagine how many times I went over that same information with students over my teaching career. I can only hope and pray that this will be a bit more widely disseminated as a result of the publication of this volume.

Several of these professional papers were published in somewhat obscure journals, and Dr. Marlowe has done the academic community a service by making them available in a convenient volume. Read these essays carefully and critically, but also with an open mind. Remember, this is God's Word and it is imperative that we hear the message that he has revealed to his people. Casual reading and devotional reading, while critical for growth toward maturity in Christ, cannot take the place of careful exegesis in opening up God's truth to the people of God today. Read these essays with the attitude of the disciples from Berea who "received the word with all eagerness, examining the Scriptures daily to see if these things were so" (Acts 17:11).

DR. EDWARD M. CURTIS
Professor Emeritus of Old Testament and Hebrew
Biola University and Talbot School of Theology

Acknowledgements

Special thanks go to the editorial boards and/or editors of the journals/books named above who first, published, and second, allowed me permission to reprint these previously published articles for the purposes of this book as a compendium of some of my past and most provocative exegetical research. Thanks also to Wipf & Stock for believing my articles deserve to see the light of publication at this level. I also should thank my Dean, Prof. Dr. Andreas Beck, of the Evangelische Theologische Faculteit, Leuven, for his repeated urging that I undertake this effort. Finally, I express my gratitude for those who have agreed to participate in this publication via contributions to preliminary and introductory matters above.

Abbreviations

AD	Anno Domini (in the year of our Lord; = CE Common Era)
BC	Before Christ (= BCE Before the Common Era)
ca.	approximately
C./c.f.	compare (not "see")
chap.	chapter
E/ed.	edition or edited by
E./e.g.	for example
EB/EBs	English Bible/s
esp.	especially
et al.	and others
etc.	and so forth
ff.	following page/pages (only used within a direct quote)
gen.	general
HB	Hebrew Bible
Heb.	Hebrew
i.e.	that is
loc.	location number
masc.	masculine
NB	*note bene* (note well)

ABBREVIATIONS

n./nn.	[foot]note number/numbers
n.d.	no date
n.p.	no page number
p./pp.	page/pages
pl.	plural
R/rpt.	R/reprint
sing.	singular
S/supp.	S/supplement
s.v.	*sub verbo* "under the word"
T/trans.	T/translator; translated by
UK	United Kingdom
USA	United States of America
v./vv.	verse/verses
V/vol./s.	V/volume/s
vs.	versus; opposed to
X C/	chiasm; chiastic

Sources

ANE	Ancient Near East[ern]
ANET	*Ancient Near Eastern Texts* (Pritchard)
BDB	Brown-Driver-Briggs, *Hebrew Lexicon*
BHS	*Biblia Hebraica Stuttgartensia*
BHS-T	*Biblia Hebraica Stuttgartensia* Tagged
BKAT	*Biblischer Kommentar: Altes Testament*
CAD	*Chicago Assyrian Dictionary*
DCH	*Dictionary of Classical Hebrew*
FOTL	Forms of Old Testament Literature (series)
HALOT	*Hebrew and Aramaic Lexicon on the Old Testament*

LXX	The Septuagint (Greek Old Testament)
MT	Masoretic Text
NICOT	New International Commentary on the Old Testament (series)
NIDOTTE	*New International Dictionary of Old Testament Theology and Exegesis*
NT	New Testament
OED	*Oxford English Dictionary*
OT	Old Testament
OTA	*Old Testament Abstracts*
P&R	Presbyterian and Reformed Publisher
SBL	The Society of Biblical Literature
SCM	Student Christian Movement Publisher
Soncino	*Soncino Books of the Bible*
SPCK/S.P.C.K.	Society for the Propagation of Christian Knowledge
TDOT	*Theological Dictionary of the Old Testament*
TWOT	*Theological Wordbook of the Old testament*

Bible Versions (cited or quoted)

ASV	*American Standard Version*
AV	*Authorized Version (= KJV[S])*
CEV	*Contemporary English Version*
DR or Douay	*Douay-Rheims Bible* (Vulgate translation 1844)
ESV	*English Standard Version*
ETNT	*Eight Translation New Testament*
GNT	*Good News Translation/Bible*
JB	*Jerusalem Bible, The*
KJVA	*King James Version Apocrypha*

ABBREVIATIONS

KJV/B/S	*King James Version/Bible*
Lamsa	*Holy Bible: from the Ancient Eastern Text, The* (Peshitta)
LB (Taylor)	*Living Bible, The*
NAB	*New American Bible*
NASB	*New American Standard Bible*
NEB	*New English Bible.*
NETS	*New English Translation of the Septuagint*
NIV	*New International Version*
NKJV/NKJB	*New King James Version/Bible*
NLT	*New Living Translation*
NRSV	*New Revised Standard Version, The*
NRSVA/-	A *New Revised Standard Version Apocrypha, The*
Peterson (TM)	*Message, The (the Bible in Contemporary English)*
RSV	*Revised Standard Version*
Tyndale (TNT)	*William Tyndale's Translation* (1525)
Vaughan,	*New Testament from 26 Translations, The*
Wycliffe (WB)	*Wycliffe Bible* (1384)

Introduction

EXEGESIS, or biblical interpretation based on the original languages, in context, is an art and a science. It is also often an act of courage. The exegete, if true to the historical, cultural, and literary contexts of a passage, will—especially if working within a conservative or traditional environment—encounter push back when one reading his or her commentary senses that the observations or conclusions challenge a long-held or cherished view, thought to have been solved or upon which other perceptions or practices have been based. Agreement with the new view means change, but worse, means admission of past error. This is hard for a conservative because conservation is at the heart of being conservative. All change is to some degree liberalization, although much about traditional interpretation of the OT can be challenged exegetically, without necessarily leading to liberalization (theologically). But too many steps in an opposite direction can lead to sleeping with the enemy. I speak as one within the evangelical world as broadly as that title and term can be extended exegetically and theologically. Where the line is that separates conservative from progressive to liberal is not known exactly. Different people will find it in different locations along the continuum. I have experienced not just being called (to my face) a "liberal" or "too progressive," at times, by some of my evangelical "buddies," but accused of not being a real believer or Christian, based not on alignment with one of the classical and contra-fundamental positions of liberal theology, but based on approval of a historical-cultural contextual explanation of a biblical phenomenon held by others (although not the majority) within the evangelical camp. Understandably, fundamentalists or conservatives are afraid of too much change (since at some point one is no longer conserving or fundamental enough), but this mentality can become counter-productive for necessary exegetical, translational, interpretive, and theological growth. Gratuitous developments are not the goal, but the best possible understanding of what OT texts are communicating to their audiences is. Improvement and correction in this realm ought to be welcomed with open arms by every user of the Bible. I hasten to add this comment is not a suggestion that I think my own exegesis has fully answered all questions or is even clearly a corrective at every turn, but it contributes an honest and open-minded attempt to move in a direction away from what may be explanations that are more colored by tradition, convention, assumptions, and dated data than by a less presuppositional and theological or even ecclesiastical-political agenda. Our esteemed theological predecessors like Luther, Calvin, and Wesley, may be giants with whom we should walk interpretively, but not apart from critical (and if needed, corrective) conversation. They, as all biblical commentators and translators, operated within a certain time period, limited by what was known scientifically, exegetically, and archaeologically. What we think we know for sure today may (and probably will if history is a guide) become less certain in the future, as new information emerges. We only can say today what is discernable about a biblical text in light of all pertinent data we know based on current tools and assumed truths, and we, like those before us, do this within a community that may demand certain lines not be crossed. Scholars are also servants.[1] An irony of the local church versus academy (pastoral versus professorial) tension we have today (or always have had) is that what many think of as a negative activity of critical, academic reading of biblical passages (supposedly independent of the Spirit's touch) results in new (not necessarily more accurate) ideas because, in fact, it is usually more (not less) *submissive* to the biblical texts as revealed in their God-ordained literary, linguistic, and life settings. As a young theological student, I was often reminded that to be a good preacher and teacher of the Scripture I needed to exegete, I needed to "let the text speak" and not be an eisegete by speaking for the text, by putting ideas in the text not there to begin with. The study of the original languages of the Bible was justified on the basis that the text meant what it said in relation to its contextual linguistic and literary realities per the author's communication as guided by God to an ancient audience within a historical/cultural setting. A text without a context is a pretext. Words do not have meanings, meanings have words. This approach should lead to

---

1. Many are not aware that the hood that is placed on someone just after successfully defending a PhD dissertation is linked to monastic clothing symbolizing humility. Its purpose is to remind its wearer that his or her duty is service to the church. Advanced learning is not for a prideful position but hard academic work of submission to the divinely revealed text in order to help others better understand God's will.

an objective-as-possible understanding of "what a writer meant by what he said" (which of course is what God is saying through him verbally in a chosen language operating by its then current rules). Of course, the process of interpretation of such texts is human, so complete accuracy is not a guaranteed result. I found, however, after I took this to heart and tried to implement it as correctly and consistently as possible, that when my results challenged cherished conclusions (which I announced seemed to be at odds with "what the text actually says"), I was told at times (and my proposal was not a challenge to a historic doctrine, rather how some words might be better translated), not how my exegesis was faulty but that great minds had already spoken. I certainly cannot claim a great mind, but I am committed to deriving theological and biblical propositions and praxis from exegesis. Before beliefs are derived, systemized, and applied, the biblical texts have to be analyzed in the original languages and in their historical-cultural contexts. Words have no meaning until so contextualized. Verses do not stand alone but as part of larger communicative sections. I recently was lecturing in a school in Eastern Europe, and when I explained how a certain OT text actually said something different than it seemed to say in some translations, one student replied, "I would rather just believe the Bible." So would I. That is why I go to the trouble of reading it in line with the objective realities of its languages and literature in context. It fascinates (actually frustrates) me that sometimes I get less push back on stressing contextual meaning from laypersons than from university students. All this is to explain why I have spent a career focused on trying to derive the best possible readings of OT passages based on the biblical communicative context and ANE/OT culture. What follows are some selected essays that reflect this hobby and habit I have tried to improve over the years. Whether or not these findings are an improvement is still open to discussion and debate, but I've enjoyed the ride. I now invite you to think along with me. Some will agree and some will not; no one will likely agree with every idea. Regardless, these ten chapters provide an example of what it means to apply contextual exegesis to OT texts and topics that (seemingly to many) have already been solved. Maybe not. You be the judge. But above all, be an exegete and let the text speak!

CREIGHTON (CREIG) MARLOWE
04 February 2019

PART I

Exegetical and Contextual Insights in Genesis

1

The Poetics of Genesis 1:1—2:4[1]

Introduction

DEBATES over the purpose and propositions of Genesis 1 continue to be concerned with its poetic nature.[2] Some evangelicals squirm when a poetic profile for this chapter is proposed because they fear this might undermine its historicity.[3] John Walton observed that some have taken a poetic interpretive and literary approach that means this creation document "should not be taken as any sort of scientific record."[4] That this text is not poetry per se but elevated narrative has been the scholarly consensus for some time. Von Rad concluded, "There is no trace of the hymnic element in the language."[5] Yet Wenham called it a hymn—not pure poetry but rather elevated prose.[6] More recently, however, attempts have been made to characterize Genesis 1 in terms closer to pure poetry. At the SBL Annual Meeting in Boston in 2008, Robert Robinson presented a paper on "The Poetry of Creation" wherein he proposed a poetic character for Genesis 1:1–3. This, however, was not based on parallelism (the typical quintessential feature of Hebrew poetry), but on the presence of stylistic features such

1. Originally published as Marlowe, "Patterns, Parallels, and Poetics in Genesis 1," 6–27. Stylistic and corrective (but no substantive) changes have been made.
2. Willems, "Evolving Evangelicalism," n.p.
3. Johnson, "Genesis Is History," 8–9.
4. Walton, *Lost World of Genesis*, loc. 974.
5. Rad, *Genesis*, 47.
6. Wenham, *Genesis 1–15*, 10.

as assonance and word-play.⁷ Such distinctions depend on how poetry is defined, strictly in formal terms such a Hebrew *parallelismus membrorum*, or more generally in functional terms, as just cited, wherein poetry is the presence of poetics of powerful words that move the audience to deep feelings. For the purposes of this paper, Old Testament poetry is understood as the use of parallel lines.⁸ These demonstrably exist in places in Genesis but have not been shown to dominate the entire creation week so as to make it a Hebrew poem. Even if it reflects a later adaptation of an original poem that, in itself, would not necessarily imply anything about an intent to inform the audience about the actual time used to form the material universe.⁹ Authors choose particular literary genres for their medium of communication that best fit their purposes and audience. The concern with Genesis 1 in the present paper is its structural patterns and the degree to which they may add poetic/structural color to the text, which may be considered elevated prose. But how elevated? A close look at the patterns that emerge reveals ignored parallels and poetic flourishes.¹⁰ Neither a complete hymn,

---

7. Robinson, "Poetry of Creation." Robinson cited Culler, *Structuralist Poetics*, 161. Features like assonance may often be found in narrative or prose. Some kind of parallelism must be present to establish formal Hebrew poetry. Otherwise one is only talking about poetics, which can characterize much of the OT, and on that basis would make a distinction between prose and poetry impossible or vague. But if such poetic features are present *en masse* then a text might be classified as poetic, which could also distinguish a text like Genesis 1 from Genesis 12, even apart from parallelism. If parallelism is present, then the case for Genesis 1 as poetry is all the more assured.

8. However parallelism is explained, it remains the most objective means of identifying the presence of poetry in Classical Hebrew. This pervasive structural feature is a, or the, major distinction between books like Proverbs/Psalms and pentateuchal/historical ones, chapters like Jonah 2, and 1, 3, 4, and prose and verse portions of the Prophets. Per n. 7 above, poetry today can be viewed as a passionate, as opposed to factual, presentation of information, yet if applied too generally and subjectively to the OT then all becomes poetic making nothing poetic.

9. See Walton and Sandy, *The Lost World of Scripture*, in toto. Here, the authors demonstrate that biblical communication was originally and principally oral in nature. The need to maintain Scripture mentally rather than in written form indicates why texts with poetic or musical memory "hooks" were the concerns of ancient communicators. The question of the text's purpose to present a six-day creation literally is not answered by appeals to poetry or prose or the meaning of יוֹם, but more likely by culturally contextualized readings as investigated by Walton in *The Lost World of Genesis* (see n. 4), or Walton, *Genesis 1*, 2011. In these books Walton argues for a functional rather than material cognitive context of the OT author in line with his ancient Near Eastern setting.

10. "Poetics" refers to the various kinds of word-plays or rhetorical devices (phonetic, morphological, or structural, e.g., chiasmus) which are applied to any text of the Hebrew Bible. Lowth notwithstanding (the father of the renewal of modern parallelism study for

poem, nor historical narrative emerges. What is suggested is a text with repetitions reminiscent of a song with stanzas.

The Creation Week, 1:1–31

The creation week narrative per se will be viewed as Gen 1:1-31. Technically, the end of the entire creation narrative (including the final day of rest from creation) is debated as either 2:3, 2:4, or 2:4a.[11] Genesis 1:1-2 is proposed as part of the first day because the beginning of 1:3 ("then/so he said/commanded") makes little sense apart from its direct connection to what is described in v. 2 (the state of disorder and darkness). The statement in 2:4a provides an inclusio with 1:1 (making of "heavens and earth"—perhaps better understood as "sky and land"—started [1:1] and ended [2:4a], leaving 1:2-5 for the first day; see Table A below[12]). These opening verses deal with the initial state of creation.[13] Whether one says "When God began

---

Christians; Bishop Robert Lowth [*De sacra poesi Hebraeorum*, 1753], in which he postulated three major categories: symmetric, antithetic, and synthetic); O'Connor observed the absence of specificity in defining OT parallelism based on the absence of a single identifying feature (O'Connor, *Hebrew Verse Structure*, 89). His title seems to exhibit how some restrict "poetry" to verse only (rather than prose) if it merits enough literary beauty and power. Caution received, still his attempt to base parallelism on syntax has not become consensus, so I will approach parallelism as multidimensional (contra Kugel's assertion against Lowth's three, of only one type, A then B). I applaud Clines' criticism of this as too limiting for the possible diversity between lines A and B (see Kugel, *Idea of Biblical Poetry*, in toto, and Clines, "Parallelism of Greater Precision," 95). A clear difference in style exists between a text like Genesis 1 and a historical narrative like Genesis 12 (see Zogbo and Wendland, *Hebrew Poetry*, 11-60, for a detailed discussion of the various features of Hebrew poetry).

11. The 1:1—2:4a section is supported by Soggin, *Das Buch* Genesis, 15, and Westermann, *Genesis I*, 16, 21-28. Cf. also Pirson, *Belichting het Bijbelboek Genesis*, 28. Genesis 2:4 is separated from 2:3 in NIV, NRSV, and NASB. In KJV (as Latin Vulgate) 1:31 is separated from 2:1. In LXX and ESV 1:31 is separate from 2:1 and 2:3 from 2:4. Cf. Nobel, *Gods gedachten tellen*, in toto, which offers an argument against delimitation after 2:4a or 2:4. Cf. also Hilbrands, *Zehn Thesen zum biblischen Schöpfungsbericht*, 7-26. Mathews opts for 1:1—2:3 (Mathews, *Genesis 1—11:26*, 27), as does Collins (Collins, *Genesis 1-4*, 39-43).

12. Tables that are referenced more than once are placed at the end of this chapter, rather than inserted multiple times in the text for ease of access.

13. Whether the expression "and the earth was" in verse 2 means immediate or subsequent ("became") action is a conclusion dependent on decisions made about the nature of 1:1 as independent or dependent on verse 2. The grammatical form itself does not dictate the answer but rather is interpreted in light of larger issues of the purpose of 1:1,

to create" or "In the beginning God created" (but beginning of what? v. 1), the concern seems to be with the first phase of creation (1:1/2–5), which is focused on the condition of the land: unfinished and unfilled (תוהו ובהו), disordered, dark, and stormy (v. 2)[14]—hence, the need for light (vv. 3–5). The MT places a sign (פ) for a major paragraph break at the end of verse 5 but also at the end of 2:3. The probable presence of a striking parallelism in verse 2 is significant: and-the-land was תוהו ובהו (2a):

A	[B]	[C]	D	E
And-darkness[-from]	[*Elohim*]	[hovered]	over-the-surface-of	the-deep-[water] (2bi) //
A'	B	C	D	E'
and-a-wind-from	*Elohim*	hovered	over the-surface-of	the-[deep]-water. (2bii).

The inclusio in 1:1 and 2:4a does not require 1:1 or 2:4a to be an independent sentence. It merely marks the beginning and end of the complete creation story of seven days (1:1–5, 1:6–8, 1:9–13, 1:14–19, 1:20–23, 1:24–31, 2:1–4a), which includes the creation week or event of six days.[15] The author seems theologically to establish the Sabbath and its observance as a regular rhythm of created human life (which might explain his *functional*

---

or 1:1–2 in light of 1:3—2:4. Even if "then the land became תוהו ובהו" is chosen, nothing need be read into that other than the creation of sky and land was initiated and out of that process (however long and via whatever means) an incomplete and un-illumined condition emerged. If the first "day" involved only the command for light and its instantaneous appearance and then naming it "day" and the darkness "night" (which already existed in v. 2), then even a day of twenty-four hours is quite empty (since these actions would have taken only seconds or minutes).

14. This appears to be a standard bi-colon, so it parallels darkness (חשך) and spirit/wind (רוח). This genitive construct ("wind/spirit of God") has to be interpreted. Is it possessive ("spirit belonging to God"), appositional ("spirit that is God"), or agent ("spirit from or by God")? Also, רוח can be spirit, wind, or breath. If this is a case of restatement in parallel lines, then the darkness over the deep water is best restated as a windstorm over the seas. So, the best interpretation in context is a wind sent by God, not the (Holy) Spirit belonging to God.

15. For the more traditional view, Stipp has made a careful syntactical study of 1:1 in light of related OT determinatives and concluded that ברשית ("in the beginning") is inherently determinative, needing no morphological indication, and that 1:1 is an independent motto verse. He argues the Tiberian text is not consistent with the nature of the conditions in Genesis 1:1. Cf. Stipp, "Anfang und Ende," 188–96.

purpose in using a week to picture the creation of all things).[16] A chiasm may be constructed not around six or seven days but around ten stages or phases that comprise the six creational days in light of the respective length of each of five steps:

A   light + sky, land (days 1–2; ninety words) two phases
    B   seas + land and plants (day 3; sixty-nine words) two phases
        C   sun, moon, and stars (day 4; sixty-nine words) one phase
    B'   fish and birds + blessing (day 5; fifty-seven words) two phases
A'   animals + humans + blessing (day 6; 149 words) two/three phases (two phases could be seen if animals and humans are grouped as "land animals").

If this is, in fact, the case, why would the planets/stars be central? It may be in the ancient Near East religious context it would align nicely with the importance of establishing that those things worshipped as gods by the Canaanites and others are, in fact, cited as mere creations distinct from the true Creator God, *Elohim*. A more satisfying analysis might be made between two different types of creation: non-*nephesh* material and *nephesh* material (נפש as "spiritual" or "spirited") each with five phases:[17]

---

16. The number of words (Hebrew) used for each day (disregarding *maqqeph* and counting the direct object marker) by this scheme are: 52, 38, 69 [or 25/44], 69, 57 [or 38/19], 149 [or 32/54/63 (animals/humans/blessings)], and 39 (but 34 if 2:3 is taken as the end of the narrative). Within the six days, ten stages may be seen (days 3 and 5 each have two stages and day 6 has three); see Tables A, B, C1-2. The framework hypothesis (days 1–3 are forms and days 4–6 are respective fillings, 1//4, 2//5, 3//6) does not work because the sky/expanse is named on day 2 but fish are created on day 5, yet the seas are created and named on day 3. Sky/heavens is day 2 but sun, moon, and stars are day 4 not 5 as expected, although day 5 has birds to fill the sky. If 1:1–5 is day 1 then land, sky, and light are involved on that day. On day 3 land appears when the seas are formed and then vegetation, which means a form and a filling are on the same day. The lines marking forms and what fills them are blurred and dotted, fluid not solid or categorical.

17. For the lack of better terminology this distinction is between material (living and non-living) things (without a נפש) and "spiritual" beings (living "souls" [נפש חיה] as describes animals in Genesis 1:20, 24 and humans in 2:7). "Spiritual" is better than "soulish" since it avoids the problem of mistranslating נפש (which speaks of a living being) as the immaterial being separate from its body. In Leviticus 2:1 נפש is translated as "someone." These creatures, unlike plants, are animated by God and in that sense are material and "in-spired." The influence of God's spirit (רוח) would be another stage of spirituality. It is interesting that this נפש nature of humans is not mentioned in Genesis 1. נפש can mean "neck" (see Jonah 2:6) and both humans and many animals breathe in life through a mouth/neck/lung system.

Creation of the material world (Days 1–4) 228 words

   A sky + land + light   day 1
     B sky   day 2
       C land + seas   day 3
         D plants   day 3
           E sun, moon, stars   day 4

Creation of the "spiritual" world (Days 5–6) 95 words

   A fish and birds   day 5
     B blessing   day 5
       C animals   day 6
         D humans   day 6
           E blessing   day 6

Days 1, 2, and 4 have one part while days 3, 5, and 6 have two to three parts (see Tables A–D below, pp. 20–22), totaling ten parts or movements. Framework theory (see n. 16 above) notwithstanding, the proper division comes not between days 3 and 4, but 4 and 5, between the creation of inanimate (material) objects and animate (spiritual) beings. The latter are described as "living" (חיה) and "moving" (רמש) or as "soulish" or breathing beings (נפש). Plant life is not so designated (third day) and is food for both animals and humans (1:29-30). A well-known chiasm occurs at 2:4, which explains the reversal (earth and heavens) that some question:[18]

   a of the heavens
     b and the earth
       c when they were created
       c' in the time when YHWH God made
     b' the earth
   a' and the heavens

---

18. See Collins, *Genesis 1–4*, 41. This chiasm shows that such structures have been recognized previously and points to the possibility, if not probability, of others. Some who oppose this chiasm as an editorial intention conjecture that the "heaven and earth" expression could be a scribal error.

The Use of the waw Consecutive

Some have appealed to the use of the *waw* consecutive in Genesis 1 as evidence of historical narrative.[19] Hebrew grammars have long recognized that this form expresses "succession in time," temporal or logical.[20] At the same time subsequent past actions (e.g., subsequent yet oppositional action) resort to the *qatal* (see 1 Kgs 2:8).[21] The *wayyiqtol* (inverted form, or more popularly the *waw* consecutive + *yiqtol*) also finds a place in Hebrew poetry (e.g., Ps 3:5 [3:4 English text], ויענני "and then he answered me"). While not strictly historical prose, poetic genre can contain historical references. Consequently, a creation document such as found in Genesis 1 may present sequential actions. Poetry by definition does not necessarily exclude the use of past events in space and time. The information the author conveys can be discovered within his ancient literary and religious context more than appeals to OT lexicography and verbal syntax.[22]

In Genesis 1 the consecutive verbs (with God as subject) are distributed as follows. The *wayyiqtol* ("then God said") appears ten times, but these do not align with the ten phases (see nn. 23–24 below).[23] These stages are initialized with "then God said" (ויאמר) or "then God blessed [ויברך]

---

19. See Sarfati, "Theologian: Genesis means what it says," specifically p. 19.

20. Joüon-Muraoka, *Grammar of Biblical Hebrew*, 357, 361, 363. I concur with Muraoka's preference for the title "*waw* inversive" (rather than "converted") for the *wayyiqtol* and *w-qatalti* due to inversion of meaning (succession instead of future) and syllable stress (final), respectively. See p. 357.

21. Joüon-Muraoka, *Grammar of Biblical Hebrew*, 363.

22. Such grammatical issues are vital for proper translation, which is interpretation, yet they have to be evaluated in light of the cultural and communicative contexts. A word or phrase does not dictate the meaning of its larger context; to the contrary, how a verb or noun or clause is understood is decided in light of the immediate contexts (pericope or book section, audience, cultural setting, etc.). One does not begin an essay based on a word but on a topic, which theme or purpose dictates the content, and then words are chosen to best introduce and develop the chosen subject. A writer first decides *how* to begin a text and that determines what word or sentence to use. Exegesis can be deceptive because it begins in reverse of how communication works. A text is broken into pieces to be studied but the exegete may forget that the pieces individually did not create the text, rather the text and its contexts dictated what pieces to use to obtain the author's intended ideas. A word only has a meaning in a context. יום unarguably is used in Genesis 1 as a "day of a week" (a normal day), but why the author used a week to portray the creation even enables us to decide if he intended to teach a literal 144-hour creation, or if his purpose was function (rather than mechanical) or theological (rather than historical). See Barr, *Semantics*, in toto, and Silva, *Biblical Words*, in toto.

23. 1:3; 1:6; 1:9: 1:11; 1:14; 1:20; 1:24; 1:26; 1:28; and 1:29.

and said [ויאמר]" or "then God blessed [ויברך] by saying [לאמר]."²⁴ On day 1 God commanded (said), then saw, then separated, and then named (the day begins with "he created" if 1:1–2 is included). The implied *we . . . qatal* form in verse 2 (היתה . . . ו) "and [the land] she/it was") could better have been a *wayyiqtol* followed by the subject ("and it was, the land") if the intention was "and then the land became."²⁵ On day 2 he commanded, then made, then separated, and then named.²⁶ On day 3 he commanded, then named, then saw/realized, then commanded, and then realized. On day 4 God commanded, then made, then separated, then saw/realized. On day 5 he commanded, then created, then saw, and then blessed by saying. On day 6 God commanded, then made, then saw, then commanded, then created, then blessed and said, then commanded, and then saw/concluded all was good (see Tables A–D below, pp. 20–22). No doubt the narrative presents the week of creation in logical or temporal order of consecution. Whether the author intended this to be historical or theological, the same verbs could have been used. That chronology or the age of the earth was his concern depends on much more than verb forms and functions.

---

24. 1:3 (day 1); 1:6 (day 2); 1:9 (day 3); 1:11 (day 3); 1:14 (day 4); 1:20 (day 5); 1:22 (day 5); 1:24 (day 6); 1:26 (day 6); and 1:28 (day 6). Another ויאמר comes in 1:29 as part of the extended blessing. The blessing on day 5 is *wayyiqtol* + infinitive construct (blessed by saying) but on day 6 is *wayyiqtol* + *wayyiqtol* (blessed and then said). Regardless of form, the movement from command creation to blessing breaks days 5 and 6 into parts. Day 6 has three parts based on movement from animal creation (1:24) to human (1:26) to blessing (1:28). Day 3 has two parts based on movement from developmental command for water and then land. Here, creation by divine word is not seen; rather, God calls material already created to act. In fact, jussive verbs are used with the sense "allow the waters/land to be gathered/produce vegetation," respectively. The creational activity is set in motion by God (not spoken into existence from nothing) and allowed to finish in its own time.

25. Consequently, consecution is not in view here (cf. the gap theory that the completed creation in 1:1 later fell into chaos; 1:2). The land created in 1:1 was in an incomplete state initially (1:1–2).

26. God "made" is Hebrew עשה, which is used interchangeably with ברא here in Genesis 1–2. The sense "create from nothing" is not a meaning of ברא but is communicated if the context describes creation from nothing (*ex nihilo*). That ברא only has God as a subject in the OT is not determinative because in written or oral language outside of the OT in the ancient Jewish world, the term likely was used with different subjects. The OT only offers us a slice of Hebrew usage overall. In Psalm 51:10 (12 MT) ברא is used in the sense of re-creation or renewal (making something new out of existing material).

The Use of Thematic and Structural Features

Each creation "day" is subdivided into six creational acts and a closing formula, although all six are not always present or in the same order. What is consistent is the opening "God said/commanded" for each day and each of the ten stages, as well as the closing formula ("evening and morning" for each day). The six creational activities are: (1) God said/commanded or said/blessed, (2) saw/concluded, (3) separated/distinguished, (4) gathered, (5) called/named, and (6) made/created.[27] On no day do all of these appear. Day 4 has the most with five: commanded/blessed, separated, made/created, named, and concluded/saw. Notably, this day may be a fulcrum for a chiastic structure (see above, pp. 7–8). Four of these six acts, but not the same four, appear on days 1, 2, and 3. After that, except for day 4, only three, and the same three, appear on days 5 and 6, although days 3, 5, and 6 have multiple stages (see Tables A–D below, pp. 20–22). Speaking to create or bless appears first on each day or phase of a day. God's "seeing" or approval or recognition of good appears on every day except the second (when sky is created). Separation/distinguishing (בדל) occurs only three times: light and dark on day 1, waters above and below on day 2, and then light from dark on day 4. The fact that light and dark are separated twice might suggest an inclusio for the first four days (the period of inanimate creation).[28] Both day 1 and day 4 describe a separation of light and dark (also named day and night).[29] Only days 1–4 use four to five of the six possible creational acts. The only difference between days 1 and 4 is that the latter names the lights as sun, moon, and stars. The order for light to exist on each day differs only in the change from singular light (אור in 1:3a) to plural lights (מאורות in 1:14a). On day 1 the light merely distinguishes day and night, but on day 4 it also marks time (seasons of days and years). Read

---

27. This analysis was made before I had ever read the commentary by Kenneth Mathews, whose previous analysis is similar. See Mathews, *Genesis 1—11:26*, 115.

28. Suggesting no animate life in the universe?

29. This un-chronological depiction of creation points to a theological rather than technical purpose of the creation account. Consequently, Waltke calls for a literary reading of Genesis 1 (cf. Waltke, "First Seven Days, 46). Theological purposes have led to chronological rearrangements elsewhere in the OT, e.g., Genesis 10–11, where chapter 10 seems to belong after 11 since 11 has one language in use and 10 has many; however, the absolute one-language theory of Genesis 11:1–9 is highly debatable; cf. Marlowe, "Sin of Shinar," 29–39. Cf. also Youngblood, *Book of Genesis*, in toto, and Clines, "'Sons of God,'" 9.

literally, a "day" could not be marked off in hours until the fourth day. All this could indicate a rhetorical purpose:

Day 1 (1:1–5) heavens and earth created (planets and stars implied)
    sky and land enlightened (day and night)
Day 2 (1:6–8) sky (waters above) named
        Day 3 I (1:9–10) earth: land and seas (waters below) named
        Day 3 II (1:11–13) land: vegetation called to grow
Day 4 (1:13–19) heaven and earth enlightened (planets and stars added)
    times calculated (day and night)

This fits with the emphasis throughout the creation story on the land and its principal inhabitant, humanity. After announcing the initial creation of land and sky (1:1) the text moves immediately to the land's darkness and need of light (1:2–5). Then there is the sky over the land with rain clouds (waters above) to make the land fertile (1:6–8), followed by the organization of the earth into areas of dry land and seas (waters below). A result was that the land could now produce vegetation to sustain life. Then finally on day 4 seasons (related to planting and harvesting to sustain life) are regulated. So, it seems the movement is from day and night being established (day 1) to day and night being effective (day 4). The stars existed from 1:1 (*Elohim* created the heavens and earth).[30] After day 4 the narrative is mainly concerned with the emergence of animate life, the pinnacle of which is human life, man and woman, who are to rule the other animals and eat from the plants.[31] Days 5 and 6 exclusively focus on God creating creatures and

---

30. The deep waters of 1:2 also represent what we know as the oceans, technically not created until day 3. So "waters below" already existed when ostensibly formed in 1:7. This reasoning naturally fails if it can be shown conclusively that 1:1–2 is an introduction or topic statement and not part of the literary creation sequence.

31. It could be argued that this rule assumed using the animals as well for food. Perhaps the plant life is fronted as food because the man and woman (*Adam* and "his woman" later named *Chavvah*? ["Eve" in English]) are allowed seed-bearing plants for food (fruits, nuts/berries, and vegetables?) and the other animals every green plant (1:29–30). Later, the man and woman will be disallowed (on pain of death) to eat from a certain tree (moral knowledge tree) in the garden in Eden where they live (2:15–17). The author of Genesis explains the central location of two trees in 2:9b. The tempter of 3:1 asks if they were forbidden to eat from *any tree*, but the woman replies (3:2–3) that they can eat *the fruit* (not mentioned previously) from any tree but *cannot eat the fruit from or touch* the tree *in the middle* (which God did not mention to Adam) of the garden without dying as a result. It can be assumed that the tree in 2:15–17 was a fruit tree, although that is not stated in those verses. Or did the tempter and woman add that detail improperly?

commanding their multiplication through procreation, and deeming this good[32] (see Table D below). Man and woman are distinguished equally as bearing God's image, which in the immediate context is defined solely as mastering (רדה) and subduing (כבש) the animal world of fish, fowl, and all else (1:26–28). The text does not say animals cannot be food, only that plants are food.[33] Chapter 1 could be framed as man's world (1:1–19) and man's work (1:20–31). Semantic support for this formation is found as follows:

A-B Statement	C Climax	B'-A' Restatement
Day 1 heaven-earth light-dark Day-Night separated [expanse implied]		*Day 4* expanse light-dark Day-Night separated heaven-earth
	Day 2 Sky = expanse separating waters above and waters below	*Day 3b* Land [under the expanse] produces vegetation with waters below
	seas anticipated	dry ground activated
	Day 3a Lands (dry ground) & Seas gathered (= Earth)	

Regardless, it seems 1:29–30 anticipates chapters 2–3.

32. Not to be missed is the use of jussive verbs by which God allows the "land to bring forth [יצא] living beings [*nephesh*]," (1:24) which suggests a lengthy process as opposed to an instantaneous act of creation by divine fiat. Cf. the previous day when God says "allow the land to sprout green" (1:11) and 1:20, where God says "allow the waters to swarm with 'living beings [*nephesh*]."

33. These humans seemingly have to have witnessed animal death to understand the warning about death resulting from disobedience. Animals are not directly forbidden as food; the comment is that *all* seed-bearing plants are edible (save one later on). Eventually, people will sacrifice animals in worship to offer them as food to God or the gods.

In addition to the previous six structural (but random) themes, plus closing formula for each of ten stages (or five themes with standard opening and closing formulae for each of six days),[34] one can observe six structural features in a near-standard order: command, result, evaluation, disunity/unity, naming, and numbering/closing formula for a weekday (see Tables B and C below). Command and result are always first and second in order and numbering is always last. Evaluation and naming are usually in the third or fifth position. Disunity/unity (separating or gathering) is almost always fourth. Days 1 and 2 are almost identical in this regard, only evaluation and disunity/unity are reversed. Again days 1–4 use all six features and in a similar, though not exact, order. Days 5–6 use only the first three features and always in the same order (as day 1) in addition to the numbering or typical closing statement ("evening and morning"). The days involving the creation of animate life do not involve things being separated/gathered or named. Later, the human names the animals (2:19–20).[35] A significant shift is again clear between days 4 and 5, as has been seen between 3 and 4.

Metric and chiastic symmetry is found in a place like verse 9:

A Creative Act Introduced: God said (v. 9a)   *wayyiqtol* (preterite)
  B Command for the sea to form: Let gather!   (v. 9b)   jussive
  B' Command for the land to form: Let appear!   (v. 9c)   jussive
A' Creative Act Concluded: And it was (v. 9d)   *wayyiqtol* (preterite)

Another kind of tri-colon could be suggested, but regardless of whatever pattern we accept, the obvious nature of this text is purposeful patterns:
    And God said "let the waters be gathered // (twelve syllables)

---

34. "Then God said/commanded/blessed . . . And there was evening and morning," leaving five other medial options of seeing, separating, gathering, calling, and making/creating. See Tables A and B below.

35. God named the parts of creation, which showed his authority over them (Gen 1); then Adam named the animals in line with his delegated dominion over them (Gen 2); and then Adam named the woman (3:20), which contextually, in terms of text and tradition, posits Adam as having some authority over the woman in line with ANE conventions. Such information is accurate in relation to history but hermeneutically is not required to be read as an authoritative proposition regarding the nature of women for all ages. Mathews believes God naming the animals defined their existence and gave signification based on ancient customs (per Mesopotamian and Egyptian creation texts where there was no name before something came to be); and in light of Genesis 2:19–20 and other passages in Genesis, as well as the naming of the stars (Ps 147:4 and Isa 40:26), naming demonstrated superiority (Mathews, *Genesis 1—11:26*, 120, nn. 29–30). Does this apply in full to Adam naming the woman?

Under the skies into one place // (twelve syllables)
And let dry land appear [likewise]"; and it was so. (twelve syllables)

Verses 11–12 have a bi-colon followed by a tri-colon, creating an a-b-c-d // a'-b'-c'-d' structure:[36]

Stage verses	Key Verbs & Nouns	Theme		Stage verses	Key Verbs & Nouns
A 11a	(Jussive) let the land produce (דשׁא) [God's desire]	Vegetation on earth		A' 12a	(Preterite) and the land produced (דשׁא) [the earth's cooperation]
		Plan	Production		
B 11b	(Participle) yielding (זרע) seed	Plants on earth		B' 12b	(Participle) yielding (זרע) seed
		Result			
C 11c	(Participle) making (עשׂה) fruit with seeds	Trees on earth		C' 12c	(Participle) making (עשׂה) fruit with seeds
		Result			
D 11d	And it came to be (wayyiqtol/preterite) [the earth's result]	Confirmation		D' 12d	And God "saw" good (wayyiqtol/preterite) [God's commendation]
		Realization	Evaluation		

Verse 13 ends day 3 with the same sort of bi-colon as day 2 in verse 8b. Another chiasmus is present in verses 26–28:

A God's decision to make humans co-managers of the animals (26)
Wishing through cohortative/jussive verbs.
   B God's creation of humans as co-managers (fulcrum; 27)
     Acting through *wayyiqtol/qatal/qatal* (past-tense) verbs.
A' God's decree that humans be co-managers of the animals (28)
Transition with two *wayyiqtol* (preterite or past-tense) verbs.

Demanding through five imperative verbs (jussive verbs are used with an imperative force in Genesis 1; e.g., "let light exist!").

The first bi-colon of verse 28 is highly symmetrical:

---

36. Plus tag "and it was so" in verse 11 and "God declares it 'good'" in verse 12. Verse 12 simply reaffirms verse 11, also chiastic (with bi-colon followed by tri-colon), and adds God's approval (which substitutes for the 11d tag), with the statement about seeds "on the earth" assumed from verse 11d.

a	b	c	//	a'	b	c
and-he-blessed	them	*Elohim*	//	and-he-said	to-them	*Elohim*.

He "favors" (ברך) them by speaking to them and revealing his will that they prosper and have purpose. This bi-colon (28b) is also likely a conceptual chiasmus of four imperatives:

a	b	//	b'	a'
Bear fruit!	Become many!	//	Fill the-land!	And-subdue-it!
[be productive]	[multiply]	//	[multiply]	[be productive]

1:28c tells how they are to do this: "rule" (the fifth imperative) over all creatures.

Parallels and Parallelism

The most objective evidence of Hebrew poetry or a poem is the pervasive presence of *parallelismus membrorum*. This does seem obvious in at least one if not a few places in Genesis 1. But it does not characterize the entire account, although proposals can be made for parallels and parallelisms not previously accepted. At least one attempt has been made to reconstruct the remains of an ancient poetic text from Genesis 1.[37] The case of 1:2 has already been discussed (see above pp. 3–4). As noted, the consecutive verb at the beginning of verse 3 is linked to the previous verses ("so [then] God said"). As a unit verses 1–5 could be translated:[38]

---

37. Polak, "Poetic Style," 5, n. 13 citing Loretz, "Wortbericht-Vorlage," 279–87. Polak looks not so much at reconstructed parallelisms per se, although he notes some parallelisms between consecutive lines (Polak, "Poetic Style," 23–26), but at syntactic, semantic (lexical registers, fixed phrases or word pairs typical of poetry elsewhere in the OT), and rhythmic repetitions, also in light of source criticism. He speaks of something less than full parallelism, which he calls "balanced coupling" (p. 22), and emphasizes the need to recognize informal characteristics, which he sees neglected in previous works like de Moor, "Narrative Poetry," 149–71, and de Moor and Watson, *Verse*, in toto. See Polak, "Poetic Style," 4, n. 11.

38. Waltke noted that in favor of this grouping is the classic grammar by Gesenius-Kautzsch-Cowley. See Waltke, "First Seven Days," 42. Yet he thinks the presence of syntagmes like "heaven and earth" present an insurmountable obstacle to this approach. He argues that this hendiadys means "the entire organized universe" and as such is at odds with verse 2, where the earth is now chaotic. But the author of Genesis 1:1 could

First *Elohim* created [ברא] the sky and the land //[39]   1
And this land was [initially] an unfilled/unfinished form.   2a

---

observe that God created everything and not necessarily mean that it was all finished and perfected (Childs' observation [quoted by Waltke] notwithstanding that this word pair can only speak of an ordered world). Still the sky and the land could be begun and remain unfinished without being necessarily disordered or chaotic in some negative sense. Again, the dependent nature of 1:1 is suggested in that such problems disappear with the reading "When God began to create everything, the land was unformed/unfinished." 1:1–2a makes a pleasing initial statement before the introduction of the parallelism in 1:2b. That "heavens and earth" should be "sky and land" is also further supported by these data. The narrative turns to a focus on the land per se in verse 2a. See also Waltke, "Creation Account," 216–28. Waltke therein convincingly sets aside the so-called "Gap Theory" (that the initial verb of 1:2 is a pluperfect, "then it became") noting (1) the stative nature of היה in 2:5 and 3:1 (having parallel circumstantial clauses); (2) the "was" meaning of similar structures in Jonah 3:3; Zechariah 3:2–3; and Judges 8:11; (3) no ancient or modern versions translate היה as "became" in 1:2; and (4) the unlikely beginning of a narrative with a pluperfect (Waltke, "Creation Account," 228). However, one must admit this last reason is based on an assumption that 1:2, and not 1:1, begins the narrative per se. Also, the argument about versions historically is weak in view of the reality that translators have been typically conservative (tending to be literal, leaving interpretation to the reader).

39. The verb ברא is used in this narrative at 1:1, 21a, and 27. It initiates the creation of inanimate and then animate things (again suggesting an intentional structure of days 1–4 then 5–6). *Elohim* created the sky and land (the empty forms needing filling) and then made/fashioned (עשה) things to fill them in stage I; and then in stage II he created sea life, but this had already been explained as God calling on the water and then the air to allow fish and birds to fill them (v. 20). Everything multiplied according to its kind (v. 21b). The same process occurs with humanity in verses 26–27 ("Let us make [עשה] humans … so God created humans [ברא]). However, ברא also initiates days 5 and 6 (animal then human creation). So, God creates (1) inanimate things, (2) animate non-human life, and (3) animate human life. But why is ברא used just for sea life? Also, day 6 divides animate life on land further into non-human and human creatures. Perhaps to make a stronger break between animal life on land, the non-human life is "brought forth [יצא] from the land" while humans were "created" (ברא). This verb could be applied to sea life at the beginning of the animate section (days 5–6), because human life could not be confused with fish as with other land animals; but of the land animals it needed to be stressed that humans were distinct, especially because of God's image (while all had the breath of life or *nephesh*, which is better "life" than "soul" since the latter evokes thoughts of disembodied spirits; by the same token, "Holy Ghost" needs to be discontinued). The sea life "swarmed" from the water (v. 20) and then was created (v. 21; ברא); the land animals (non-human) were "produced" by the land (v. 24) and "made" (v. 25; עשה). Humans are "made" (עשה) by God (1:26; ["let us make" is a rhetorical device like the royal "we"]) then poetically "created" as human (v. 27a), and as male and female (v. 27b). The non-human sea and land life emerge from the water or land and are created and made, but humans are just created or made (although in Genesis 2 the male is fashioned from the mud and the female from the side of the male). See Table D below.

And darkness was [covering] the surface of the deep [seas] //   2bi
While a wind from *Elohim* was blowing over the waters.   2bii
So [then] *Elohim* commanded, "Let light come into existence!" //   3a
And light then came into existence.   3b
Then *Elohim* recognized the light as good //   4a
So, *Elohim* distinguished the light from the darkness.   4b
And *Elohim* named the light "Day" //   5ai
And the darkness [*Elohim*] named "Night."   5aii
And then evening arrived, //   5bi
And then morning arrived; /   5bii
the first day [ended].   5c

Already well-known and undisputed is 1:27,

A	B	C	D	
so-he-created	*Elohim*	the-man	in-his-image	//
D	B	A	C'	
in-the-image-of	*Elohim*	he-created	him.	

A fairly obvious bi-colon and tri-colon can be proposed for both verse 6 and 7, respectively:

	a	b	c		e	f	
(6)	And-he-said	*Elohim*	"be	an-expanse		in-the-midst-of the-waters" //	
[a]	[b]	c	d'	e'	f	f'	
[And-he-said]	[*Elohim*]	"be	a division	between	waters	from-waters."	
a	b	c	d				
(7) So-he-made	*Elohim*	the-expanse	and-he-separated,	/			
e	f	g	h	i			
between	the-waters	which	(were)	under	the-expanse	//	
e	f	g	h'	i			
and-between	the-waters	which	(were)	above	the-expanse.		

Others can be proposed more or less convincingly. But this is sufficient to demonstrate that parallelism, while perhaps not comprehensive, is present in Genesis 1. An original poem could be imagined, of which the present text is a re-creation.

Conclusion

This exploration of the various structures and themes of Genesis 1 in terms of patterns and parallels has indicated several possible ways in which the narrative is characterized by intentional rhetorical and poetical devices. While not a historical narrative per se, it does present the creation event in a series of sequential or subsequent (logical or chronological) steps, stages, or phases. At the same time some of these may be chiastic, so a linear set of steps is not necessarily presented, rather a literary means of fronting or focusing on certain key or theological perspectives seems evident. These data suggest that the nature of this story is highly stylized and structured and does not present itself as an obvious linear movement of creational acts.[40] The author of Genesis 1 was principally concerned with the meaning (theology), not the mechanics (chronology) of creation. Such poetics do not disallow a text's ability to express historical and factual information (as some psalms demonstrate), but the use of a normal work week of six days does not preclude the author from having a functional, theological, or symbolic purpose for that image. A rigid, literal hermeneutic is not the only valid option for reading this passage. Whatever its purposes or propositions, its style is sublime. Genesis 1 embodies no simple string of successive or consecutive acts, although consecutive verbs predominate. These latter show sequence consistent with the author's plan to use a week from day 1–7 to encapsulate his creation theology but do not have to be used to communicate chronological acts in history. The answer to *why* the author employed a normal week of seven days (six creational ones) may be as much functional or theological as mechanical or temporal. The mere presence of *waw* consecutive or use of יוֹם as a normal day does not prove that the author's purpose was the time of creation. Similarly, the use of numerous poetics does not prove that his purpose was non-historical or only theological or symbolic. One may conclude, on the basis of what has

---

40. Clare Amos speaks of the "song of seven days" regarding the creation week of Gen 1:1—2:4a (Amos, *Book of Genesis*, 1–14).

been shown, the text combines highly poetic informality with a degree of formality.

Table A: The Days and Stages of Genesis 1:1–31[41]

Day	Verses	No. Verses	Creative Word	Creative Stages
1	3–5	3	God said	1. Light (Day)
2	6–8	3	God said	2. Sky ("dome")
3	9–11	3	God said	3.1 Earth and Sea (Continents and Oceans)
	12–13	2	God said	3.2 Vegetation
4	14–19	6	God said	4. Sun, Moon, and Stars
5	20–21	2	God said	5.1 Fish and Fowl
	22–23	2	God blessed saying	5.2 Multiplication (be fruitful)
6	24–25	2	God said	6.1 Land Animals
	26–27	2	God said	6.2 Humanity
	28–31	4	God blessed saying	6.3a Multiplication (be fruitful)
			and said	6.3b All animals and plants for food

Table B: Order and Appearance of Thematic Features in Genesis Creation "Days"

Themes ↓	יוֹם	1	2	3 I	3 II	4	5 I	5 II	6 I	6 II	6 III
God said/ Blessed		1	1	1	1	1	1	1	1	1	1
God saw		2	—	4	2	5	3	—	3	—	2
God separated		3	2	—	—	2	—	—	—	—	—
God gathered		—	—	3	—	—	—	—	—	—	—

41. Cf. Mathews, *Genesis 1—11:26*, 117, n. 13.

Form	1	2	3-I	3-II	4	5-I	5-II	6-I	6-II	6-III
God called	4	4	2	——	4	——	——	——	——	——
God made/created	——	3	——	——	3	2	——	2	2	——
Evening/Morning	5	5	5		6	4		4		

Table C1: Six Deeds: Order and Appearance of Structural Features in Genesis Creation "Days"

Form ↓	יום	1	2	3 I	3 II	4	5 I	5 II	6 I	6 II	6 III
Command		1	1	1	1	1	1	1	1	1	1
Result		2	2	2	2	2	2	——	2	2	2
Evaluation		3	4	5	3	5	3	——	3	3	3
Disunity/Unity		4	3	4	——	4	——	——	——	——	——
Naming		5	5	3	——	3	——	——	——	——	——
Numbering		6	6	6		6	4		4		

Table C2: Six Decrees: Structure of the "Days" of Creation in Gen 1:3–31

Form ↓	יום	1	2	3 I	3 II	4	5 I	5 II	6 I	6 II	6 III
God said or blessed saying		3	6a	9a	11a	14a	20a	22a	24a	26a	28a, 29a
God saw		4a	——	10c	12b	18b	21b	——	25b	31a	
God called		5a	8a	10a	——	16c	——	——	——	——	——
God created or made		——	7a	——	——	16a	21a	——	25a	27a	——
God separated		4b	6b	——	——	4b, 18a	——	——	——	——	——
God gathered		——	——	10b	——	——	——	——	——	——	——

Table D: Sequence Schematic of Things "Created" from Yom 1–6

יוֹם	Ref.	Created (ברא) or Made (עשׂה)	Commanded to be or Controlled
Intro.	1:1–2	What follows is after the creation (ברא) of the unfinished and dark sky, land and sea:	
1	1:3–5		Light; Day and Night named
2	1:6–8	Expanse made (עשׂה)	Expanse named Sky
3	1:9–10		Water gathered and Dry Ground exposed: named Sea and Land.
	1:11–13		Vegetation produced by the Land
4	1:14–19	Sun, moon, and stars made (עשׂה)	Seasons signified; light for the earth provided in the Sky; day and night governed.
5	1:20–23	Fish and fowl created (ברא) by kind	Water and Sky to teem with life. Be fruitful and multiply.
6	1:24–25	Animals made (עשׂה) by kind	Animals produced by the Land.
	1:26–30	People made (עשׂה) to rule. People created (ברא) with gender.	People to rule over animals "in God's image." Be fruitful and multiply. Subdue earth and eat plants.
	1:31		All made (עשׂה) declared good.
Outro. 7	2:1–4a	What preceded was about how the Land and Sky were completed and created (ברא). *Elohim* rests from creative work.	Rested from work he did (עשׂה). Rested from work of creating (ברא) he had done (עשׂה).

2

The Form and Function of Genesis 6:1–4[1]

Introduction

GENESIS 6:1–4 is well-known for its mysterious בני האלהים ("sons of the God [gods?]") and נפלים ("giants"? or "fallen ones") and the variety of interpretations they have evoked.[2] Mathews called this text "the most demanding passage in Genesis for the interpreter,"[3] and as Speiser noted, "Its

---

1. Originally published as Marlowe, "Gen 6:1–4," 129-44. Stylistic and corrective but no substantive changes have been made.

2. The traditional notion of these as fallen angels in light of Job 1:6 and 2:1 is doubtful. The same expression can develop very different usages and meanings over long periods of time. If Job and Genesis share the same time of composition, the contexts are still different. But also, instead of Job proving Genesis 6 is about angels, it may show something else, if it demonstrates anything at all. The beings that come before YHWH in Job have an adversary (Heb. שטן) with them. He came from earth (1:7; 2:2) which suggests these "sons of the gods/God" (בני האלהים) did also. Those who see this שטן as Satan understand these "sons of God" as angels but on the basis that Satan is thought to be a fallen angel. So circular reasoning is often involved. The *satan* is mentioned only in Job 1-2, 1 Chronicles 21:1, and Zechariah 3:1-2 in the OT. Texts like Isaiah 14 and Ezekiel 28, popularly thought to be about Satan, say nothing about a שטן or angels (מלאך literally "messengers"; "angel" being merely a transliteration and not a translation of the Greek ἄγγελος). If these OT texts are not about Satan, then they also say nothing about his moral fall from heaven. Again, circular reasoning occurs when people say we know these texts are about Satan because he is a fallen angel and we know he is a fallen angel because of these same chapters.

3. Mathews, *Genesis 1—11:26*, 320.

problems are legion."[4] This study, rather, is concerned with the structure and central sense of this powerful yet petite pericope. It proposes a chiastic structure for these verses, but with no promise of settling such unresolved exegetical questions. The realization of a chiasm, however, may provoke new speculations about the characters involved in this short story. Previous and substantial commentary on these strange verses has focused much more on its setting than structure. Wenham already observed a palistrophe, but of verses 5–8.[5] If a chiasm highlights a central point as the author's main focus, then verse 3 (YHWH's determination to limit the duration of fleshly life) fits well with the surrounding narrative (i.e., the contrast of wickedness needing judgment in vv. 5–7, 11–13 with Seth's line leading to Noah in chapter 5 and with Noah's selection for salvation in vv. 8–10, 14, as the most righteous person alive at that time). The notion of a chiasm was hinted at by the recognition of the verb ילד appearing only in the opening and closing of the text (vv. 1 and 4b) and of the parallel, respectively, between men birthing daughters and daughters birthing men. Verse 3 contains unique content; that leaves verses 2 and 4a, where the sons of God are mentioned as well as the נשים and נפלים, respectively. These נשים are glossed over in many versions. So, it remains to expose more fully the chiastic nature of this story.

Genesis 6:1–4 as an Independent Unit

A clear break is observed before 6:1 and after 6:7 or 8. Noah is the focus of the end of Genesis 5, the beginning of 6:8, and following. The 6:1–7 section is bracketed by the existence of Noah as uniquely righteous in his time. Chapter 5 depicts Noah as a descendant of Adam through Seth (Cain's new

---

4. Speiser, *Genesis*, 45.
5. Wenham, *Genesis 1-15*, 136.

    A The LORD sees mankind (5)
      B The LORD regrets (6)
        C The LORD says "I will wipe out" (7)
      B' because I regret
    A' The LORD sees Noah (8)

Cf. commentaries on Genesis by Franz Delitzsch, Victor P. Hamilton (NICOT), John E. Hartley, Kenneth A. Matthews, Gerhard von Rad, Nahum M. Sarna, John Skinner, E. A. Speiser, Bruce K. Waltke, Gordon J. Wenham, and Claus Westermann (who includes a specific section on literary form). None of these propose or reference a chiastic approach to Genesis 6:1–4.

brother) and other predecessors with notable spiritual pedigrees. Among these, two are highlighted: Enoch, who "walked with *Elohim*" (5:22) and then "was not" because *Elohim* took him (5:24), and his son Methuselah, who lived longer than anyone (969 years; 5:27).[6] Noah was his grandson (if the genealogy is read at face value, assuming no gaps; 5:25-29). Noah also had a number of brothers and sisters, produced over some of the remaining 595 years of Lamech's life (5:30). That he died at age 777 could be numerically symbolic. Noah's fathering of three sons ends chapter 5 and is repeated in the opening verses of the account of Noah, which begins in 6:9. The mention of Noah in 6:8 can be seen best as a transition statement to this new section or "generation" (תולדות). This heading has begun two previous sections in 2:4 (the second creation account) and 5:1 (the genealogy of Adam through Seth).[7] All this leaves 6:1-8 as a defined and independent pericope. But what about 6:1-4 and 5-8?

6. The traditional idea is that Enoch was so righteous that God could not wait for him to die naturally so God brought him to heaven while still alive, allowing him only 365 earth years. The text does not say this exactly. All it says is that after following God 365 years he was no more because God took him. One could just as easily suggest this is an idiom for death (which actually we use today when someone dies). Enoch was no longer around because he died and was buried and went to be with God. The main problem with this view, however, is that it goes against the tenor of the passage, which tries to show that those who were most righteous lived very long lives. Of them all, only Enoch "walked with *Elohim*" (at least this is stated only about him (twice!) [vv. 22, 24] while it could be assumed for the others); yet, he died young (relatively). At the same time, it is an odd notion that God would remove a very righteous person from the earth, especially during such wicked times in need of a righteous witness. While Methuselah lived the longest, nothing is said about his spirituality. Only Noah is also said to have "walked with *Elohim*" (6:9b), and God did not anxiously whisk him away for fellowship. Regardless, Genesis 5 is concerned with Noah's ancestry as Adamite, Sethite, and Enochian. This is a line (opposed to Cain's) of men obedient to God. The only previous similar statement about walking is when YHWH-*Elohim* walked in the garden, where lived Adam and his wife (3:8). Later expressions were used like the exhortation Moses gave to the Hebrews to "walk in all the ways YHWH your *Elohim* has commanded" (Deut 5:33, cf. 8:6; Judg 2:17, *inter alia*).

7. This heading is only used to introduce information about the righteous line from Adam. First (2:4), it heads the second creation account where the emphasis is on the perfect paradise and partners in Eden. Then (5:1), it begins the line of Adam (being in God's image) through Seth (in Adam's image) leading to Noah. Next (6:9-9:29) is the story of Noah, the most righteous man on earth. After that comes the announcement of an accounting of the lineages of Shem, Ham, and Japheth (10:1), but only for Shem (ancestor of Abram) is this repeated at the start of his genealogy (11:10). The Shemite line continues to be highlighted with the account of Terah (father of Abram; 11:27). Among Abraham's sons there is a תולדות or account for both Ishmael (25:12) and Isaac (25:19, the son of promise). Then for both of Isaac's sons, Esau (or Edom; 36:1) and Jacob (or

That the MT places a disjunctive sectional marker (פ) after 6:4 supports a major break between verses 1–4 and 5–8, although the two are connected thematically. The former section is about a specific kind of evil which caused YHWH to threaten human longevity or existence, and the latter is about YHWH's decision to destroy humanity (with one exception) due to its thorough wickedness. Both sections begin, as would be expected, with a *wayyiqtol* verb of past consecutive or sequential action ("then it came to be that" and "then YHWH saw"). Notably, 6:9 reverts to *Elohim* as the divine name (although later YHWH appears). YHWH is the divine being of 6:1–8. Previously in chapter 5, *Elohim* is predominant, except for verse 29, where Noah is introduced, and his name explained as a sign of relief (נחם) in the midst of hard toil (and a reference is made back to 3:17–19, where YHWH-*Elohim* cursed the ground to be resistant as a result of Adam's disobedience).

There is some question if 6:1–8 should rather be divided as 6:1–3 and 4–8. This is because verse 4 begins with a *qatal* verb ("they were"). The main verb of verse 1 also is a *qatal* "he began" (the initial *wayyiqtol* "it came to be" a typical literary device to open a new story).[8] Throughout 6:1–3 the action is carried by consecutive verbs and verbs other than היה ("and they saw"; "and they took"; "and he said"), but with verse 4 comes "they were" (*qatal*); however, the main action of this verse is another *wayyiqtol*, "then they gave birth" (fronted by the state of affairs that נפלים were present at that time). So, 6:1–4 maintains a structural unity as an independent prelude to verses 5-8. Typically, היה in these early chapters of Genesis is used after a new sequence is introduced by a verb of action (e.g., 4:2, "then she *gave birth* [*wayyiqtol*] to Abel; and Abel *became* [*wayyiqtol*] a shepherd, while

---

Israel; 37:2). This ends all the "accounts" in Genesis. The Abraham-Isaac-Israel-Joseph line gets most press in Genesis, but the infamous sons, whose descendants become Israel's enemies, are recognized in passing since these later nations figure prominently in Israel's history.

8. The root חלל is used for "begin" or "to profane." See *HALOT*, s.v. חלל. Cf. 4:25, where this root is used in the comment, "then he began [some versions say "men began"] to call on the name YHWH." Some have suggested the meaning "men profaned the name YHWH." Genesis 6:1-4 could be seen as a continuation of such rebellion against God's authority. But "begin" is the more likely sense in each case because another verb is used for the actions begun. Another interesting potential parallel between these events is that the "sons of God" are thought by some to be the godly line of Seth just listed in Genesis 5, and in 4:25 "he began to call" could link to Seth or his son Enosh just before their genealogy from Adam is outlined (5:1-27, leading to Noah in 5:28-32, the righteous man solely saved from the flood of judgment on all others, who reappears on the heels of the sons of God story in 6:1-4 and the details of human wickedness in 6:5-7).

Cain *became* [*qatal*] a farmer").⁹ Its use in chapters 1–2 is related to results of previous creative acts. In 3:1 this new episode about temptation, sin, and punishment is introduced with a *qatal* of היה for the sense "now the serpent was." A state of being is fronted before the main action verb is used, "Then he said [to the woman]." Only the *qatal* of היה appears in chapter 3:1, 5, 20, 22.¹⁰ The MT marks a major division (ס) before 4:1. The new story begins with a *qatal* followed by three consecutive verbs ("And *Adam knew Chavvah*, his woman, and *then she became pregnant, and then she bore, and then she said*"). Then in 4:2a, "*then she bore* Abel his brother." With 4:2b and 4:3 comes היה as a *wayyiqtol*, "then it came to be." No break is to be made with 4:2 or 4:3 because היה or *wayᵉhiy* (= *wayyᵉhiy*) is not a sign of a new section necessarily or at all in these chapters. Although the MT places a divisional ס after 5:31, the next verse (5:32) does not start a new section because both verses begin with the subordinate *wayᵉhiy* followed by *wayyiqtol* actions ("It came about that *he died*" . . . "It came about that *he fathered*"). But 6:1 fronts a *wayᵉhiy* and then employs a *qatal* as a main action verb ("It came to be that humanity *began* to increase").¹¹ The divisional marker in the MT after verse 31 indicates that verse 32 provides a transition to a new section. Noah had three sons, and this sets the stage for humanity producing offspring in 6:1. Noah having these sons is repeated in 6:10 and 6:10–13 mirrors 5:32—6:3 (Noah's sons are born into a world so wicked that God decides to punish humanity). The *qatal* in 6:4 (from היה) is subordinate to

---

9. Translations often gloss over the verb "to be" in 4:2b. The two instances could be translated "and Abel *was* [*wayyiqtol*] a shepherd of flocks, but Cain *was* [*qatal*] a tiller of the soil," or alternatively, as pluperfects or past conditionals, "and Abel had become/ became . . . but Cain had become/became." This touches on the discussion over the option of translating והארץ היתה (*qatal* of היה) in 1:2 as "but the earth had become" or "and then the earth became" instead of the traditional "and/but the earth was." The *qatal* in 4:2b follows the mood set by the previous *wayyiqtol*. In 1:2 the *qatal* begins the statement. The *qatal* of היה in Genesis 1–6 appears in 1:2; 2:24; 3:1, 5, 20, 22; 4:2, 14, 20, 21; 6:3, 4, 9, 21. In 2:24 the form *wehāyū* (same as in 6:3b; pp. 37–38 below) is a *weqataltiy* (inverted perfect), meaning "they will become" (cf. 3:5, 20). In 2:25 the *wayyiqtol* means "were" (since they did not then "become" naked but already were so). In 3:1 the serpent did not become but was (*we* . . . *hāyāh* just as in 1:2) crafty. 3:22 requires "has become" not "became" (היה without preceding or prefixed *waw* unlike 1:2).

10. Respectively, "he was" (*qatal*); "you will be" (*w-qataltiy*; equivalent to a *yiqtol*); "she was [or 'would become']" (*qatal*); and "he has become" (*qatal*). Note the three different possibilities of tense for the *qatal* (past indicative, present conditional, and perfect indicative). See n. 9 above.

11. In 5:31 Lamach lived (*wayyiqtol* of היה) and then he died (*wayyiqtol*). In 5:32 Noah lived (*wayyiqtol* of היה) and then he bore (*wayyiqtol*).

the main action that daughters "bore" (*wayyiqtol*) mighty men, as *wayᵉhiy* is subordinate in 6:1 to the main actions that humans "began" (*qatal*) to increase and daughters "were born" (passive *qatal*). So, 6:4 belongs with 6:1–3 thematically and grammatically. The use of a *wayyiqtol not* based on היה ("then he saw") in verse 5 marks a new emphasis but not a new topic.

Genesis 6:1-4 as a Chiasm

The recognition of a chiasm in Genesis 6:1–4 is generated by the clear demarcation of verses 1–4 as a unit and the unique nature of verse 3 as the climax. Along with this is the observation that verse 1 parallels 4b and 2 mirrors 4a.

Lexical/Conceptual Symmetry

Comparable words, expressions, or ideas exist in the parallel parts of these verses. In verse 1 the statement that "men" (אדם) began to increase (or become important) is mirrored in 4b by the information that mighty and important (שׁם; "name") "men" (אישׁ) were born when the "sons of God" were having sexual intercourse with human women. Note that אדם does appear in 6:1, 2, 3, 4a, and 4b with the chiastic order of subject-adjective-direct object-adjective-subject. While the "men" of verse 1 are humans, those of 4b are males, but only human ones. Whether they are or are not the same as the נפלים in 4a, they are human. At the same time, the humans (male and female) of verse 1 and the human males of 4b are notable in terms of quantity and/or quality. The former produce human daughters (בנות האדם; explained in v. 2) and the latter are born to the same daughters (v. 4aii). The parallel is that both parts of the unit speak of numerous or notable people and their connection to these human women. Although the full idea of "human daughters" is spelled out in verse 2, the "daughters" of verse 1 are the same kind. Therefore, these human daughters appear in verses 1, 2, 4a, and 4b (although 4b has "them": daughters [v. 1]; human daughters [v. 2]; human daughters [v. 4a]; they [v. 4b]). This is a kind of chiasm, leaving verse 3 as unique in not referring to these daughters.

A	daughters (unspecified)	1
B	human daughters (specified)	2
B'	human daughters (specified)	4a
A'	they (unspecified)	4b

Only verses 2 and 4a mention the "sons of God." These two parts bracket the exceptional verse 3, the only place YHWH is mentioned. Here is the fulcrum of the unit, the only place where YHWH's response to the behavior of people is recorded, and it is placed in the center of observations about human sexual activity. In 6:2 these "sons/descendants of God/the gods" (whoever they are) "take" women at will.[12] This suggests rape and capture. In verse 4a they impregnate these women. The "children" (literally "they [the daughters] birthed [males] to them [the sons of God]") highlighted in verse 4aii are restricted in 4b to "mighty males" (גברים, איש). Verses 2 and 4a (the B and B' elements) not only are restricted to the sons of God but also to the mention of the נשים ("women; wives") and נפלים ("fallen ones; tall ones"), respectively. Could this rare term נפלים also be feminine plural originally as is נשים? In 6:2 these "women" were taken by the sons of God. In 4a the "fallen/tall [females?]" were existing in the land when the sons of God were lusting after beautiful women to marry or with whom to fornicate and produce offspring. Women taken and raped might

---

12. Translations say they "married" any they desired, but the text (while marriage could be assumed) only says these women were taken, any and all these "sons of God" wanted, due to their beauty. The implication is that only the most attractive were taken by force, suggesting a lustful motive, so some were likely wives (in a polygamist setting) and most or all became pregnant. Conversely, VanGemeren explains this "taking" as the normal Hebrew idiom for legal marriage, so could not indicate unnatural unions (VanGemeren, "Sons of God," 321–34). However, here, the "taking of women" is further defined as "any and all they chose." This at best is polygamy and at worst enslaved women or concubines with whom intercourse was by force or resignation. Clines depicts the "dynastic ruler" view of the "sons of God" as involving despots engaged in forcing women into royal harems or indiscriminate rape. For Clines this approach has the merit of taking the phrase just mentioned in Genesis 6:2 seriously. In reference to Westermann, Clines mentions the violent lust of the "sons of God" having OT antecedents or parallels (where perhaps beauty of women led to immorality) in Genesis 12:10–20, 2 Samuel 11, and especially Lamech's taking of two women (Gen 4:19), which diverged from God giving Adam a woman. He cites Bonhoeffer's expression of unrestrained sexuality as well, making a parallel with Genesis 11. See Clines, "Significance," 339–43. See also Westermann, *Genesis*, 494–97; and Bonhoeffer, *Creation and Fall*, 80.

have been considered fallen (morally) as women already not virgins.[13] The lexical chiasm is as follows:

A *Numerous* (great; רבב) humans, *birthed* (ילד) *daughters* 1
  B "Sons of God" lust after ("see") *daughters* 2ai
    and take נשים 2aii
    C YHWH impatient with humans (spirit vs. flesh) 3
  B' נפלים in the land 4ai
    "Sons of God" impregnate ("came to") *daughters* 4aii
A' *Birthed* (ילד) males 4aiii
= *Notable* (great name; שם) males, heroes (גברים) [*born*] 4b

The verb ילד "to give birth" is used only in verses 1 and 4. In verse 1 daughters were born (*yullᵉdū*) to men and then in verse 4 they had children born (*wᵉyālᵉdū*) to them after being impregnated by certain men. In 6:2 men took any woman they desired and in verse 4 these same men went (after) these women. Also, in only verses 2 and 4 are these men identified as the בני האלהים. The marriage or rape mentioned in 6:2 implies the birth of children, but 6:2 uniquely names and describes these offspring as הנפלים and famous warriors (הגברים). Verse 3 stands alone describing YHWH's disappointment with humanity and his determination to render judgment upon all humans. The verse therefore sets between the bookends of 6:1–2 and 6:4. All of the verses mention humans (אדם). It is used as a direct object only in verse 3 (the chiastic center), as an adjective only in 6:2 and 6:4a, on either side of the center, and only as a subject in verse 1 (which is implied in v. 4b), forming the A/A' border. Also, ארץ "earth" appears only in 6:1 and 4.

Grammatical Symmetry

The opening *wayyiqtol* ("then it came to be") and the *qatal*, with temporal כי, plus infinitive ("when they began to increase"), provide an introduction (1a, before *athnach* disjunctive) to the narrative, which begins properly with the passive *qatal* "they were born." This parallels the reliance on the *qatal* form in verse 4. No *qatal* form appears in verse 3 as it does in all

13. Greek *numphē* ("bride, young wife" later "beautiful young women" and "beautiful young goddess") and Hebrew *nepiliᵞm* share enough letters to beg the question if the etymology of the Greek word is Semitic so that one ancient use of *n-p[h]-l-m* was for youthful and beautiful (morally fallen?) women. See discussion below on p. 34. In ancient Greek, *numphē* meant "bride." Cf. related terms at http://www.etymonline.com.

THE FORM AND FUNCTION OF GENESIS 6:1–4

other verses of this section about the בני האלהים. 6:1b-2, therefore, comprises the first level of the narrative and the chiasm. This is followed by a verse (3) in which a *w^{e}qataltiy* verb uniquely appears as well as a future/jussive ("should") *yiqtol*. These mark verse 3 as structurally and verbally independent, providing the fulcrum for the chiastic arrangement: A(1–2)/B(3)/A'(4). The *yiqtol* of verse 4 ("they came") seems out of place since a past-tense is required, but a consecutive (*wayyiqtol*) would not work in a temporal clause ("the *n^{e}pili^{y}m* were in the land at that time and afterwards, when the בני האלהים came) Consequently, to preserve the symmetry with 6:1b–2, a *yiqtol* was chosen for aesthetic reasons. Also, the *yiqtol* allows for a precative (subjunctive, "would") sense that fits better in the temporal setting: "whenever the בני האלהים would come." The *yiqtol* of verse 3 may also be interpreted as a precative future ("my *rûaḥ* should not remain") preceding the indicative future *w^{e}qataltiy* (perfect of certitude; "the days must be"). A *yiqtol* forms the center for the three main verbs in 6:3 and 4 and a *wayyiqtol* for 6:1b–2. LXX does not follow the chiastic nature of the verb forms in the MT:

V.	X		MT Hebrew Verb	MT Form	MT Function	LXX Greek Verb	MT Translation
1a	A	a	ויהי	*wayyiqtol*	preterite consecutive	aorist indicative	"Then it was"
		b	החל + לרב	*qatal* + infin. const.	past temporal	aorist indicative + infinitive	"when they began to add"
1b1-2	B	a	ילדו	*w ... qatal*	past indicative	aorist indicative passive	"and .... they were born"
		b	ויראו	*wayyiqtol*	preterite consecutive	aorist participle	"Then they saw"
		b	ויקחו	*wayyiqtol*	preterite consecutive	aorist indicative	"then they took"
		a'	בחרו	*qatal*	past indicative	aorist indicative	"they wanted"
3	C	a	ויאמר	*wayyiqtol*	preterite consecutive	aorist indicative	"Then he said"
		b	ידון	*yiqtol*	future jussive	aorist subjunctive	"it should [not] remain"
		a'	והיו	*w-qataltiy*	future certainty	future indicative	"they must be"

4a	B'	a	היו	qatal	past indicative	Imperfect active indicative	"they were"
		b	יבאו	yiqtol	past subjunctive	Imperfect active indicative	"they would come"
		a'	וילדו	weqatal	past indicative	imperfect active indicative	"they fathered"
4b	A'	[a]	[היו]	[qatal]	[past indicative]	Imperfect active indicative	"they were"

Metrical Symmetry

In addition to lexical parallels, numerical symmetry may be found between the stanzas. The word count of 6:3 is fifteen, while verse 4 contains only three less words (twenty-three) than 6:1–2 combined (twenty-six). This creates a 26/15/23 chiasm, but if 6:4 is viewed in two parts an 11/15/15/15/8 word-count chiasm results:

A 11 words   v. 1 (ending at *soph pasuq*)
 B 15 words   v. 2 (ending at *soph pasuq*)
  C 15 words   v. 3 (ending at *soph pasuq*)
 B' 15 words   v. 4ai (ending at *zaqeph qaton*)
A' 8 words   v. 4aii-b (ending at *soph pasuq*)

The division of 6:4 conceptually and numerically is best accomplished by making the first major disjunction at *zaqeph qaton* (4ai). The next two Hebrew words ("they-birthed to-them"), before the *athnach*, fit with the following text until the *soph pasuq* (4aii–4b). This results in:

A Men (humans) increase and daughters are born   v. 1
 B Sons of God see daughters and   v. 2a
     take women (*nashiym*)   v. 2b
  C YHWH decides to punish fleshly people   v. 3
 B' Sons of God go to the daughters   v. 4aiβ
     at time of fallen ones (*nepiliym*)   v. 4aiα
A' Important and heroic men (males) are born   v. 4aii–4b

Syllable count, consequently, results in a 26, 34, 34, 37, 21 chiasm:

A	26 syllables	v. 1 (ending at *soph pasuq*)
B	34 syllables	v. 2 (ending at *soph pasuq*)
C	34 syllables	v. 3 (ending at *soph pasuq*)
B'	37 syllables	v. 4a (ending at *zaqeph qaton*)
A'	21 syllables	v. 4b (ending at *soph pasuq*)

The Content of the Chiastic Levels

A//A' Many Men//Mighty Men (vv. 1//4aii–4b)

The outer levels ostensibly speak of mankind (being numerous, v. 1) and certain males (being renowned, v. 4b), but the emphasis in verse 1 on having daughters (as opposed to only sons) in light of this parallel could indicate a focus on "male" humans in 6:1 as well as in 4b. Fathers were having daughters (further defined in v. 2 as בנות האדם, human daughters) and these daughters gave birth to men/males of (אנשי) "name" = "fame." The men of 6:1 were becoming "great" (Heb. רב; apparently in number but perhaps also or alternatively in size, power, and/or wealth).[14] The males (אנש) of 6:4 are *gibborim* and perhaps also *nephilim*. But 6:4a parallels 6:2 (both about the human daughters married to or at least impregnated by the "Elohimites"), so, setting aside the *N/nephilim* for the moment, the males in 6:4b that parallel those in 6:1 are "strong/powerful" or "mighty" and perhaps "tyrannical," "large," or "brutal" (גבר *gbr*).[15] 6:1 and 4b may mirror each other as great/important men having daughters and then daughters having great/important men.

B//B' Sons of the Gods::nashim //
Sons of the Gods::nephilim (vv. 2//4ai)

The בני האלהים appear only in 6:2 and 4a, also bracketing the focal point of 6:3. These are being understood as polytheists or followers of only *Elohim* ("El, the most powerful One"). They also could be descended from Cain (elsewhere called Kenites).[16] In 6:2 they "took" any human woman they

---

14. See the possible meanings of רב (from רבב) in *HALOT*, s.v. רב.

15. See the possible meanings of גבר in *HALOT*, s.v. גבר.

16. The traditional view of these as "angels" has received what should be an exegetical death blow by VanGemeren, who defends the Sethite view ("sons of *Elohim*";

wanted and in 6:4aii they fathered children/sons by these women born to the great men of 6:1 and perhaps 4b. The attempts to make "took" mean "raped" are appealing but not proven. The women could have been taken into marriage (as most translations prefer) as an acceptable idiom. Since they bore children by these men who took them in 6:4aii, marriage is again suggested although not required. Also, these "Elohimites" are not characterized as "strong" or "brutal" as the great men in 6:1 and 4b (who are their sons—so has the apple fallen far from the tree?). Neither are the N/*nephilim* "fallen ones" equated with these possible polytheists but are another social entity or also the mighty ones who are sons of the "Elohimites."[17]

A curious aspect of this parallel between 6:2 and 4ai is the possible juxtaposition of the "women" (נשים) and the נפלים ("fallen ones"; giants?). Ancient Greek νυμφη (*nymphē*) was "bride" (see n. 13 above). A number of translations do not represent the presence of the word "wives/women" except to say something like "they married any they chose." In this case, "married" stands idiomatically for the longer phrase in the text "they took to themselves women." So נשים is often unnoticed in translation. Yet it is there in the MT and suggests a parallel with נפלים, except that the latter has a masculine form so is understood to represent males. However, the word for "women" in this case also has what appears to be a masculine location yet derived from אישה, which is feminine. In 6:4 the word for "men of" is אנשי (from אנוש; absolute counterpart is אישם "men" or אנשם "males" in other places in the OT). The words man/male and woman/female should not be confused and have different, although uncertain, etymologies. Ugaritic

---

VanGemeren, "Sons of God," 332–34, but esp. 343–48). This is contextually supportable except that a chiastic structure and other data suggest "sons of the gods" or polytheists are being described. The Cainite interpretation is advanced in the commentary by S. D. Luzatto (see Spero, "Sons of God?," 16, n. 4). Spero also lists at least five ways "sons of ha-ʾelohim" has been interpreted over the years as noted by Rabbi David Tzvi Hoffmann (Spero, "Sons of God?," 16). The "angel" view is surpassed contextually, historically, and exegetically by all others. Bible readers of all theological persuasions need to abandon it.

17. John Day argues against any Mesopotamian or Greek background for one fully Canaanite. The "sons of God" motif derives from the "sons of El," and the term *nephilim* is retrospective for *rephaim* (originally meaning "dead"; cf. Ugaritic *rpʾum*), indicating that these unusual beings ("giants"?) have died away. See Day, "Sons of God," 427–47. S. Spero speaks of the women being rapaciously abducted, but also goes so far as to imagine that the "sons of God" were *homo sapiens* and the "daughters of men" female Neanderthals. The predatory males interbred with these fair women causing a breakdown in the genetic process and leading to ("gigantic"?) offspring like these and the "sons of Anak" who terrorized and tyrannized others. See Spero, "Sons of God?," 17.

for "wife/woman" is ʾatt and for man/male" is *mt, bmš* or ʾadm.[18] There is interchange among letters in some Semitic languages (e.g., Ugaritic *t* can become š/שׁ [= sh] in Hebrew). The final "t" on Ugaritic "woman" is a standard feminine ending, but in Hebrew the form in the plural took on the -*im* as the male plural. In terms of structure, the author had the opportunity to mention the *nāšîm* in the section counterpart to that with *nᵉpilîm*. Perhaps this underscores that the "fallen ones" were the result of sexual union between the sons of אלהים ("gods"/God?) and the נשים (the women they "took") as is reiterated in verse 4aii. This observation could settle the confusion often shown when commentators say that the identity of the Nephilim as the children mentioned in the same verse is not obvious; i.e., it could be that the Nephilim existed when these children were born but are not necessarily to be equated with them.[19] But if they are distinct, is there a solution?

Nᵉpilîm is a rare and mysterious term and it may not have the same history as the term in Numbers 13:33, since Genesis 6 reflects pre-flood mythology. Could it be that the word in Genesis was a loan word from another language? Could a later editor have paired it with *nāšîm* due to the similar endings for poetic purposes? Several social units are in this passage, actually or potentially: the Adamites, the Nashim, the Elohimists, the Nephilim, the Yahwists, and Gibborim. The proposed chiasm (see above, pp. 29–33) parallels the *nashim* ("women"?) with the *nephilim* ("fallen [man and/or women]"?). The syntax of verse 4 is awkward, all admit, making it unclear if these *nephilim* are, or are not, the result of the interbreeding between the "Elohimists" and the *nashim* (daughters of the Adamites). Note also, while it could be said that the *îm* ending of *nephilim* is masculine, the word for "women" has the same ending. All this being the case, *nephilim* could be another designation for the *nashim* (so v. 4a, where "fallen ones" exist, can restate v. 2, where women are taken). So, is it possible that the text speaks of fallen women or forced brides? Alternatively this נפל may have nothing to do with the regular Hebrew root, and may have entered the ancient vocabulary from other related languages.[20] These data could make

---

18. See Segert, *A Basic Grammar*, 178, 180, 193; Segert, "A Short Vocabulary"; and Bennett, *Comparative Semitic Linguistics*, 136, 227.

19. This proximity is recognized by Day, "Sons of God," 427–47, as well as admitted as a valid option by VanGemeren, "Sons of God," 334.

20. The ancient Greek word for "bride" is *nymphē*, so *n-ph-l* could have been loaned into Greek or from proto-Greek into ancient Semitic, making *n-ph-l-m* an alternative word for "women that are made brides" and, hence, available as a parallel counterpart for abducted *nashim* ("women; wives"). Greek types of language are dated before the

the women perhaps taken by force into marriage in verse 2 restated by the *n-ph-l* term in verse 4 as "[forced] brides," which is consistent with the possibility this word is a *niphal* of פלל indicating "subdued ones" to parallel the earlier women (taken by force). This interpretation assumes the difficult syntax of verse 4 is not equating the *nephili[y]m* with the *gibbori[y]m*. Rather the author merely recognizes that the former were on the earth at the same time.[21]

---

later Greek Empire of Classical Greek as far back as the mid-third century BC. Classical Hebrew did not have separate words as we do in English to distinguish "woman" and "wife" (unless *nephish/nephilah/nephilim* did exist for that purpose). In the OT a single woman is a woman and a wife is a man's woman. A woman is also a "female man" (a man is an 'ish and a woman an 'ishah; cf. English "man" and "wo-man"; based on the biblical assertion in Genesis 2 that she would be named "woman" for she "came out of" the "man"). Such ideas reflect the ancient chauvinism but do not prescribe it merely because the OT accurately records how people thought. 'adam means either "Adam" or "human" or "the [male]-man." *Nāshiym* ("women") is the plural of 'ishah ("wo-man"). In Genesis 6:4b another word for "man [male]" other than 'adam is seen, "men of" 'anshēy (from 'ish). This is merely the plural of 'ish. In the OT, 'enōsh is also used for "human being" and also the name of one of the sons of Seth (cf. Ugaritic *ansh* "be manly"). Bn-'nsh "son of human" led to *bunushu* "human being" in Akkadian (cf. Arabic 'insān "human"; see *HALOT*, s.v. אנוש).

21. From the viewpoint of ancient mythology, the text might recognize legends about both "giant" (in name, number, or stature) women (Amazonian?) and men (Herculean?). This is not to say the author wrote later than these Greek myths but that earlier literary prototypes of such legendary and giant warriors of either gender may have existed. Related is the LXX translation of נפלים as γίγαντες. In Greek mythology the mention of *gigantes* goes back to the sixth-century BC. Mosaic the Hebrew text goes back as much as nearly 1,000 years, but in its final edited form could approximate the Greek poets. Some relate the "falling" idea to the concept of "giants" that resulted from divine miscarriages and were hurled down to earth. Others see this as pointing to heroes fallen in battle or supposed large inhabitants of Canaan spied by the first Hebrews to enter (Num 13:33; linking them to or with the Anakim, ענקים; see *HALOT* s.v., נפלים). The Greek "giants" were not necessarily huge in size but could also be in significance, strength, or their striving (see Muraoka, *Greek-English* Lexicon, 130). In the mythology they fought the Olympian gods and were born of the (Mother) Earth after it/she was impregnated with blood from the castrated (Father) Sky, but others say Tartarus was the Father (see Hesiod's *Theogony*, http://www.perseus.tufts.edu/ hopper/text?doc=Hes.+Th.+185). The Greek OT at Genesis 6:4 says these *gigantes* "were on the earth at that time." This coupled with the fact that *gigantes* suggests "earthborn" in the *Theogony* may indicate that the Greek translators had a connection to Greek mythology in mind, which should not be read back uncritically into the Hebrew author's world view. Over centuries of Greek literature these "giants" gradually grew less and less human (see Zimmerman, *Dictionary*, 111, 126, 264–65). There remains the possibility of disregarding the MT pointing and reading the Hebrew word not as based on *n-p-l* but *p-l-l* or *p-w-l*, or a bygone homograph *n-p-l*, reflecting a Semitic root pre-dating and loaned into Hebrew. But no extant semantic

Notably, men/mankind is always ’*ādām* until this last verse, where the idiom "men of name" occurs. This is because humanity is in view in each case until these particular male heroes are mentioned. This casts doubt on a strict parallel between humans as males in 6:1a and male warriors in 4b. But even if we think of humanity in 6:1a, the focus still seems to be on the fact that fathers had daughters, although of course they do not produce daughters without help (so ’*ādām* in v. 1 allows for this reality). The word גבר has been related to Arabic *jabbār* meaning omnipotent (God), giant, or Orion, leading to "tyrant" in regard to Isaiah 49:25.[22] A connection to "angels" was based on "mighty ones of strength" (גברי כח) in Psalm 103:20, which there parallels "messengers" (מלאכים). It has to be noted that the translation "angel" prejudices such a term as "messenger" (which may or may not refer to a heavenly or spirit being), so a cross reference to a translation of Psalm 103 could be misleading in terms of clarifying Genesis 6.[23]

C YHWH's Response (v. 3)

The fulcrum or climax of the chiastic pericope of Genesis 6:1–4 is verse 3. It begins with ויאמר יהוה "Therefore YHWH said [due to the indiscriminate taking (raping?) of (multiple?) women]" (v. 3ai). What he said was "My *rūaḥ* [S/spirit?] will not always [עולם] remain [דון] with the אדם in that also he [is] flesh [בשר]" (v. 3aii). The final part of the verse begins with *wᵉhāyū*, which could be taken formally as either a *weqatal* (past tense) or *wᵉqataltiy* (future tense; see n. 13 above). Is the initial *waw* the sign of an inverted tense (on the analogy of the *wayyiqtol*) or merely the conjunction prefixed to a suffixed-conjugation form? The subject either way is "his days" (meaning

---

data are useful. Akkadian *palālu* means "supervise" (*HALOT*, s.v. פלל, citing von Soden, *Akkadisches Handwörterbuch*, 813); but cf. older *CAD*, XII:50–51. A theoretical *hapax* Hebrew root *p-l-l* (although formally masc. pl.), if a passive form, would mean perhaps "the subordinated ones." The word הנפלים could be taken as an arthrous *niphal* (masc. pl.) participle absolute of [פלל].

22. *HALOT*, s.v. גבר, where "brute" is conjectured. Nimrod was a *gibbōr* on the earth and a *gibbōr* of hunting (game) in Genesis 10:8–9. Often 10:8 is translated "mighty [warrior]" as a proposal, and some have asked if he hunted people or animals or both. In Isaiah 49:25 these "mighty ones" are parallel with עריץ "ruthless [tyrants]" and are taken captive.

23. Some translations of Ps 103:21 have "heavenly hosts" when the term heavenly is actually not in the text. The term צבא "host" is restated by "servants" and is sometimes translated "warrior." Some relate "גבר of strength [כח]" in Ps 103:20 to "angels" since the phrase parallels "his messengers" (מלאכים).

mankind's time span). But are these men just the transgressors described in 6:1–2 or every living human at that time in history or the story? And is this time period the length of (years of) an average human life or the time left until something yet undisclosed happens (or something that has already transpired)? The use of the future-tense *yiqtol* "will [not] remain" suggests a future orientation is best for the last statement of this verse.[24] When the past tense with the verb is intended the author places the subject first and then the verb as the start of verse 4, without the conjunction *waw*: הנפלים היו "the Nephilim [they] were." Also, as a *wᵉqataltiy*, it is the only time this verb form appears in the pericope, highlighting this unique center-point verse (3) around which the chiasm and content of 6:1–4 revolves. Yet as a future tense the question remains what exactly is being forecast in verse 3b. How will these human's time be restricted to 120 years? The meaning has to be related to what is said in 3a, which itself is open to interpretation.

Traditional versions use "spirit" for *rūaḥ* in 3ai (some add the upper-case "S" to indicate the Holy Spirit; however, this cannot be what YHWH would have intended to say to this author since he could not have perceived such a Trinitarian idea.) Yet what is YHWH's "spirit"? How would it not remain with these humans? Some translate this verb "contend" (NIV) or "abide" (NRSV) to avoid the awkward notion of this divine "spirit" being in or with men who have committed such terrible crimes. In this way, "spirit" is an attitude, something like YHWH's tolerance.[25] For Childs, "regardless of what the original meaning of the [120] years was, in its present position one cannot help seeing some connection with a period of grace before the coming catastrophe."[26] If, however, 6:3b is about longevity then "breath" for *rūaḥ* would make more sense (i.e., the breath of life given by God would not remain in these [all?] humans [on average?] more than the years specified). A problem with the longevity view is that the threat seems to be applied specifically to humans alive at that time, and specifically those womanizers, who were idolizing external beauty and impregnating (see v. 4) multiple women by force. Another problem is that a life-span of 120 years was not experienced by the survivors of the flood and the next generation or so

---

24. Day proposes deriving ידון from דנן "be strong" rather than the traditional דין "abide." For Day this supports the interpretation that humans were seeking immortality from divine marriages, so God plans to punish them and not allow them to obtain this spiritual strength or power (Day, "Sons of God," 427–47).

25. Some equate God's "spirit" *rūaḥ* with his "breath" *neshāmāh* in Genesis 2:7. See Clines, "Significance," 349.

26. Childs, *Myth and Reality*, 58.

(Noah lived to be 950, 9:29; Terah, 205, 11:32; Abraham, 175, 25:7). When we get to humans who began to experience 120 years on average, this interpretation means that the punishment of 6:3b is applied to a much later and innocent (of the crimes of 6:1–4) generation. The words of 6:3b are spoken as an indictment on humanity living at that time, living in a manner that upset YHWH and led to his sorrow over creating these humans (6:5), ultimately deciding to wipe them all out (save Noah's family) with a flood (6:6–8, 11–18). Taking all this into account, the most reasonable explanation of the warning given in 6:3b is that YHWH's moral sensibilities would not indefinitely (עוֹלָם) tolerate such (violent; cf. 6:11–13) abuse of women, so humans would be allowed 120 years more (until judgment day; i.e., again justified in 6:5–7 and described in 6:8—8:14, with the literary transition to Noah in 6:7–8).[27]

Conclusion

This examination of Genesis 6:1–4 has observed a number of features that argue strongly for an intended chiastic structure in general of A (6:1) B (6:2) C (6:3) B' (6:4a) A' (6:4b). The main supports for this are the parallels between (1) men of number and men of name in verses 1 and 4b, and (2) the sons of God and daughters of men in verses 2 and 4a, leaving verse 3 isolated and unique as the climax of the chiasm, wherein the intolerable conditions of 6:1–2 and 4 are judged with the plan to end current humanity within 120 years. The possibility of understanding the נפלים of verse 4a (B') in light of 6:2 (B) is provided by the proof of a chiasm, yet what exactly is clarified by this parallel (especially between the נשים and נפלים) remains uncertain. A very tentative conjecture regarding the curious and controversial הנפלים of Genesis 6:4 was based on ignoring the MT vocalization and proposing a *niphal* participle of II פלל ("subdued ones" // the "taken

27. If, however, one views this text as representative of early ANE mythological (religious/theological) thinking, Genesis 6:1–4 can be taken more at face value as an etiology of how people came to have shorter life spans, spirit beings no longer had intercourse with humans, and why the great flood happened. The "period of respite" is favored over the "human longevity" view also by Clines (Clines, "Significance," 349-50). He points to the Atrahasis epic, where the span of time between certain catastrophic events and the catastrophic climax of the flood is 1,200 years. The numbers 120 and 1,200 may both be sourced in the Babylonian sexagesimal system. That both myths have the sequence of creation, human multiplication, and flood suggests that the biblical 120 years had the same time gap function as the 1,200 in the Babylonian flood tradition. See also Lambert and Millard, *Atrahasis*, 66-73; and Millard, "New Babylonian," 13.

women" of v. 2; B//B' in the chiasm), this Hebrew verb being a proposed *hapax legomenon* and homograph on the analogy of Akkadian *palālu* ("to supervise; subdue," allowing for "subjugate"). Contextually and culturally, the 120 years of verse 3b is best understood as the time remaining until the flood comes in light of a similar time gap used in the Babylonian flood myth. The *rūaḥ* in 6:3a is used for God's temperament (such immoral activity as in vv. 1–2 will not be tolerated "indefinitely" [עוֹלָם]). This verse is isolated as a fulcrum or climax by the presence of a one-time *wᵉqataltiy* verb (perfect or *qatal* with inversive *waw*).

3

The Sin of Shinar in Genesis 11:4[1]

Introduction

THIS article was sparked by P. J. Harland's observation that, "The account of the building of the Tower of Babel in Gen. xi presents an enigma. In contrast to the other stories of the primeval history the sin which the people commit is not made explicit."[2] Harland discusses the two different traditional views: (1) the Christian interpretation that the sin was that of human pride trying to take power from God, and (2) the Jewish explanation that the sin was failure to comply with God's mandate after the flood (Gen 9:1) to disperse and fill the earth. What follows will challenge the popular understanding of the sin committed by the builders of the tower of Babel as religious rebellion, i.e., disregard for the command given in Genesis 9:1 to populate the earth and/or pride and self-sufficiency that led the Shinarites to "storm the heavens" and rival God by erecting a tower so tall as to threaten God.

According to Chrysostom, the people who migrated from the East to found Babylon were motivated by ambition and pride. He saw this text as a warning to those who seek fame through building mansions for themselves. Augustine interpreted this pride in terms of defiance of God's power,

---

1. Originally published as Marlowe, "Sin of Shinar," 29–39. Stylistic and corrective but no substantive changes have been made.

2. Harland, "Vertical or Horizontal," 515. Luther also thought that "This chapter [11] does not indicate clearly wherein the sins of the builders of the Tower of Babel consisted" (Pelikan, *Luther's Works*, 2:210).

and Dionysius said they were giants, whose power worried God, who were seeking salvation by human means.[3] None of these seem to find a connection between the sin of Shinar and God's command to fill the earth, as is now so popular. Augustine seems to be the fountainhead of the idea that the transgression was essentially religious in terms of aggression against God's rule directly. Defying God may be a logical assumption but not the only possible one, and likely not the most probable. The text shows them behaving ungodly but not necessarily anti-godly.

We agree with Skinner, "the idea of storming heaven and making war on the gods, which is suggested by some late forms of the legend (cf. Homer's *Odessy* Xi. 313ff.), is no doubt foreign to the passage"[4] and with von Rad, "That men wanted to storm heaven, God's dwelling place [cf. Isa 14:13] is not said."[5] Man's self-exaltation is checked by God, as Skinner notes, but the issue is what kind of prideful purpose was involved.[6] Isaiah 14:13 is about an Assyrian king's ambition to be deified and sit among the divine council on the sacred mountain top (which is another setting than the ziggurat). We suggest pride in Genesis 11 was exhibited through power: violence and oppression against humanity. The problem was first and foremost horizontal (which is inevitably vertical). Of course, warfare and enslavement of others had become their focus by already having abandoned any religious instructions they may have had about the sinfulness of such behavior.

The idea that Genesis 11:1 places the story at a time when one and only one language was in existence globally will be questioned.[7] The pur-

---

3. See Louth, *Ancient Christian Commentary*, 166-70, citing Catholic University, *Fathers of Church*, 14:495-99; 48:170; 67:66-67; 78:138-39; 82:222-29; 91:147-48; Pseudo-Dionysius, *Pseudo-Dionysius*, 282; and *Corpus Christianorum*, 128:79.

4. Skinner, *Genesis*, 226.

5. Rad, *Genesis*, 149.

6. Skinner, *Genesis*, 229.

7. For related literature see Jubilees 10:18; *Sibylline Oracles* 3:100 in Charlesworth, *Old Testament Pseudepigrapha II*, 76, and *Old Testament Pseudepigrapha I*, 364; Josephus, *Antiquities*, 1:118, 57; for rabbinic views: Pearl, *Commentaries*, 39; Milton, *Paradise Lost*, XX; Westermann, *Genesis 1-11*, 734; Wenham, *Genesis 1-15*, 245; Hamilton, *Book of Genesis*, 356; and others, in addition to the famous painting by Pieter Brueghel (which has probably influenced popular belief more than the Bible or any book, except Bible books for children or lectures, and is likely equaled by fundamentalist sermons). See Hiebert, "Tower of Babel," 29, citing Kugel, "Tower of Babel," 228-42 (for a review of early interpreters); Hiebert, "Babble or Blueprint?," 127-45, for a review of interpretations until the present. Westermann, *Genesis 1-11*, 719-21, warns against an interpretation that focuses on a particular place or tower, yet also traditionally says their sin was forcing their way into God's presence.

pose of this article is primarily to show that the current and common view still leaves important questions unanswered or not answered satisfactorily. A secondary goal is to make a modest proposal for a valid alternative understanding that the sin of Genesis 11:4 that led to God's dispersion of these people was not religious but ruthless: a preoccupation with military might and violence. The view that the sin was something other than or more than religious is not original, but I hope to add more fuel to the fire of the debate, reawaken it, and demonstrate some weaknesses of the traditional view as well as strengths of this proposal.[8] The argument of this article is that a prideful desire for world conquest is the evil that God judges, not pride that tried to reject or resist God per se; so the tower was for military not religious purposes (although ironically if it was a temple to rival or replace God, or engage in idolatry as some claim [cf. Genesis Rabbah], then that in a sense would be an irreligious purpose by definition, i.e., men making

---

8. Besides Harland's approach (see n. 2 above), Hiebert has made the proposal that this story is about the tension between cultural solidarity and diversity (cultural injustice; Hiebert, "Tower of Babel," 29–58). He argues that Genesis 11:1–9 has no focus on pride and punishment but exclusively explains why the world has a diversity of cultures. It has even been suggested that Jesus had this story in mind when he taught his disciples about counting the cost of discipleship. He told his disciples the parables of the tower builder and the king going to war (Luke 14:25–33), which interestingly combines a story of building of a tower with one about warfare. See Jarvis, "Expounding Parables," 196–98. Jacques Ellul gave a brilliant treatment of the meaning of such a city in the ancient world. He spoke of the inevitability of the city, due to the motives for its creation, needing to conquer the "country" and of its necessary spiritual power for good or evil. Nimrod accomplished his "hunting" of men through city building. In the same context of the building of Babylon in Shinar in Genesis 10 is also the reference to Nineveh in Assyria (also "built" by "Nimrod"). According to Nahum 3:1, Nineveh was a city of falsehood, violence, and plunder. This is the legacy of city building in human history. See Ellul, *Meaning of City*, 8–22.

themselves divine, a religious yet false religious activity.)⁹ Whoever these people were, they could be held accountable for violent behavior.¹⁰

One Language and Travel from The East (11:1–2)

Chapter 11 begins with the statement not that the entire global world had one language only but that an entire specific region ("the land") somehow came to have "one tongue and a common vocabulary."¹¹ Even the mention of tribes moving out across כל–הארץ should be viewed as only the expansion of various people groups as delimited by Genesis 10 to a large region of the earth, yet not the entire earth. This would suggest already a number of

---

9. Some non-traditional views on the nature of the sin regard the tower not as a ziggurat but a siege or watch tower (see Uehlinger, *Weltreich und "eine Rede*," 231–36, 503–13, 534–36, who argues against the temple idea and sin of religious pride, indicating the sin was an attempt at world domination). Uehlinger compares the language of world domination found in Assyrian rhetoric, specifically inscriptions dealing with the failure of Sargon II in conquering the known world. Pride is said not to be the issue for Genesis 11, but pride can be or most certainly is involved whether people are trying to rival God or run over fellow humans. See Harland, "Vertical or Horizontal," 518 citing Uehlinger, who cites Genesis Rabbah. Empire building as an interpretation was also promoted by Croatto, "Reading of Story," 203–23. Others explain the sin as social injustice, e.g., Reimer, "Tower of Babel," 64–72. Cohen, "Tower of Babel," 25–29, compares the tower story to loss of jobs for NASA scientists in spite of their grand schemes and abilities to reach the skies and asks for social solutions for those unemployed.

10. Ephrem the Syrian (born ca. AD 306) suggested that after confusion set in, a war erupted in which Nimrod was victorious. He then scattered the population of the city and set himself up as king of Babylon. See Louth, *Ancient Christian Commentary*, 166, 187.

11. Orally, T. Muraoka (Hebrew and Semitics professor emeritus of Leiden University) suggested the meaning "one dialect" for the phrase ודברים אחדים. The entire statement שפה אחת ודברים אחדים is enigmatic as illustrated by the various ways it is translated in the Bible versions and interpreted in the commentaries. Perhaps the connective *waw* is not conjunctive syntactically ("and also") but explicative ("especially"), or pleonastic (stylistic). Possibly the two clauses are appositional ("that is"). This could be a hendiadys. It sounds quite odd or redundant to say "one language and one speech" as if two very different things are meant, unless Muraoka is right about the latter being a dialect. If the point in history was when only one language was being used it would suffice to just say "everyone spoke one (or 'the same') language." Why add this next comment about "words"? To say "one language and a shared vocabulary" is redundant, unless meant appositionally or explicit as a restatement ("that is, a shared vocabulary"). But then Hebrew does possess some redundant features. Regardless of what exactly is meant, the added phrase and the context (see comments on 11:2 above) seem not to place the event historically at a point of development when communal life was so young that no linguistic or dialectical changes had occurred.

languages in use. The author could only speak of his known world and not the global earth of many societies with very ancient roots we know today. Hamilton's argument, based on Gordon, that the unique wording of 11:1 means a *lingua franca* is the best explanation.[12]

What is most important here is the mention of people traveling "from" the East. Some translations say "to" the East, but the preposition used, *min*, is normally "from." If this is correct, then the story is placed at a point in time far enough past the early movements of Noah's sons, such that people have gone eastward and then back again. This is highly significant because it suggests or establishes a lapse of time that would most likely be long enough for various dialects if not languages to have developed. Since Shinar is by scholarly consensus an area in Mesopotamia, moving there from the East would mean people groups were already at least as far east as what in ancient times became Persia. But even if מקדם means "eastward," we still have the problem that multiple languages are already mentioned in chapter 10. If 11:1–4 is about a time when only one language was in use (at least in this region or the world) then chronologically the story has to be placed between 9:28 and 10:1. Some would say it coincides with 10:25, which speaks of the time when the land/earth was divided. The problem is that various languages are already in existence in 10:5–24. So, any division into multiple tongues could not be what is mentioned in verse 25.

A Plan to Build a Great City with a Greedy Purpose (11:3–4)

This event took place at some point after brick-making technology was perfected. This would seem to suggest a time when more than one language was in use on the earth, although not necessarily in a particular province. Regardless, now we get to the heart of the matter. Verses 3–4 conclude the opening pericope regarding the Shinarites and act as a fulcrum for moving to the second and final pericope about God and his response. Here, the focus is on the motives of these people. The tower is a minor part of the story. They plan to build a city with a tower, which was normal for that period of history. If we focus on the tower per se then we miss that fact that

---

12. Hamilton, *Book of Genesis*, 350–51, nn. 7–8 citing numerous articles and chapters by C. H. Gordon, especially Gordon, "Ebla as Background," 295. He also cites an argument that this language was Sumerian and the scattering is linked to the Ur III period in DeWitt, "Historical Background," 15–26.

the intention was to build a city and, even more, a reputation so intimidating that they would be safe from attack (which could lead to defeat and dispersion).[13]

The expression "a tower and its head in the heavens" does not necessarily mean they planned to make the tower so high it would reach the clouds (although clouds might form this low), much less the stars or God. It may only be a way of saying "tall." The term "heavens" (שמים) is used in the OT for "H/heaven" or "heavens/sky" depending on context. Pre-scientific theologians thought in terms of something like nine miles high.[14] First of all, the ancients had no such technical ability, and neither does anyone today. (The ancients equated heaven with heights like mountain tops, not a place beyond distant galaxies as we do today). Second, scholarly consensus is that this tower was what we know as a *ziggurat*,[15] and these pyramids were not

---

13. Gordon Wenham (*Genesis 1–15*, 239) suggests a hendiadys here ("city tower"?), which takes the city out of the picture (unless it is "towered city"). But a city tower presupposes a city, so even if the focus is on the tower per se, we still have to ask its purpose. If the reader does not know about ziggurats it is reasonable to conclude this is a watch or siege tower. As a religious structure, however, it could still fit a warfare situation as far as the story goes. A ziggurat would have been used for inviting the gods' blessings on their battles. The purpose of a ziggurat could have in no way enraged the gods. YHWH would have been upset by idolatry, but these are not Hebrews and the text does not describe the problem this way. The sin would have to be something that was universally viewed as sinful, like gratuitous violence.

14. Luther spoke of medieval folklore that placed the tower at nine miles high. See Pelikan, *Luther's Works*, 2:211.

15. Therefore, DeWitt could confidently assert: "It is common knowledge now that the tower is the ziggurat of the lower Tigris-Euphrates basin" (DeWitt, "Historical Background," 15). In the *Archaeological Study Bible* it says, regarding Genesis 11:4, "Ancient cities were dominated by a temple complex, including a tower. . . . Ziggurats were dedicated to particular deities. Their design made it convenient for a god to 'come down' to his temple, receive worship from his people and bless them" (*NIV Archaeological Study Bible*, 20). On sacred space in the ancient world, see Hurowitz, *I Have Built*, in toto. DeWitt plausibly argues that the date of the tower event is best related to the fall of the Third Dynasty of Ur, the end of the Sumerian civilization ca. 1960 BC. He connects the division of languages in Genesis 11:7 with the time of Peleg when the earth was divided (10:25; cf. 11:18; DeWitt says 10:18 [sic?]). His defense of the tower of Genesis 11 as a temple uniting heaven and earth is based mainly on the wording of 11:4 (mentioning the heavens) for which he finds parallels in ancient Mesopotamian texts which speak of ziggurats or temples as links between heaven and earth. See DeWitt, "Historical Background," 21. However, these texts use the term "house" not "tower," although structurally these temples were often seven-stepped pyramids of ca. thirty feet (ten meters) high. Extant towers range from sixty to two-hundred feet per side. See Walton, *Ancient Near Eastern*, 119.

erected to dizzying heights. Furthermore, the purpose of a ziggurat was not only to reach the gods but to provide a gateway for a god to come down to the people.[16] So the *ziggurat* interpretation precludes any idea that building this tower was a superhuman construction of a super skyscraper and some kind of attempt to "storm heaven" and rival or resist God.

Yet if this tower was not a ziggurat, what was it? The only other ancient tower we would associate with the building of a city would be a watch or siege tower, and the latter has already been suggested by early Jewish exegetes,[17] who did not conclude that this passage indicates some kind of treachery against God via a tremendously tall tower, which modern readers somehow think is obvious. I suggest that we have been conditioned to think this way, so we see in the passage what we expect, which is much more than it actually says. Although the KJV and even the NIV both use phrases that speak of this tower reaching heaven (KJV) or the heavens (NIV), this verb in fact is not part of the Hebrew text.[18] This interpretation is erroneous in that it violates both the purpose and nature of the ziggurat. A house for the gods was placed on top of these pyramids to promote contact with them or one of them, and such contact was intended for communion with the deity, not for confrontation. A tower with a heavenward top is therefore to be understood as describing the purpose of the tower as religious.

If the tower was not a ziggurat then it had a military purpose (offensive or defensive) and had nothing to do with God or the gods. So, either way (for worship or war), the traditional interpretation of a ridiculously high tower opposing God fails. The explanation of this tower as a watch or siege tower is hard to prove, but we can note first that the term (מגדל) is often used of a watch tower in the OT (although its use in Gen 11 seems to favor

---

16. As André Parrot concluded, a *ziggurat* was "a *bond of union*, whose purpose was to assure communication between earth and heaven"; therefore, a "giant step-ladder by means of which a man may ascend as near as possible to the sky" (Parrot, *Tower of Babel*, 64.) Such a definition on the surface seems to align well with the words of Genesis 11:4a.

17. See *inter alia* Walton, "Mesopotamian Background," 155–75; and Walton, *Ancient Near Eastern*, 121.

18. Luther was influenced by such wording, as many still are. He concluded it was a place of worship. See Pelikan, *Luther's Works*, 2:213. He may have been influenced by the Vulgate as were the KJV translators. The Vulgate in verse 4 reads: *et dixerunt venite faciamus nobis civitatem et turrem cuius culmen pertingat ad caelum et celebremus nomen nostrum antequam dividamur in universas terras* ("And they said: 'Come, let us make a city and a tower, the top whereof may reach to heaven: and let us make our name famous before we be scattered abroad into all land'"; D-R).

the *ziggurat*), and second that the concern with a city and a tower to defend against deportation is consistent with a military motive for the tower.

The major issue here is the people's desire to "make a name for themselves," that is to build a fierce reputation. This second aspect of their building program is what is directly connected to their purpose: "so that we will not be captured and carried away to other lands."[19] The plan was first to build a city with a central pyramid for the gods (to ensure divine help) and second to build a reputation strong enough to deter would-be attackers, so that they could hopefully avoid being conquered and enslaved. Perhaps this involved the legislation or imposition of a *lingua franca*. Perhaps they had forced the people in the area they had subdued (Shinar) to adopt their language in place of their native tongue. Such measures were and are typical when a new kingdom is established. The reader must wonder who the Shinarites feared might invade and enslave them. This reality suggests a time in history when a number of "nations" existed as enemies, which implies the existence of at least several dialects if not languages.[20] The traditional view is not concerned with this observation because usually it understands the fear of dispersion as a fear that God would scatter them in light of his plan and command to Noah and his sons as stated in Genesis 9:1: have children and fill "the earth [הארץ]"! (Although again it could be argued that "earth" is not necessarily the globe as we understand it but as Noah would have understood it, i.e., the land area of which he was aware.) Nothing in the text from 9:1—11:4 clarifies that these settlers were worried about God making them perpetual travelers and/or parents. In fact, the text taken at face value says that they have travelled from the East to get to Shinar. And logically their ancestors first had to travel eastward before they could travel back westward. They have to be a sizable community in order to build a city, so they had no compulsions about bearing children. Nothing suggests they were opposing God's ideal of filling the earth except the assumption they

---

19. Cf. KJV punctuation: "Go to, let us build us a city and a tower, whose top may reach unto heaven; and let us make us a name, lest we be scattered abroad upon the face of the whole earth"; and NRSV, "Come, let us build ourselves a city, and a tower with its top in the heavens, and let us make a name for ourselves; otherwise we shall be scattered abroad upon the face of the whole earth."

20. An alternative approach is not to worry about such inconsistencies (e.g., only one language and one set vocabulary but various nations) and admit the story is a fable meant to teach a valid lesson not validate historical details. But the presupposition of this study is to understand that a historical event is behind the story, and its intention is to interact with a traditional interpretation that is held by those who accept this text as historical and divinely authoritative.

were aware of Genesis 9:1 and were resolved to disobey. Even if they were not from the East but had travelled eastward and were cognizant of the command to fill the lands with people, the very fact they have just arrived in Shinar at journey's end is evidence of following that order. Certainly, people had to settle somewhere at some time, and just because these people finally get to a desirable place is no reason to say they settled down out of an evil motive to disobey God.

Furthermore, these apparently Mesopotamian (or pre-Persian?) people would not necessarily know about God's words in Genesis 9:1. That is only the case if we assume they are so close in time to Noah's sons that the command was still fresh and being taught. But if they are living at a time when enemy nations could plunder them, they likely have no knowledge of YHWH or his commands. And if they do, there is still nothing that makes a solid connection between their actions in 11:4 and the divine command in Genesis 9:1. The only possible connection textually is that while 9:1 promotes "global" migration, 11:4 indicates a desire to avoid being scattered.[21] The question then becomes, of what were they afraid? The tone of 11:4 is not that of a resolution to defy God. These Shinarites are not talking to God or responding to anything about him in verses 1–3. They are discussing why they need to build a city. City building had not been divinely forbidden, so building a city is no proof of a plan to bypass 9:1. All that the text of Genesis 11 says so far is some people were moving about the Middle East and increasing their population to the point that when they discovered a suitable place they settled down and set about building a city with a tower, most likely a *ziggurat* for contact not conflict with the gods or God.

Another issue that is often overlooked is the fact that many slaves would be needed to achieve the building of this city, especially the kind of tower the traditional view envisions. Still many workers, most likely slaves in the ancient Near East, would be needed to build the typical *ziggurat* enclosed by a city with walls. This indicates that the people who moved to Shinar from the East must have enslaved people along the way or conquered an already existing civilization in Shinar upon arrival, possibly—as was common—by destroying an existing city and rebuilding it. The pride and power of 11:4, then, is not a matter of rejecting YHWH but of ruthless military aggression. Religion or dependence on their gods or chief war deity would

---

21. The verb used for "scatter" in 11:4b (פוץ) is similar to but not the same as that found in 9:19, where Noah's sons are mentioned as those whose descendants were scattered (נפץ) over the "earth."

have been part of this, as the building of a *ziggurat* shows. Spiritual sin comes into play here only in that they worshipped false gods; but the text in verses 4–6 that highlights the problem that entreated YHWH's wrath was the Shinarites' attitudes and actions of building a reputation ("name") of which the building of a city was just one example—not the building per se but *why* and *how* they built it. Their main purpose was to guard against being scattered (v. 4b), and God's verbal response (v. 6a) involved a concern about them being "one people with the same language." YHWH was angered by how these Shinarites had been and were planning to use their unified power. All this points to a problem related to gratuitous and aggressive military might. This view fits with what had been the principle sin of mankind throughout the early chapters of Genesis. Sibling rivalry led to murder in the first family (Gen 4:1–8). The flood was sent to judge a world or region "filled with violence" (6:13). Ham's descendants were destined to become slaves of the descendants of his brothers (9:25–27). Nimrod, the founder of the earliest settlements that became Babylon and Akkad (among other cities) in *Shinar* (10:10), was a "mighty warrior 'in the land' [בארץ]" (10:8), and "mighty hunter before YHWH" (10:9). Even some traditional interpreters of Genesis 11 have taken this phrase in verse 9 to mean "hunter of men,"[22] presumably in light of 10:8 which describes him as a warrior. Regardless, he was a warrior and is credited with activities leading to the

22. People's pride and pursuit of power inevitably led to battles between cities for more prestige. This usually ends in the defeated population being dispersed or deported (scattered and enslaved). God allows this to continue as the natural consequence and punishment for gratuitous violence against neighbors. Interestingly, a Puritan commentator speaking of Nimrod said: "By hunter here is not meant an hunter of beasts, but an hunter of men" (Whately, *Prototypes*, 87). Luther said about verse 4 that: "The descendants of Ham had invaded the region of Shem . . . Because they were inclined towards despotism, they had a desire not only to drive out the descendants of Shem but also to establish [as Satan does] a new government and a new church" (Pelikan, *Luther's Works*, 2:219). Cf. Ellul, *Meaning of City*, 10–13, who makes a case for "hunter before the LORD" meaning "plunderer" or "conqueror." I would add the parallel with "mighty warrior" supports this as a military statement not one about hunting game. Ellul speaks of this reflecting the establishment of the first military empires by one whom God knows about but who does not know God as did Moses. Being "before YHWH" is a negative assessment in this case. The city is a center from which war is waged (Ellul, *Meaning of City*, 11–13). Josephus wrote: "They were incited to this insolent contempt of God by Nebrodes [LXX term for Nimrod], grandson of Ham the son of Noah, an audacious man of doughty vigour [*sic*]. He persuaded them to attribute their prosperity not to God but to their own valour [*sic*], and little by little transformed the state of affairs into a tyranny, holding that the only way to detach men from the fear of God was by making them continuously dependent upon his own power" (Josephus, *Antiquities IV*, 55).

establishment of cities known for their conquests and cruelty as well as architectural accomplishments.

Interestingly, only the narrator mentions or names God as YHWH. It is not clear if these people worshipped YHWH as God or a god. If so, it does not fit with what we know about the earliest Sumerians or Babylonians. (Most scholars connect these civilizations to this story, except literalists who place the story very soon after the initial migration of Noah's sons, before a new language could develop and even before *ziggurats* first appeared, making the relationship to 9:1 reasonable, and making the tower an unbelievably high structure in order to defy God and demonstrate their self-sufficiency.) Nimrod is associated with YHWH in 9:9, but the meaning is unclear. The author recognizes YHWH's knowledge of Nimrod but whether or not Nimrod knew about YHWH is uncertain.[23] He was a descendant of Ham (10:6–8),[24] whose descendants were cursed to be slaves (9:25), so he was not part of the line of people leading to those chosen and blessed by God (Shem), which would indicate he was likely at odds with YHWH. What is clear is that he was associated with settlements in Shinar and with warfare.

Those who hold to the *ziggurat* view of the tower and still say the sin was religious in nature have the burden of proof to show how a structure intended to appease the gods is evidence of sinful pride. The problem seems clearly not to be the tower but the motive of building a city so that the inhabitants could be secure from external threat. They are not trying to avoid migration but subjugation. Whether or not only one or several languages existed at this time, whether or not "a region of the earth" or "the entire earth" is in view in verse 1, and whether or not the tower is a religious or military one, unity and the power and prospects it brings was both the goal of these people (v. 4) and what concerned YHWH (v. 6). And whatever the sin of Shinar was must and will be established on grounds independent of these decisions. How we understand Genesis 11:1–4 is crucial, because it explains why God is so angered in verses 5–8. Also, what is emphasized in verse 6 may be the clue to understanding verse 4.

---

23. The Sumerians worshipped Anu (meaning "sky" or "heaven/s") as the chief deity. Ellul refers to the distance between YHWH and Nimrod, who was "before the LORD" (Gen 10:9; Elllul, *Meaning of* City, 11–12). YHWH was not sanctioning Nimrod's prowess; rather Nimrod was separated from YHWH while a part of his omniscience.

24. In Genesis 10:8 he is called a son of Cush (a son of Ham in v. 6), but in Micah 5:6 he is Assyrian.

The mentioning of "one lip" (שפה אחת) in 11:1 in contrast to multiple tongues (ללשנתם) in 10:31, and the mentioning of Babel in 11:9 and Shinar in 11:2 in contrast to Babylon and Shinar in 10:10, have raised controversy over the chronological relationship between these chapters and over the possible literary placement of the "one language" and "one people" in chapter 11 after the territories, nations, clans, and tongues in chapter 10. There is no chronological problem or question if the proposal made in this article is correct. Chapter 11 focuses on one example where a particular people (perhaps led by Nimrod in the earliest settlement of Babylon) subjugated a region and enforced linguistic and political unity with wicked and wanton desire for power, prestige, and prosperity. This explains how "it came to be" (ויהי) in 11:1 that this land had one language at some point in the multiplying and migrations of chapter 10. Otherwise, the traditional view that 11:1 speaks of, a time before new languages developed, is hard pressed to explain why the tower story follows the spread of nations and languages and to position it between chapters 9 and 10. If only one language existed in the world in 11:1, the story cannot fit with Nimrod and the founding of Babylon in 10:8–10 or with Peleg (פלג) and the dividing of the earth in 10:25, since multiple tongues are in use. That chapter 10 speaks of "tongues" and 11 of "one lip" and "shared words" (dialects?) is best taken as synonymous ways to speak of language, but perhaps it indicates the author of the tower story had something unusual in mind. Again, the word for "divided" (פלג) in 10:25 is not the same as that for the dispersion (פוץ) in 11:4, 9. To what 10:25 is referring is a mystery, but if we did equate it with the builders of the city in Shinar (as some holding the traditional view of 11:1 do), the understanding of 11:1 as limited to the time of the original human language is (ironically) weakened. That violence was at the heart of the Shinarites' quest for a name and defensive posture better explains YHWH's anger and anxiety as expressed in the next half of the story (vv. 5–9).

YHWH's Opinion of These Plans (11:5–7)

The most significant feature of verse 5 is the reference to God coming down. This is consistent with what we know about the function of the *ziggurat* as a means of contact between people and their principle deity. It was not for them to go up to meet him but for him to have a place to dwell in, yet above their city, and possibly to descend the steps to meet with them or for priests to ascend to him. Yet the entire atmosphere and attitude was one of communion. From the narrator's point of view, YHWH is the one and only true God, so only he could respond to what people do, whether they know his name or not. This verse indicates his concern with the city and tower, but nothing negative is yet revealed. That comes in the next verse.

In verse 6 the concern shifts from the city and tower to the real problem: this people's unity both political and philological, along with their methods and motives. God's response and solution in verse 7 is also aimed at their linguistic unity. So, this is the key. Something about their power and potential in concert with their psychology alarmed YHWH enough that he needed to stop them (vv. 6-7). Interestingly, this return to a statement about the "one language" since 11:1 makes use only of the first element (11:1a, "one lip") and not the second (11:1b, "unified words").

What is ambiguous yet vital for understanding this text is the statement in verse 6, "and this to begin them to do [וזה החלם לעשׂות]." The versions translate this as "and this they have begun to do" (cf. NIV; KJV; LXX) or "this is only the beginning of what they will do" (e.g., NRSV). But the question the translations do not answer (seeking to be more literal than interpretive in such cases, even the dynamic equivalent ones like NIV) is what this "this" is. What is it exactly that they have begun to do that upsets YHWH? The city and tower are almost finished. This is based on 11:5, which says God came down to see the city and tower these people "had built [בנו]," likewise LXX (ᾠκοδόμησαν), although some versions have "were building" (e.g., NIV). Yet there is an apparent contradiction in verse 8, which says that YHWH's intervention led to a halt in the construction of the city (which is why some translations seek to harmonize the text with "were building," although the verb used does not say that). A solution is to translate the verb in verse 5 as "had built [so far]." They may have built the tower first as a priority. Verse 8 says they stopped building the city but does not mention the tower—although the tower could have been included as the central feature of the city, as understood by ancient readers. It may be also that verse 8 indicates continued building beyond the first phase of a city with a tower. This could be an indication that the people were excessively consumed with greedily and mercilessly advancing their kingdom at all costs (although not the megalomaniacs some suggest), which would explain God's great grief over their actions and swift punishment.

Still what they had begun to do that bothered YHWH as sinful was not the construction project per se. The problem must be related to the nature of the unity created, which was driven by sinful, selfish motives and enabled by having a city, especially but not necessarily if the tower was a military one. The city was a tool, morally neutral like an ax but capable of being used with malicious intent.[25] If these people are not stopped, they will apparently continue to abuse their privilege of having a unified population. But the odd thing here is that unity is normally something positive in the Bible and in the eyes of YHWH. Linguistic unity is something we would typically see as a blessing because we experience our linguistic barriers as troublesome for the communication of the Bible's good news. Here, however, linguistic and societal unity is sinful. So, YHWH confuses their communication (v. 7). Jacques Ellul wrote, regarding this phenomenon of miscommunication even, when people speak the same language,

> A humanity capable of communicating has in its possession the most terrible weapon of its own death: it is capable of creating a unique truth, believed by all, independent of God. By the confusion of tongues, by noncommunication, God keeps man from forming a truth valid for all men. Henceforth, man's truth will only be partial and contested.[26]

The expression "let's go down" (v. 7a) is a pun meant to ridicule the people who had said "Let's go build" (v. 4a). God mimics their words: If you try to go up, I will just come down. This use of "let us" when God is speaking brings to mind statements like we see in Genesis 1:26, "Let us make man in our image." The "us" has been interpreted as God and the angels or as the Trinity. But this similar use in Genesis 11 indicates that such an expression is just a figure of speech like the editorial "we." In 11:7 YHWH says "Let us" not due to a plan to work with the angels but merely as a play on words to make fun of the people's frail plans—however majestic in their own eyes.[27] Regardless, the point of verse 7 is that YHWH's solution to the problem or sin of Shinar is to create misunderstanding and confuse their communication. It must be observed that nothing is said specifically about the creation of new languages. That is one possible logical deduction to make but not the only one. The rest of the passage only says that something

---

25. In the previously published version of this article, the editor used "evil" to replace "sinful" and "malicious," but I do not think we should any longer use "evil" in English unless the deeds are diabolical or supremely hideous and hateful (because current English usage tends to restrict "evil" to matters devilish or very depraved and no longer, as in older English, to a disaster or any and every crime or sin).

26. Ellul, *Meaning of City*, 19.

27. Likewise, such a statement in Genesis 1:26 is probably just a literary convention of the author and nothing theological should be taken from it.

happened to bring urban sprawl to a halt and the people were scattered (vv. 8, 9b). As a result, the place was ridiculed as "Babel" (a pun between Babylon, *babel*, and Hebrew *balal* "to mix up") because of their inability to communicate (v. 9a). The author or editor is writing after the rise of Babylon or maybe even Neo-Babylon in order to poke fun at this idolatrous empire. The LXX translates *babel* as Babylon. Verse 9 speaks of confusion and scattering throughout the כל-הארץ, which again may be taken in context to mean "all the land" (a particular region of the earth not the entire globe).

YHWH's Punishment of These People (11:8–9)

The punishment fits the crime. Gratuitous conquest was solved by confusion and the incapacity to unify in order to occupy and oppress. It cannot be missed that the confusion of language is related to כל-הארץ. Since the story is about what happened in a limited location, Shinar, the linguistic confusion cannot be extended to "the whole earth" but only to the "whole region." The verb used does not indicate that at that time God divided these people into different languages, only that they were rendered unable to understand each other enough to continue cooperating and constructing.[28] Only by a presupposition and a jump in logic can these words be extended to mean that numerous languages were supernaturally created. Something happened that led to miscommunication and chaos and eventually to these people being deported or dispersed. The narrator presents YHWH as directly punishing them, but the Old Testament mindset was such that even if they were conquered and taken captive, YHWH would be seen as orchestrating the events of history. So the wording would be the same even if an enemy nation was the direct cause of their scattering. The word "scattered" does not intrinsically mean "to the four winds"; that is merely a default meaning in modern English due to the traditional teaching. Being scattered in a number of Old Testament texts speaks of how Israel will be conquered and captured by other nations (Deut 4:27; 28:64; Jer 9:15; Ezek 11:16, et al.). "Over the face of the earth/land" may alternatively picture being dragged

---

28. A widely accepted chiasm of Genesis 11:1–9 makes a parallel between "had one language" (b; 11:1b) and "the LORD confused the language" (b'; 11:9b). This would suggest that the one language was confused not divided. See Fokkelman, *Narrative Art*, 13–22. In this chiasm the center point or climax, for which there is no corresponding line, is "The LORD came down" (11:5a).

away over the ground by a foreign power rather than splitting up and traveling in many directions.

Conclusion and Application

"Babel" does not mean "confused"; it just sounds like the word that has that meaning. The Israelites could not miss this opportunity to take a pot-shot at the pompous Babylonians. Parts of the story are intended as humorous and heuristic and overall to promote holiness by encouraging the readers not to follow the bad example of these Shinarites. Genesis 11:1–9 picks up on 10:8–10 and the tales of Nimrod.[29] However, it could be surmised that 11:9 was added by a redactor so that the original story was not intentionally related to the origins of Babylon. The same word (בבל) is employed for Babylon in 10:10 and Babel in 11:9. Either way the story as we now have it contains a final commentary on why the city was named Babylon or Babel, i.e., because it was confused (בלל). Yet the etymology of Babel (Akkadian *Bab-ilu*) is from the Sumerian meaning "gate of the god," presumably due to a sacred gate at the end of the procession street in Babylon.[30] (Yet the house at the top of a *ziggurat* was also considered a gate for the gods' entrance into the human realm). The Babylonian, and later the Assyrian, empires were known for their cruel treatment of those conquered and captured. The mention of one language in the land likely hearkens back to a period when a particular *lingua franca* like Sumerian or Babylonian was in force

---

29. Wenham's view is that that 11:1–9 explains the diversity and dispersion of chapter 10, but he does not tie it specifically to Nimrod (Wenham, *Genesis 1–15*, 242–44). My proposal is also that 11 explains 10 but not in terms of how the diversity of tribes and tongues arose. However, the view that violence is the sin of verse 4 does not depend on how the language of verse 1 is understood. Whether or not 11:1–9 fits chronologically before 10 or early in it, the attempt to make a name is reasonably defined by the narrative in its immediate and Old Testament context, not as attacking God or avoiding migration but pride that led to an abuse of power. The story shows they had no problem with migration and reproduction. And nothing indicates God was angry about the tower per se but rather about the motives behind the city. The tower was evidence that they sought God, but the Ten Commandments had established God's resolution that a right relationship with him was related to a right relationship with humanity. Jesus summed up the Old Testament and its two greatest commands as love God and your neighbor as yourself (Luke 10:27). Cf. 1 John 4:20, "If anyone says, 'I love God,' yet hates his brother, he is a liar. For anyone who does not love his brother, whom he has seen, cannot love God, whom he has not seen."

30. S.v. בבל in *HALOT*. David C. Mitchell notes the derisory nature of the translation of Babel ("Gate of God" in Aramaic; see Mitchell, "God Will Redeem," 373, n. 30.

(11:1). The region of Shinar was discovered, perhaps invaded, and inhabited (11:2), and eventually a brick city (Babel, typical of Mesopotamia) was built with a *ziggurat* as a central feature, meaning the gods were called upon for assistance (11:3–4a). But the people's motives were not pure. They built a fortress and sought the chief deity's help in order to establish a fierce reputation so that no other nation would defeat and disperse them (11:4b). So, YHWH was concerned about what they were doing (11:5); he was worried about the potential problems if their unified power (militaristic and linguistic) went unchecked (11:6). He so orchestrated events that they became confused; through miscommunication and chaos their unity was weakened (11:7). As a result, they were defeated and their empire building ceased; they were deported and dragged away to another region as captives (11:8). Epilogue: This is why the city was named Babyl[on]: because the area under its control became confused, mired down in miscommunication, and YHWH used another nation as his instrument to bring judgment and scatter this once proud and powerful, but too proud and powerful, people who violently misused their privileged position.

What then is the value of this text for the modern reader? It is an example of one of the dominant themes of the Old Testament: God's repeated judgment of those who act violently and abuse power. The issue is not the tower but the *power* of Babel. The narrative in Genesis 11:1-9 gives every indication that the problem was not votive (religious) or volitional (refusal to migrate) but violence (a reputation built on power, real and perceived).

PART II

Exegetical and Contextual Insights in Psalms

4

The Form of Psalm 23[1]

Introduction: Is Psalm 23 a Chiasm?

APPROACHES to this psalm are legion: theologians, teachers, preachers, seminarians, linguists, free-lance writers, death-bed counselors, spiritual shepherds, and even a literal shepherd have all "looked" at Psalm 23.[2] Of course, "looked" is euphemistic for interpreted, and so *many* have looked that a new angle does not seem possible or desirable. But although it seems every exegetical trend has been employed to unlock the secrets and sense of this psalm, somehow it has almost entirely escaped the chiasmic craze—until now (sadly or happily depending on the reader's perspective). While I sympathize with those who are skeptical about literary license looking for chiasm at every turn in the biblical text, I have become convinced of the contextual and structural reality and intentionality of this literary device in Psalm 23.

The outline or literary structure of this psalm is a major issue over which interpreters continue to disagree. Leupold laments the psalm's history of fragmentation by commentators, but Craigie reminds his readers that its structure is "difficult to define with clarity or certainty."[3] Is there

---

1. Originally published as Marlowe, "No Fear!," 65–80. Stylistic and corrective but no substantive changes have been made.

2. See Keller, *A Shepherd*, in toto. Keller grew up in East Africa surrounded by herdsmen and also spent eight years as a sheep owner and rancher (n.p., from the "Introduction").

3. Leupold, *Exposition of Psalms*, 208.

only one metaphor being employed by the psalmist (i.e., the shepherd) or are there two, three, or more, e.g., shepherd, guide, and host? Almost every approach imaginable has been tried in terms of an analytical and linear outline of one or more sections with one or more metaphorical images, but not that of a conscious and careful, conceptual chiasm. The unresolved confusion and conflict among commentators over this matter suggests that a new, non-linear, and more extensive explanation is necessary as a possible solution to the debate over this psalm's intended literary form.

Interpretation of Psalm 23 as a Chiasm

An Interpretive History of the Literary Structure Psalm 23

To date, only general and topical chiastic outlines have been hinted at on rare occasions,[4] and a detailed metrical chiasm has been worked out[5] but not a detailed conceptual chiasm with a central, unrepeated climax as the solution to the debate over this psalm's structure. These conceptually and structurally suggestive chiastic interpretations of Psalm 23 in its relatively recent and mostly scholarly literary history will be reviewed next, followed by the non-chiastic treatments.

Chiastic Considerations

Clarke's commentary (1976 edition) exhibits a chiasmus, although this pattern (A-B-B-A) is not mentioned per se as characteristic of the literary structure: provision (vv. 1–3), protection (v. 4), protection (v. 5), and provision (v. 6).[6] Y. Bazaq's 1981 stylistic and structural analysis interpreted verse 4 as a center-point around which the rest of the psalm circles. A pattern of phonological and conceptual parallels was observed between verses 1 and 4, 2 and 5, and 3 and 6.[7] The present proposal maintains the same verse (4) as the theological fulcrum or thesis of the poem, but otherwise sees a chiastic pattern of similarities in purpose between verses 1–2 and 6, and 3 and 5. Gerstenberger hinted at a chiastic nature for Psalm 23 in 1988 by saying that the final verse "returns to objective, confessional language," after

---

4. See comments on Clarke's commentary below (p. 68) and in n. 6.
5. See pp. 63 and 75 and n. 9 below.
6. See Clarke, *Analytical Studies*, 78–79.
7. Cf. Bazaq, "Psalm 23," 370–77, and cf. Greensphan, Review of "Psalm 23," 161.

explaining that it opens with a confessional.[8] In 1990 L. F. Bliese selected Psalms 1–24 for study, seeking to show that intentional structural symmetry rather than randomness guided the psalmists. This author was satisfied that either metrical chiasmus (twenty-eight times) or metrical homogeneity (twelve times) is clearly present in these psalms and should be expected in much of OT poetry. In the former case (chiasmus), the lines of the poem or of each stanza of a poem (working from the outside to the center) have the same number of word accents successively. For Psalm 23 the chiasmic meter is 4655 6 5564:

A   (v. 1 = 4 beats)
  B   (v. 2 = 6 beats)
    C   (v. 3 = 5 beats)
      D   (v. 4a = 5 beats)
        E   (v. 4b = 6 beats) = a marked peak
      D   (v. 5a = 5 beats)
    C   (v. 5b = 5 beats)
  B   (v. 6a = 6 beats)
A   (v. 6b = 4 beats).

The isolated central line or lines then become(s) its marked peak. In the latter instances (i.e., those of metrical homogeneity), the accents per line are the same throughout a given psalm, leading to a marked final (rather than central) peak.[9]

Non-chiastic Considerations

In 1982 R. Ahroni wrote on the unity of Psalm 23, arguing against what is viewed as forced attempts to show unity through emendations, and seeking to establish an imaginative, conceptual, and emotional unity. In line with but more specific than Bazaq,[10] Ahroni identified verse 4b as the key thought around which the rest of the psalm revolves: the "rod and staff"

---

8. Gerstenberger, *Psalms*, 114–15.
9. Bliese, "Structurally Marked," 265–321, and cf. Dempsey, Review of "Structurally Marked," 396–97.
10. See p. 62 and n. 7 above.

representing God's justice and mercy.[11] R. S. Tomback reconsidered verse 2 the same year and used Mesopotamian backgrounds to explain this verse in a manner consistent with the master (LORD) and shepherd of verse 1. While this study was not concerned with the overall structural implications of this interpretation, the chiastic character of Psalm 23, which this current paper seeks to defend, depends on the close association of verses 1–2 and their collective disassociation from verse 3 in contrast to the modern tendency[12] to disregard the strong masoretic disjunctive accent (*rebia mugrash*) of verse 1 (while inconsistently following it in verse 3), and thus create a bi-colon with verse 2a, leading to the need to harmonize the text by producing another bi-colon from verses 2b and 3a, and yet another from verse 3b.[13] In 1985 a focused essay by C. O'Connor on the structure of Psalm 23 appeared, taking into account the metrical system developed by M. O'Connor. Results were: (1) sixteen lines: 1b[1 line], 2a–b[2 lines], 3a–b[2 lines], 4a–d[4 lines], 5a–c[3 lines], and 6a–d[4 lines]; (2) two sections or stanzas of eight lines each: 1b–4c and 4d–6d; and (3) four strophes or paragraphs, each of related material, of four lines each—two per stanza: I. 1b–3a and 3b–4c, then II. 4d–5c and 6a–d.[14] This still suggests a hinge purpose for verse 4 but splits its contents between 4c and 4d, making the former the close of section I and the latter the opening for section II. The verse is transitional as demanded by a chiasm, but the development of thought as viewed by O'Connor is linear rather than cyclical, since the verses of each strophe are seen as related, or intra-related, but not inter-related with verses in other strophes. He offers few clues for a chiasm.

But chiastic or other similar structures in Hebrew poetry in general, and in the Psalms in particular (but not Psalm 23 per se), were being noticed in the mid-1980s. J. Bazak spoke of concentric circles characterizing the shape of Psalm 25 and concluded, after an analysis of Psalms 25, 34, 37, and 145, that similar shapes were either synonymous or chiastic.[15] At the same time, J. S. Kselman put forth a chiastic interpretation of Psalm 101, one exegetical significance of which was to suggest that the question

11. See Ahroni, "Unity," 21–34, and Urbrock, Review of "Unity," 165–66.

12. Cf. recent translations like the NIV and NRSV and the edited page of *BHS*.

13. Since verse 3b contains the same strong disjunctive as verse 1, this is possible. But another better alternative is to see 3b as a bi-colon following and fitting with the monocolon 3a to create a type of synthetic "tri-colon."

14. See O'Connor, "Structure," 206–30, and Miller, Review of "Structure," 185.

15. Cf. Bazak, "Structural Geometric Patterns," 475–502; and Collins, Review of "Structural Geometric Patterns," 185–86.

posed in verse 2b was answered by verse 8.[16] Then P. Auffret questioned the traditional assumption of great literary artistry in Psalm 23. Yet his study, while noting previously overlooked structural features, was based on its traditional, linear two-part structure: verses 1–4 (part one) and verses 5–6 (part two).[17] In the following year (1986), K. K. Sacon applied a literary-structural analysis to Psalm 113 and arrived at a chiastic colometry.[18] This supported the assumptions that Bliese would make four years later.[19]

Related to the relationship of verses 2 and 3, which issue has bearing on the chiasm proposed in this paper, T. M. Willis in 1987, while not concerned with the outline or structure of Psalm 23, argued grammatically for a thematic connection between verses 2–3a. These three lines describe three functions of a shepherd.[20] The next year M. S. Smith evaluated the traditional bi-partite outline of Psalm 23 and the attempts to reconcile the seemingly conflicting images of God as first a shepherd (vv. 1–4) and then as a host (vv. 5–6). He concluded that unity is found only in the psalmists perspective of a spiritual journey, wherein verses 1–4 present what a pilgrim would see on a journey to the temple and verses 5–6 what happens at the end of his pilgrimage.[21] In the same year, Y. Mazor defended the traditional, gradual shift from shepherd to host (vv. 4–5) as a compliment to another, earlier and sudden shift (vv. 3–4) from sheep (believer) to shepherd (God).[22] Mazor claimed this results in an integrated, rhetorical unity that pictures God's grace through twin images of "the stern protector and the generous host."[23] By great contrast, also in 1988, D. P. McCarthy took a deconstructionist approach (à la Derridá), concluding that Psalm 23 contains inherent contradictions that account for the interpretive confusion that has characterized the scholarly study of these six verses to date.[24]

---

16. Cf. Kselman, "Psalm 101," 45–62, and Halligan, Review of "Psalm 101," 187.

17. Cf. Auffret, "Essai sur," 557–88, and Avalos, Review of "Essai sur," 288.

18. Cf. Sacon, "Methodological Remark," 26–42, and a review in *OTA* 10 (February 1987) 64.

19. See p. 63 and n. 9 above.

20. Cf. Willis, "A Fresh Look," 104–6, and a review in *OTA* 10 (October 1987) 270.

21. Cf. Smith, "Setting and Rhetoric," 61–66; and Halligan, Review of "Setting and Rhetoric," 67.

22. Cf. Mazor, "Psalm 23," 416–20; and Wright, Review of "Psalm 23," 184.

23. Cf. Mazor, "Psalm 23," 420; and Wright, Review of "Psalm 23," 184.

24. Cf. McCarthy, "Not-So-Bad," 177–92; and Deeley, Review of "Not-So-Bad," 184–85.

In 1989 C. Gilead gave another approach to the standard double-stanza division of Psalm 23. Each stanza was observed to contain three bi-cola and a conclusion, to be distinguished from the introduction and conclusion of the entire poem. Its literary and linguistic substance and style were seen as a result of influence from the shepherd's hymn via the contemporary Jeremiah.[25] The same year witnessed the publication of van Uchelen's 1989 article in which he sought to solve the problem of the diversity of interpretations of this psalm's imagery and structure by looking for linguistic features that could provide empirical evidence to point out the proper path to understanding the text. Structurally, however, he still speaks of two different metaphorical halves.[26] Noteworthy for the purposes of this present article is van Uchelen's conclusion that verse 4 (for grammatical reasons) provides the key to the basic meaning of Psalm 23. This study's proposed chiasm centers on this verse as the main and unparalleled point of the psalm as well. Finally, in a 1999 return to Psalm 23 exegesis, Robinson adds little new for structural studies, presenting it as a unity of two parts, verses 1–3 then verses 4–5. Verse 6 is deemed a conclusion.[27]

An Interpretation of the Literary Category of Psalm 23

Psalm 23 should be viewed as an extended confession of trust, in form-critical terms.[28] The praise psalm flows in principle from the vow of praise, which is a typical feature of the classic and complete lament psalm. In practice, it comes from the reality of release from ruin and its resulting resolve to recognize God's goodness and greatness before others. Once saved, the psalmist swears that public and vocal testimony will be given as praise before the congregation. Likewise, the standard petition section of a lament can lead to a single psalm devoted to prayer. So, the confession of trust section, found in many or most laments, gives rise to an externally but not existentially independent psalm, which (like the twenty-third, for example)

---

25. Cf. Gilead, "Psalm 23," 341–47 [Hebrew]; and Greenspan, Review of "Psalm 23," 184.

26. Cf. van Uchelen, "Psalm XXIII," 156–62; and Pitard, Review of "Psalm XXIII," 170–71.

27. Cf. Robinson, "Pastures New," 2–10; and Redditt, Review of "Pastures New," 461–62.

28. Cf. Gerstenberger, *Psalms*, 113–16. Robinson calls it a "Psalm of Confidence" (see Redditt, "Pastures New," 461).

is categorically an extended confession of trust in YHWH as a certain savior and sustainer of life. This is a confession to YHWH that the psalmist still believes that he is his only true source of strength, sustenance, and safety. Logically and functionally and necessarily this comes before the psalmist has experienced God's present promise and provision of victory, when it looks like defeat or death is possible or even probable. Based on the consistent character of God and conduct and commitments on behalf of the psalmist and other believers in the past, the psalmist determines to hang onto YHWH as his only help, even if he fears the situation is hopeless.[29]

A Summary of the Debate Over the Structure of Psalm 23 and the Significance of a Solution

A major difference in interpretive approaches has been over how to explain the last third of the psalm (vv. 5–6), where the poet shifts to imagery which seems to have nothing to do with shepherds and sheep, at least on the surface. Some, therefore, try logically to explicate the visual changes from pastures (vv. 1–3) to a dark or deadly predicament (v. 4) to being pampered before enemies and eternally protected (vv. 5–6). But others try to show how the entire context of the psalm maintains a connection to the theme of sheep and shepherd. Leupold's 1959 observation is still apt:

> Then there is the matter of the unity of the psalm or the unity of the figure employed by the psalmist. Some, the majority, perhaps, find only one figure, that of the shepherd. Of a slightly more recent date is the interpretation that finds two figures, that of the shepherd and that of the host. Others insert a third between the two, the guide. Others, giving special thought to v. 6, devise some kind of a fourth figure. By this time one is compelled to admit that the beautiful little psalm has been pretty sadly fragmentized.[30]

A selective survey of commentaries from past to present will quickly reveal this confusion. Leupold (1959)—as one would gather from his comment above—takes a unified shepherding approach which explains each part of the psalm as stating something the shepherd provides.[31] VanGemeren

---

29. Cf. Psalm 3:1–3 and 13:1–5, where, respectively, verse 3 and verse 5 are the confessions of trust.

30. Leupold, *Exposition of Psalms*, 208.

31. Leupold's outline (*Exposition of Psalms*, 209) is that the shepherd provides rest and guidance (vv. 2–3); protection (v. 4); food (v. 5); and fellowship (v. 6b). Verse 6a is

in 1991 followed the typical bipartite shepherd-host division (the LORD is my shepherd, vv. 1–4; and the LORD is my host, vv. 5–6).[32] He also notes three opposing works in regard to the subject of verses 3–4: Thierry (1963) and Briggs (1952), who see this passage as being about people, and Willis (1987), who relates it to the three tasks of a shepherd for his sheep.[33] Merrill (1965) and Eaton (1965) both give them a royal meaning.[34] Briggs sees people being treated as guests in three ways: with God as their shepherd (vv. 1–3a), guide (vv. 3b–4), and host (vv. 5–6).[35] Clarke (1979) somewhat artificially applies the shepherding metaphor throughout the psalm. He also forces the text into ten available and alliterated resources for God's human sheep (which heightens the dubious quality of his analysis): rest (v. 2), refreshment (v. 2), restoration (v. 3), regulation (v. 3), rescue (v. 4), reassurance (v. 4), reception (v. 4), rejoicing (v. 5), retainers (v. 6), and residence (v. 6).[36] Craigie (1983) recognizes the two-fold shepherd-host arrangement as the consensus but observes at least two other valid metaphorical patterns: (1) the unity of the shepherd motif throughout (à la Koehler), and (2) the lack of metaphor at all in verses 5–6 (à la Vogt, who takes these verses literally as a sacrificial banquet, which is also the psalm's setting).[37] Kidner (1973), as well, accepts the double metaphors of first the shepherd and then the friend. The shepherd by definition incorporates the functions of "guide, physician and protector."[38] In terms of *Gattüng* criticism, Gerstenberger

---

viewed as a parenthesis wherein the psalmist abandons any figure of shepherding.

32. VanGemeren ("Psalms," 214–17) calls the poem's structure both simple and complex, but his analysis reveals only the former description. He references several German articles, one French article, and some English articles, as well as one book on the structure and metaphors of Psalm 23—which are probably the source of his comment on the psalm's complexity—but he does not remark on any chiastic interpretations found therein. Sources on structure he mentions are Craigie, *Psalms 1–50*, 204–5; O'Connor, "Structure," 206–30; Mittmann, "Aufbau und Einheit," 1–23; Stenger, "Strukturale 'relecture,'" 441–55; and Vincent, "Recherches exégétiques," 442–54.

33. See VanGemeren, "Psalms," 217, citing Thierry, "Remarks," 97; Briggs, *Book of Psalms*, 207; and Willis, "Fresh Look," 104–6.

34. See VanGemeren, "Psalms," 217, citing Merrill, "Psalm XXIII," 354–60; and Eaton, "Problems of Translation," 171–76. In this regard, one should also see Eaton, *Kingship and Psalms*, 36–38.

35. Briggs, *Book of Psalms*, 207.

36. Clarke, *Analytical Studies*, 78–80.

37. Craigie, *Psalms 1–50*, 204–5, citing Vogt, "'Place in Life,'" 195–211; and Koehler, "Psalm 23," 227–34.

38. Kidner, *Psalms 1–72*, 110-11.

gives the outline of this so-called "song of confidence" in three parts, as (1) confessional statement, verses 1–3; (2) affirmation of confidence, verses 4–5; and (3) expression of hope, verse 6. Against most modern analysts he believes the psalm is structured according to liturgical needs.[39]

When Keller explained verse 5, his experience with watching shepherds compelled him to see the "table" which is being prepared by the shepherd as the "tablelands" where sheep graze. Linguistically, therefore, Keller's basis for maintaining sheep as the subject of this verse is erroneous, even if the basic idea is correct.[40] Numerous commentators, for similar or distinct reasons, are comfortable with the complete characterization of this psalm in shepherding imagery. Another example is Maddux's un-versified outline, which is typical, as Keller, of the many popular and published but oversimplified treatments of Psalm 23: the shepherd's care; the shepherd's redemption; the shepherd's presence; the shepherd's protection; and the shepherd's dwelling place.[41] While some scholars also argue for the shepherding motif throughout Psalm 23, others wonder how such imagery can reasonably be applied to sheep. As Kidner says parenthetically, "The attempt to sustain the first metaphor [i.e., the shepherd] . . . would turn it through a full circle, picturing men as sheep which are pictured as men—with their table, cup and house—which is hardly a profitable exercise."[42] As a final example, Alden (1974) followed the shepherding theme consistently through the fourth verse, and then noted there are multiple metaphors in verses 5–6.[43]

If the present analysis is correct, the reason for the changes in imagery is to be explained by the symmetric demands of the chiastic principles and parallels of the ancient Eastern poetic mind and not by the dictates of Western analytic and systematic thinking imposed on poetic literature, which has led to the false expectation of some type of outline for the psalm

---

39. Gerstenberger, *Psalms, Part 1*, 113, 115.

40. See Keller, *A Shepherd*, 104–5. He points out how the Spanish word mesa (a high plateau where sheep graze) means "table," and the same word with the same meaning appears in an African dialect. Of course, it only matters if this is the meaning of the Hebrew word David used, שׁלחן. But this OT Hebrew term appears only to be used of an ancient "table" where humans eat: either of a leather mat placed on the ground (Isa 21:5), a (usually royal) table with dishes (1 Kgs 5:7), or of a cultic table for sacrificial food or meat (Exod 25:23; Ezek 40:39). See the standard Hebrew lexica.

41. Maddux, *Psalms in Outline*, 19.

42. Kidner, *Psalms 1–72*, 111.

43. Alden, *Psalms of Devotion*, 59.

in two parts (i.e., I. vv. 1–4 and II. vv. 5–6) and the need to try and justify the transition from flock to feast.

The Chiastic Structure of Psalm 23 Exhibited

The charts that follow represent, visually, the conclusions reached in this examination of Psalm 23, pertaining to its chiastic characteristics. It seemed best to allow the reader to view the structure of the psalm suggested by this study, as a frame of reference, before diving into the exegetical details used to support it.

The Text of Psalm 23 as a Chiasm[44]

    A   23:1 YHWH is my shepherd; [therefore] I shall not want.

         23:2 He makes me lie down in green pastures; he leads me beside still waters.

      B   23:3 He restores me: he leads me in right paths for his name's sake.

        a   Even though I walk through the darkest valley,

           C (23:4) b   I fear no danger, for you are with me;

      a' your rod and your staff—they comfort me.

    B'   23:5 You prepare a table before me in the presence of my enemies; you anoint my head with oil; my cup overflows.

  A'   23:6 Surely goodness and mercy shall follow me all the days of my life, and I shall dwell in the house of YHWH my whole life long.

---

44. The adapted translation used as a convenience for this chart is that of the NRSV. The punctuation and some wording have been changed to fit the conclusions of this paper. The differences are that NRSV has (1) a comma after "shepherd" in verse 1; (2) a semi-colon after "waters" in verse 2; (3) a period after "my soul" in verse 3, which is here translated "me"; (4) a semicolon after "evil" in verse 4, which is here rendered "danger"; and (5) the traditional substitution of LORD for the appearance in the Hebrew text of the tetragrammaton (יהוה), for which YHWH has been re-substituted. Also, any words in brackets are supplied. The Hebrew word for "soul" (נפש), when used with a suffixed personal pronoun, usually refers to that person's own life or self; therefore, the pronoun itself has the same sense in English. In such cases, "soul" has nothing to do with an immaterial part of a person that lives on after death. It does refer to the life force of a person in the sense of his own life or self, and consequently, the NRSV, as other modern versions sometime do, gives a footnote for the use of "soul" in the text of this psalm and others which says "or life" or something similar.

As an inclusio, God's personal name, YHWH, is used in the beginning and ending verses. In terms of content both of these chiastic boundaries emphasize God's constant and certain care. The sovereign shepherd of souls provides spiritually for his people abundantly and appropriately.

The Themes of Psalm 23 as a Chiasm

When the previous chiastic scheme of the verses of Psalm 23 is translated into a thematic statement for each step of the chiasm, the following results:

A   Complete provision (1–2)
     B   Purposeful Restoration (3)
        a   Our need for rescue (4ai)
           C   (4)   No need for fear: b   How to wait for rescue (4aii)
        a'   His ability to rescue (4b)
     B'   Purposeful Renewal (5)
A'   Continual provision (6)

The Chiastic Significance of Psalm 23 Explained

The Metrics of the Hebrew Text

The masoretic major poetic disjunctive accents will be shown as used in Psalm 23 with the MT.[45]

(1b)[46]   A   רעי יהוה (rebia mugrash) לא אחסר // (silluq)

(2a)   בנאות דשא ירביצני (athnach) // על-מי מנחות ינהלני (silluq)

(3a)   B   נפשי ישובב (athnach) //

(3b)   ינחני במעגלי-צדק (rebia mugrash) // למען שמו (silluq)

(4ai)   גם כי-אלך בגיא צלמות (pazer) //

(4aii)   C   לא-אירא רע (rebia magnum) // כי-אתה עמדי (athnach)

(4b)   שבטך ומשענתך (rebia mugrash) // המה ינחמני (silluq)

(5a)   B'   תערך לפני שלחן (rebia magnum) // נגד צררי (athnach)

---

45. Listed in descending priority, these accents are: 1. Silluq; 2. Oley Veyored; 3. Athnach; 4. Rebia Magnum; 5. Rebia Mugrash; 6. Shalsheleth Magnum; 7. Sinnor; 8. Rebia Parvum; 9. Dechi vel Tiphcha; 10. Pazer; 11. Mehuppak; 12. Azla.

46. 1a of the MT is the editorial superscription added to the "original" psalm.

OTHER VOICES IN OLD TESTAMENT INTERPRETATION

(5b) דשנת בשמן ראשי (rebia mugrash) // כוסי רויה (silluq)

A'   (6a) אך טוב וחסד ירדפוני (dechi) // כל־ימי חיי (athnach)

(6b) ושבתי בבית־יהוה (rebia mugrash) // לארך ימים (silluq)

Metrics of Psalm 23

Levels	Chiastic Units	Syllables	Accents	Words
A	YHWH my-shepherd	4 (2+2)	2	2
	not I-want	3 (1+2)	2	2
B	in-pastures green	4 (2+2)	2	2
	he-makes-me-lie	4	1	1
C	by-waters-of rest	5 (1+1+3)	2	3
	he-leads-me	5	1	1
C'	my-life	2	1	1
	he-returns	3	1	1
B'	he-directs-me	4	1	1
	along-paths-of-rightnesss	7 (4+3)	1	2
	for-the-sake-of his-name	6 (4+2)	2	2
A'	also if-I-walk	4 (1+1+2)	2	3
	in-valley-of darkness	5 (2+3)	2	2
	not-I-will-fear trouble	4 (1+2+1)	2	3
		60	22	26
A	for-you with-me	6 (1+2+3)	2	3
	your-rod and-your-staff	8 (3+5)	2	2
	they, they-will-comfort-me	7 (2+5)	2	2
B	you-prepare for-me a-table	8 (3+3+2)	3	3
	in-the-presence-of my-enemies	5 (2+3)	2	2
C	you-anoint with-oil my-head	8 (3+3+2)	3	3
	my-cup overflowing	5 (2+3)	2	2
B'	surely goodness and-mercy	6 (1+2+3)	3	3
	they-will-follow-me	4	1	1
	all-the-days-of my-life	5 (1+2+2)	2	3
A'	and-I-will-return	3	1	1
	to-the-house-of-YHWH	4 (2+2)	1	2
	for-length-of days	5 (3+2)	2	2
		74	26	29

Next, the masoretic major poetic disjunctive accents will be shown as used in Psalm 23 with an English translation:

A   (1) *YHWH* is my shepherd (*rebia mugrash*); //
I shall not want [for adequate care] (*silluq*).
(2) He makes me lie down in green pastures (*athnach*); //
he leads me beside still waters (*silluq*).

B   (3) He restores me—(*athnach*); //
He leads me in the right paths (*rebia mugrash*), //
to protect His reputation (*silluq*).

             ai If I might wander into the deepest, darkest valley (*pazer*), /
C   (4)   aii I fear no danger (*rebia magnum*); //
                 for you are with me (*athnach*); //
           b   Your rod and staff (*rebia mugrash*), //
                 they comfort me (*silluq*).

B'   (5) You prepare a table before me (*rebia magnum*); //
in the presence of my enemies (*athnach*). //
You anoint my head with oil (*rebia mugrash*); // my cup overflows (*silluq*).

A'   (6) Surely goodness and grace will follow me (*dechi*) / all the days of my life (*athnach*);
and I will dwell in the house of *YHWH* (*rebia mugrash*), // a long time (*silluq*).

As the above treatments of the text of Psalm 23 demonstrate, this present study rejects the decision of some translators and textual emendators to "correct" the Masoretic Text by re-arranging verse 3a as the final part of a tri-colon along with verse 2a–b,[47] or as part of a bi-colon with 2b.[48] The latter makes an artificial division between 2a and 2b and forces verse 1 into the role of the initial parallel member of a bi-colon comprising verses 1–2a.[49] All these approaches require the translator to disregard the punctuation of the Masoretic Text. In this case, the text makes good sense and probably the best sense if the MT versification and accentuation are faithfully followed.

---

47. Cf. NRSV and NIV.
48. Cf. *BHS*.
49. Cf. Wendland's linguistic analysis of Psalm 23 (Wendland, *Analyzing Psalms*, 66), where he notes how many or most translations into English do not reflect the strict formal correspondence that exists between the parallel lines of this verse in Hebrew: In-pastures-of greenness he-lays-me-down // Beside-waters-of quietness he-leads-me.

This means, of the current and most popular English versions, the NKJV[50] presents and preserves the best organization and punctuation of Psalm 23, in light of the premises and proofs of this paper.

Verse 1 (ignoring the superscription attributing the psalm to David, which is a later but reliable editorial insertion) should be taken alone as a "synthetic"[51] bi-colon and not as the first line of a bi-colon with verse 2a as the second, parallel member or line. The reasons are that the MT employs: (1) most importantly, a strong disjunctive accent (*rebia mugrash*) above the Hebrew word (רעי) meaning "my shepherd," and (2) notably, the *silluq* with *soph pasuq* after "want" (אחסר) indicating the end of the verse. In effect, this verse briefly states the theme of the psalm and should be read with verse 2, which is the beginning of the chiastic poem per se and corresponds to verse 6. Another alternative, better yet than separating 2a from 2b in order to make verses 1 and 2a a bi-colon, would be to see verses 1–2 as a "tri-colon" (mono-colon plus bi-colon). This alternative approach still, however, has to ignore the strong disjunctive in verse 1 to make it a mono-colon; so the most consistent treatment is to take verses 1 and 2 together as two lines of bi-cola, which provide the first level of the chiasm, linking a short thematic preface (v. 1) with the initial thought of the following five verses, which finds its counterpart in verse 6, which is rather lengthy anyway, as a balance to verses 1–2, and ends with thoughts of "ever dwelling" (v. 6b) as a fitting mirror image of "never wanting" (v. 1b). Either way, verses 1–2 comprise the first chiastic level.

Whether verse 1 is a mono-colon or bi-colon/-cola, the parallelism of verse 2 should be retained as a bi-colon ending with the *silluq* of that verse, as in the MT, and not restructured to include 3a to produce either a bi-colon

---

50. The KJV has the same versification, naturally, and similar punctuation, but the NKJV is superior translationally (in terms of structure and poetic sensitivity) because it presents the poetic and musical nature—which is intrinsic to all members of the Hebrew psalter—through the use of poetic stanzas. The psalms are songs and the OT Psalter (book of Psalms) was eventually a hymnbook for Israel. All psalms are poetry that was eventually set to music for use in the worship that occurred in the temple in Jerusalem and, later, the synagogues. On the other hand, the NKJV, also like the KJV, does not necessarily have the best rendering for all words and phrases in this psalm; more modern versions like the NRSV and NIV win in this category.

51. This term can be meant generally (as here) for any parallelism besides whatever is "synonymous" (or static) or antithetical, or it can relate specifically to a category of parallelism when more than three types are assumed. Current scholarship is uncomfortable with "synonymous" in a pure sense, but a number of OT poetic parallels do not seem to be advanced to any clear degree by the parallel line.

THE FORM OF PSALM 23

of verse 2b with verse 3a or a tri-colon of verses 2a–3a. A very strong disjunctive accent (*athnach*) divides verse 2 into a pleasing and productive bi-colon: "He makes me lie down in green pastures//He leads me beside still waters," followed by the sign ending a verse. While MT versification is not automatically absolute, the text makes good sense as it stands, probably the best sense as this discussion will defend. The seeming bases for altering the sense of the MT here are the assumptions of a necessity: (1) to parallel verses 3a with 2b (because of the arbitrary decision to parallel vv. 1 and 2a) and/or (2) to parallel verse 3a with verse 2 because of a shared theme and since 3b can stand alone, theoretically, as a "synthetic"[52] bi-colon. However, as will be developed more later, the meaning of verse 3a fits as well, if not better, with the rest of verse 3 as with verse 2. Verse 3a is separated from 3b by another *athnach* and then 3b itself has two parts created by the strong but less strong *rebia*—the same but only accent of verse 1b, following the non-original superscription in 1a. Therefore, verse 2 should be identified as a static bi-colon and verse 3 with its major dichotomy after 3a as: (1) probably, a tri-colon composed of a mono-colon (v. 3a) followed by a "synthetic" bi-colon (v. 3b); or (2) possibly, as a synonymous or synthetic bi-colon. These options for verse 3 compare and contrast as follows: He restores me: // He leads me in right paths, / for his name's sake (or he restores me [in righteousness, for the sake of his reputation]; // he leads me in right paths, for his name's sake).

As already noted (see p. 63 above) a chiasm based on the meter of Psalm 23 has been proposed by Bliese: A:4, B:6, C:5, D:5, E:6, D':5, C':5, B':6, A':4. This scheme of nine elements was based on a verse distinction of, respectively, verses 1, 2, 3, 4a, 4b, 5a, 5b, 6a, and 6b. The present study recognizes a different versification for the thematic chiasm, 1-2, 3, 4, 5, 6, but still finds the same center. Based on this latter scheme and on one beat per word (counting words joined with *maqqeph* as one beat), the parallelism and meter of Psalm 23 may be analyzed as follows: A:10, B:6, C:12, B':10, A':10.

Verse	Parallelism	Meter	Total Beats
A (1b)	"synthetic" bi-colon	2:2	
(2a-b)	"synonymous" bi-colon	3:3	10
B (3a)	mono-colon	2:	

---

52. See nn. 13 and 51.

(3b)	"synthetic" bi-colon	2:2	06
[or 3a-b	"synthetic" bi-colon	2:4]	
C (4ai)	mono-colon	4:	
(4aii-b)	"synthetic" bi-colon	4:4	12
B' (5a)	"synthetic" bi-colon	3:2	
(5b)	"synthetic" bi-colon	3:2	10
A' (6a)	"synthetic" bi-colon	4:2	
(6b)	"synthetic" bi-colon	2:2	10

If the parallelism is split as bi-cola at *athnach* only, a clear A-B-C-B'-A' chiastic pattern also emerges for this psalm, with verse 4 having a unique meter and, therefore, consciously constructed as the center of the psalm:

Section	Verse(s)	Metric Pattern	Total Beats
A	1–2	4:6	10
B	3	2:4	6
C	4	8:4	12
B'	5	5:5	10
A'	6	6:4	10

As seen, verse 3 may be analyzed as either a mono-colon with a synthetic bi-colon, or as a synthetic bi-colon in which the first line (3a, extant as only a mono-colon) assumes a similar or related section of line 2 (3b) following "He leads me" for completion of its thought. "He leads me" of line 2 would be parallel with "He restores me" of line 1. If intended as identical or very similar sentiments, then this verse of poetry could be seen as "synonymous" rather than "synthetic." Either way—as synonymous or synthetic, or two, three, or four stanzas of poetry—if the first line (v. 3a) is a shortened corruption or creation based on an originally intended longer version (echoing or enhancing 3b), then the metrics would come out closer to 8 or 10 beats, rather than 6, which would more closely parallel the 10 beats of verse 5, its chiastic counterpart. In addition, the metric patterns 4:6 in the opening verses 1–2, and 6:4 in closing verse 6, provide an inclusio for the chiastic poem and together make a 6-4-4-6 chiasm.

For an alternative approach, if one combines 4ai with verse 3, the outcome is 10 beats, leaving 8 beats for 4aii-b as the center or peak, and creating a perfectly balanced a-b-c-b'-a' metrical chiasm of 10-10-8-10-10 beats (vv. 1–2, 3–4ai, 4aii-b, 5, 6). This outcome is pleasant, but it flies in the face of the weak *pazer* accent at the end of 4ai, treating it as a strong disjunctive. But if the MT accents are viewed as usually reliable while not absolute guides, then in this scenario, the result is a much longer B element (vv. 3–4ai) which would be seen as a mono-colon of 2 beats (v. 3a) followed by a bi-colon of 4:4 beats (vv. 3b–4ai). The C unit (v. 4aii–b) or apex would be a bi-colon of 4:4 beats (or alternatively two bi-cola of 2:2 and 2:2 beats) which fits together well, perhaps synonymously: "I fear no danger for you are [your protection is] with me! // [I fear no trouble for] your rod and your staff comfort me!" 4ai also goes well with the preceding verse 3: "He restores me: // He leads me in the right paths to protect His reputation // in case I might wander into a deep, dark valley." When in this scheme 4aii–b is taken as the center section, as with the previous proposal, it also reflects a micro chiasm within the macro chiasm of the entire psalm, although in this case a-b-b'-a' (instead of a-b-a'). Still the main idea includes God's presence which excludes all fear:

A	I fear no danger (*rebia magnum*)		2 beats
	B	for you are with me (*athnach*)	2
	B'	your rod and your staff (*rebia mugrash*)	2
A'	they comfort me (*silluq*).		2

No chiasm of the parallelism in Psalm 23 is observable. The first chart above of the metrical chiasm has the advantage of showing the three parts of verse 4, which themselves can be seen to present an a-b-a' chiasm of 4-4-4 beats. There is, in addition, another way to view verse 4, the fulcrum section of this poem. Verse 4aii, which has been presented as the central theme around which the psalm rotates and the central phrase around which this verse revolves (making a chiastic verse within a chiastic psalm), also demonstrates its centrality in another fashion.

The first phrase of this sentence ("I fear no danger"; v. 4aiiα) fits well with the preceding and initial clause of this verse (4ai), while the second phase ("for you are with me"; v. 4aiiβ [still before *athnach*]) fits with the following and concluding clause/sentence (v. 4b). This highlights verse 4aii as the point around which the other parts of verse 4 rotate and from which they depart. In 4aii, the first phrase, "I fear no danger," is in line with the preceding statement and pronoun "even though I might wander into a deep, dark valley." And, although followed by the *athnach* (a disjunctive pointing back), the second phrase of verse 4aii, "for you are with me," is in keeping with the following sentiment and pronoun "your rod and staff, they comfort me." Perhaps this is why the *rebia magnum* is used with the former phrase and the *athnach* with the latter. The *athnach* marks the end of a complete thought, yet the last part of that thought ("for you are with me") has to do double duty for what is before and after. Therefore, 4aiiα has a strong pause before moving on to 4aiiβ. And together these two phrases provide the fulcrum and foundational theme of Psalm 23: "I fear no danger; for you are with me!" Psalm 23 calls the reader to a fearless life and uses a creative and carefully constructed chiasm to do it conceptually, metrically, and dramatically.

The Mechanics and Meaning of the Hebrew Text

a. Level A, A' (Outer): (vv. 1–2; // v. 6) YHWH Shepherds with Complete and Continual Provision

Verse 1a–b: "YHWH is my shepherd; // I will lack nothing [essential spiritually]."

Verse 2a–b: "He causes me to lie down in green pastures; // He leads me [to lie down] beside quiet water."

Verse 6a–b: "Undoubtedly goodness and grace will accompany me every day of my life; // and I will return to [or "dwell in"] the house of YHWH a long time."

b. Level B, B' (Inner): (v. 3 // v. 5) YHWH Shepherds with Purposeful Renewal and Restoration

Verse 3a–b: "He restores me [physically and spiritually]; // He leads me along the right paths, /

For the sake of His own reputation."

Verse 5a–b: "You prepare a table before me in the presence of my enemies; // You anoint my head with oil, / My cup overflows."

c. Level C (Center): Climax: (v. 4) Never Fear!

Level C, –a, –a' (Outer Climax): (v. 4a, b) The Sheep's Need and the Shepherd's Nature for Rescue

All-present, regardless of the environment (v. 4ai)

Verse 4a: "Yes, even though I might wander through a valley of deep darkness," /

All-powerful, regardless of the enemy (v. 4b)

Verse 4c: "Your rod and staff, they comfort me."

Level C, –b (Inner Climax): (v. 4aii) No Need for Fear! The Divine Shepherd is Always Near

Verse 4b: "I will not be afraid of any danger, for You are with me!"

Conclusion: Psalm 23 is a Chiasm!

Psalm 23 has a chiasm within a chiasm. Its formation is both simple and sublime. The entire psalm exhibits an A-B-C-B'-A' chiastic pattern, with the climactic and center section/verse (C; v. 4) also displaying a sub-chiasm, having the pattern of a-b-a' (or a-b-b'-a'). In this way, the psalm means to help the reader to make no mistake and maybe miss the main point: YHWH's presence prevents all panic. The outer layer of corresponding verses is composed of the cluster of verses 1–2 which parallels verse 6. The inner layer of correspondence juxtaposes verse 3 with 5. Finally, the focus falls on verse 4, wherein the psalmist's fearless proclamation in the light of God's presence amidst deep darkness is framed by reflections on his perilous situation and God's powers of salvation.

5

The Function of Psalm 23[1]

Introduction

ATTEMPTS to clarify the outline or structure of Psalm 23 are not new but should continue. The author of this paper has one such study already in print.[2] But further investigation has led to some new ideas and convictions. The verbal patterns of Psalm 23 provide an interesting study, which may shed some light on its structure.[3] Based on the verbal pronouns or subjects doing the actions, the psalm divides into two parts and contains a chiasm in each, as well as an overall chiasm. These features may help

---

1. Originally published as Marlowe, "David's I-Thou Discourse," 105–15. Stylistic and corrective but no substantive changes have been made. Former appendices have become Tables in the text (see pp. 83–84, 86–87, 89 below regarding pronouns and chiastic levels).

2. An article published in 2003 focused on the entire psalm as a chiasm. At that time, I was not aware of the stem patterns I suggest in this paper and I did not find two sections each with a chiasm as here. That study based its conclusions on syllabic count, which will not be considered in this paper in relation to the two sub-chiasms of a larger chiasm. Both studies find the same center in the overall chiasm though, with different structural approaches to Psalm 23. See Marlowe, "Psalm 23," 65–80.

3. For purposes of convenience this study will speak of David as the author of Psalm 23. David is the most plausible author of Psalm 23, not simply because the editorial superscription associates it with him. The purposes of this paper do not allow a discussion of the issue of Davidic authorship in the psalms. In short, the expression מזמור לדוד, while part of the superscription, allows for the sense "a song by David" (see 2 Sam 22 and Ps 18, clearly by and about David, לדוד), although in another context this could mean "for David" or "belonging to the David[ic collection]." However, the shepherd theme and mention of "enemies" in Psalm 23 are strong Davidic features.

with the question over the apparent change in imagery from shepherding to banquet hall, which some try to dismiss and argue for a consistent shepherd image throughout.[4] The I-Thou relationship popularized by Martin Buber in his seminal work[5] is anticipated already by the sweet singer of Israel, who arranged this psalm around an I-He (vv. 1–4a) and then an I-You (4a–6) section. For what it's worth, this particular division results in two strophes of 28 and 29 word-units respectively (including the superscription). Regardless of other conclusions about images and themes, outlines, sections, and chiasms, Psalm 23 is typically divided at the end of verse 4 into two major strophes. The following will conjecture the novel idea of this major division coming in the middle of this verse.

The Name YHWH as A Structural Feature

The opening exclamation (v. 1:1b) involves the use of the Hebrew God's personal, ineffable name, YHWH. Verse 1:1a is the editorial superscription that associated this psalm with King David. God's name reappears in this psalm only in the final verse, which could be seen as an inclusio. An indirect reference to this name occurs also in verse 3, where the poet mentioned the sake of God's name as a motive for God's guidance into right living.[6] Another indirect reference may be seen as well in verse 4, where

---

4. Even going so far as to say that the "table" in verse 5 refers to "table lands" where sheep graze (see Keller, *A Shepherd*, 104–5).

5. First published in 1923 as *Ich und Du* by Martin Buber (the same year as S. Freud's *Das Ich und das Es*) and translated into English in 1937 (by W. Kaufmann) and 1958 (by R. G. Smith).

6. As an excursus the usage and meaning of the word צדק may be clarified. Traditionally rendered "righteousness" in this psalm and elsewhere, this English rendering for modern readers is problematic. The notion of being righteous is currently not a popular or positive quality. It smacks of self-righteousness or a neurotic obsession with legalistic rule-keeping to the point of being so fastidious that people are uncomfortable in the presence of what is interpreted as a "holier-than-thou" attitude. Some read "righteous" as meaning almost "perfect." So, a better translation is needed today. As for Psalm 23 it sounds strange to speak of a "path that is righteous." In light of the shepherd motif being employed, the author clearly intended to speak of God as a spiritual shepherd that guides his "sheep" (followers) along the "right" paths (i.e., those that are safe and lead to nourishment). God directs his people in right living. Essentially, then, this term as a verb has to do with doing right and, as a noun or adjective, the result of doing right. In short, a "righteous" person, if we use that word, is merely one who lives according to the right rules, which by definition in Scripture are God's rules. No one can be perfect so that is not the issue. This is why people like Noah were called "blameless" (a word sadly

the psalmist said, "You *are* with me." This is an intriguing possible parallel because this is the only place in the psalm, other than at its beginning, where the verb "to be" is understood in relation to God. One is tempted to see a pattern of four references to the divine name (YHWH), the first and the last being explicit uses of it (vv. 1, 6) and the middle two being allusions to it (vv. 3, 4). This suggests a possible chiasm and structural pattern (with vv. 2 and 5, the ones next to the first and last verses, filling in the gaps, both speaking of YHWH's appropriate provisions for the psalmist, as a sheep in the midst of wolves (v. 2), and as someone surrounded by enemies (v. 5). The psalmist's "lack of fear" becomes the center-point between statements about YHWH's presence and protection:

A	YHWH [is] my Shepherd		1
	B God provides abundant food and water		2
		C *You guide me . . . for the sake of Your Name*	3–4ai
			D I fear no "evil"⁷	4aii
		C' *for You [are] with me, You comfort me*	4b
	B' God provides a feast with abundant wine		5
A'	I will return to YHWH		6

mistranslated as "perfect" in older English versions). Therefore, we should translate צדק as something like "to do what is right/legal/just" or "what is right/legal/just" (as opposed to what is wrong). In the OT context, doing right has to do with conformity to God's laws so one could say that the mindset of "rightness" or "righteousness" was that of keeping God's legislation or maintaining justice. In that regard, we could use the translation "law keeping" or "law abiding." But then these ideas in current use also can carry negative connotations. When I was a child, there was a popular cartoon called *Dudley Do-Right of the Mounties*; it was about a Canadian Mounted policeman who was a naive "do-gooder" to the point of ridiculousness, still, he always "got his man [caught the criminal]," even if by bumbling his way along by doing right in a literalistic and legalistic manner. But maybe the current generation is so removed from those days (when also the Lone Ranger roamed and ruled the West through being a good guy in a white hat) that we can speak of "doing right" without all the past difficulties.

7. The word "evil" may not accurately represent the intended meaning of רע for the modern reader. Today, "evil" suggests mainly something demonic or despicably horrible. We no longer speak of a flood, for example, as an evil event (as was true in centuries past). In the OT, the word being translated "evil" is almost never or never about such kinds of crimes or satanic activity. The word basically is the opposite of "good" ("bad"; so, the tree of the knowledge of good and evil should more correctly be the tree of the knowledge of right and wrong). The psalmist here in Psalm 23 does not expresses his lack of fear for only what is the most wicked or devilish acts but of any harm (although in this case he does have in mind even times when he is in dangerous, dark [not deadly] circumstances; v. 4a; see n. 10 below.)

But other patterns emerge as the verbs and subject pronouns are considered. Separate patterns are found in two sections or strophes (vv. 1–4a and 4b–6): I-He and I-Thou.

I-He (Psalm 23:1–4a)

Verse 1a is the superscription and verse 1b is the first line, which is comprised of a verbless clause or sentence (1bi) followed by a statement of result employing a *qal* imperfect (*yiqtol*).[8] In the first section of this psalm (vv. 1b–4a), a pattern of verbal stems emerges: *qal* (1x)-*hiphil* (1x)-*piel* (1x)-"*piel*" (1x)-*hiphil* (1x)-*qal* (2x).[9] If the verb היה was used rather than understood in verse 1bi, it would certainly have been *qal*, so that would yield: [*qal*]-*qal*-*hiphil*-*piel*-"*piel*"-*hiphil*-*qal*-*qal* (A-B-C-B-A). "*Piel*" shows that this verb more exactly is a *polel*, but for all intents and purposes that is a *piel* variation. Additionally, the subject or object pronouns (either attached to the verb or not) correspond to this pattern, with the first-person ("I, me, my") dominating the A and A' lines, and the second-person ("you") characterizing the emphasis of the center portion (B-C-B') and climax C. Cf. these tables:

Verbal Stem Pattern (Ps 23)

	Stem	Verb	Subject	Object	Translation	State	Verse
A1	[*qal*]	[היה]	YHWH	My	[is]	——————	1bi
A2	*qal*	אחסר	I	——————	I [do not] lack	*yiqtol*	1bii
B	*hiphil*	ירביצני	He	Me	He lays down me	*yiqtol*	2a
C	*piel*	ינהלני	He	Me	He guides me	*yiqtol*	2b

---

8. The term "imperfect" is an unfortunate (and inaccurate or misleading) but now standardized way to refer to the prefixed conjugation. Preference is given in this paper for the more current and correct designation *yiqtol*, but many readers may not be as familiar with this as the traditional "imperfect," so both will be used interchangeably in this discussion.

9. If interpretation based on verbal tense or aspectual sequence seems unusual, the reader is referred to Goldingay's observation related to a chiastic pattern of fientive and stative verbs in Psalm 93:1 (Goldingay, *Psalms 90–150*, 68).

C'	polel	ישובב	He	Me	He restores (me)	*yiqtol*	3a
B'	hiphil	ינחני	He	Me	He leads me	*yiqtol*	3b
A'1	qal	אלך	I	———	I walk/wander	*yiqtol*	4ai
A'2	qal	אירא	I	———	I [do not] fear	*yiqtol*	4aii

Pronoun and Verbal Stem Pattern (Ps 23)

	Stem	Chiasm	Pronoun Content	Verse
I-He	[G]	A1	YHWH *is* my shepherd	1bi
	G	A2	I	1bii
	H	B	He	2a
	D	C	He	2b
	D	C'	He	3a
	H	B'	He ... his name	3b
	G	A'2	I	4ai
	G	A'1	I	4aii
I-You	[G]	A	You *are* with me	4bi
	D	B	They (= Your staff)	4bii
	G	C	You	5a
	D	C'	You (+ *qatal*)	5b
	G	B	They (= Your goodness)	6a
	G	A'	I (+ *weqatal*) ... YHWH	6b

Are such patterns coincidence? Perhaps, but not likely, even if created by the masoretic vocalizations added 1,000–1,500 years after the original poem. Regardless, all the verbs appear to have been imperfect since the beginning. That creates no pattern, other than a static one, but does explain the mood of the author. He reflected on YHWH's continuing and current care. He testified to present expectations based on past experiences. These are not things YHWH *will* do but *is* doing and can be trusted to do again. Where a different mood perhaps occurs is with the final two verbs, "even if I might walk" and "I will fear no רע." Because of YHWH's constant and consistent care, the psalmist could use these two *yiqtols* for, first, a mood of contingency and, second, a future tense: "if I wander off down a dark path, I will even then not be afraid of any deadly danger."[10] On the other hand, one could look at these statements more in the perfective present: "when I wander (as I often have) in a dark (or deadly) place, I do fear no danger." While verb forms in Hebrew poetry are often stylistic and cannot be interpreted by a rigid set of tenses and tones, the consistent use of the same form here probably indicates a conscious concentration on the present tense option of the *yiqtol* and its ability to carry a mood of an action that is incomplete (ongoing) or iterative (customary).

As for the pattern presented by the verbal stems, which is coordinated with a pattern presented by the pronouns, some plausible conclusions may be drawn. The opening and closing sections (A and A') both uniquely use *qal* stems and verbs with first common singular subjects. All the rest of this first section (vv. 1b–4a) uses verbs with third masculine singular subject pronouns, all meaning "he" (YHWH). It is interesting that this psalm never refers to God in any way other than with his personal name, directly or indirectly. Symbolically, he is a spiritual shepherd, but he is addressed as YHWH only. The second levels (B and B') both use *hiphil* stems uniquely in this section. Finally, the center part or fulcrum of the chiasm uniquely uses *piel/polel* stems. This leads to the following parallels.

A Since YHWH is my Shepherd, I do not have need
  B He makes me lie down in green pastures
    C He guides me beside restful waters
    C' He restores me
  B' He leads me along the right pathways
A' I wander into darkness / I fear no danger

---

10. The older traditional versions were not aware of more recent data that help students better understand the word צלמות used here (which has been thought of as a compound but is more likely an abstraction). Compounds are unknown in OT Hebrew except in names. This is not a name, so the usual explanation of it as "shadow" (צל) plus "death" (מות) needs to be questioned, especially since we are now aware of an ancient Semitic root צלם meaning "darkness." So, this is a "valley of deep darkness" not a "valley of the shadow of death." This older translation unfortunately has helped relegate this psalm to a use mainly or only at funerals; in reality, it is not a psalm composed for comforting people about the gloominess of death but a psalm very much about the joy of life lived under the care of a loving divine shepherd. Also, the word often rendered "evil," while it has that lexical option in the right context, is here not about the psalmist's fear of satanic attack or wicked influences but, as a sheep that wanders off the right path and encounters wolves, of deadly dangers.

Cf. the following table.

Verbal Chiastic Content Compared (Ps 23)

CHIASTIC LEVELS			Chiastic Content (Verbal)	Verses
A	B	C	Chiastic Content (Verbal)	Verses
A1			You are my shepherd (verbless clause)	1bi
A2			I will not lack	1bii
	B		He makes me lie down	2a
		C	He guides me	2b
		C'	He restores me	3a
	B'		He leads me	3b
A'2			I may walk	4ai
A'1			I will not fear evil	4aii
A			Because You are with me (verbless clause)	4bi
	B		They (Your protections) comfort me	4bii
		C	You prepare a table and cup for me	5a
		C'	You refresh me (*qatal*)	5b
	B'		They (Your mercies) will follow me	6a
A'			I will return to Your house (*weqatal*)	6b

The parallel between A and A' indicates a connection between God's shepherding and the "sheep's" lack of fear in any location or situation. The B and B' lines go together since they emphasize YHWH's causative force in directing his "sheep" to the right places, the right pastures, and the right paths. The right pasture is one that is "grassy" or "green" (דשא, i.e., contains sufficient food, appropriate and abundant). In the imagery of the psalm, this is "spiritual" food. The right paths are not those that are necessarily completely safe (as the next verse says, the sheep may be allowed to wander down dark paths), but also, and more so, those that give direction in right living (or "righteousness"). The psalmist must have had divine revelation in mind as the main method by which YHWH supplied his spiritual sheep with ethical and moral nourishment. Finally, the climax of this section in verses 2b–3a is centered on the refreshment and renewal offered by the shepherd. It must be pointed out that the verb for "guidance" (along calm waters; נהל) is, with only one exception, only used in the *piel* in the OT, and never in the *qal*, so in such a case the *piel* is functionally a *qal*, so this may compromise what is being asserted about its role in the structure of Psalm 23. Be that as it may, this does not negate the overall structure being proposed because it could be coupled with the previous verb as part of the B level, leaving the *polel* as the C level and climax (which does have a *qal* use, so stands out as a clear *piel* choice, unique in this section).

In fact, placing verse 2b ("guidance along calm waters") with C and not with B is problematic on other grounds, because it goes against a long-standing view (e.g., KJV and NASB) that it is a restatement of verse 2a (B; "made to lie in green pastures"). An alternative is to couple what is called C, above, with B, and have only verse 3a ("being restored") as the true center of the chiasm. On the other hand, some believe (e.g., NRSV and NIV) that, despite the symmetry in structure of 2a and 2b, verse 2b really belongs with verse 3a as a parallelism and 2a belongs with verse 1. The differences can be seen by comparing the punctuation in the NIV with the NASB and with the lineation in the NRSV (the former two are not always presented in poetic versification):

NASB	NIV	NRSV
1 The LORD is my shepherd, I shall not want. 2 He makes me lie down in green pastures; He leads me beside quiet waters. 3 He restores my soul; . . .	1 The LORD is my shepherd, I shall not be in want. 2 He makes me lie down in green pastures, he leads me beside quiet waters, 3 he restores my soul.	1 The LORD is my shepherd, I shall not want. 2 He makes me lie down in green pastures; he leads me beside still waters; 3 he restores my soul.

A different approach to the parallelism appears in each of these. The traditional treatment (NASB and KJV, et al.) presents a couplet (bi-colon) in each verse. Quiet waters are parallel with green pastures. This is hard to deny since these two lines form a strong symmetric and possibly "synonymous" (or static) parallel: a-b-c // a'-b'-c' (prepositional phrase followed by verbal phrase in each).[11] But the editors of the MT (here *BHS*)[12] do not buy it, and space the text on the page similar to what is reflected by the NRSV (cf. RSV, which reverses the semicolon and period in vv. 1–2). The

---

11. While the parallel categories of Robert Lowth are outdated, there is still an argument to be made that some parallel cola are synonymous in nature or characterized by restatement. My thesis here is not helped or hindered regardless of what nomenclature is used to categorize the various parallels.

12. See *BHS* or *BHS-T*, 1105.

problem is what to do with verse 3a. This mono-colon has to go with 2b to create a bi-colon (as NRSV), or it has to go with 3b to create a very uneven bi-colon (e.g., KJV, NASB) or tri-colon (e.g., NIV). But the answer posed by the NRSV requires that the beautiful symmetry of verse 2 be ignored or abandoned. The result is that lying in green pastures is parallel with having no needs and then being led by restful waters is parallel with being restored. While the coupling of verse 1b with 2a seems a bit artificial (no need // abundant grass), the pairing of 2b and 3a is more pleasing and natural (quiet waters // inner restoration). However, having no need with YHWH as a shepherd is, upon further thought, perfectly consistent with the provision of abundant spiritual "grass" or food. Perhaps the investigation into verbal patterns via this paper can help provide some clues to a solution. If so, then it supports the pairing of 2b and 3a more than the traditional 2a and 2b, since 2b and 3a create the center of the strophe. Either way, the chiasm being proposed works. But based on verbal stem patterns, verse 2b (*piel*) goes with verse 3a (*polel*) to comprise the C and C' elements and peak of the chiastic structure (since also the author could have chosen another verb in 2b with a *hiphil* option if he wanted it to fit clearly with 2a [the B element]). The compounding of 2b and 3a brings together the ideas of *rest* and *rest*oration as the central theme of the chiasm formed by 1b–4a. The end A'2 ("fear no danger") is a perfect counterpoint to the beginning A1 ("YHWH is my shepherd"). The pre-end A'1 (walking in dangerous places) is a perfect counterpart with the post-beginning A2 (I have no needs, i.e. I am completely prepared and provisioned).

I-Thou (Psalm 23:4b–6)

It might be surprising that a new section begins in the middle of verse 4 with the statement "for you are with me," since it seems on face value that this is a natural rejoinder to what has been proposed as the end of the first section ("I fear no danger"). People are accustomed to reading or thinking of verse 4a as it appears in the KJV: "Yea, though I walk through the valley of the shadow of death, I will fear no evil: for thou art with me." But for reasons explained below, a major shift should or could be made between "I fear no danger" and "because you are with me," despite the fact that the MT accents suggest otherwise with *athnach* on "with me" and *rebia* on "evil" (more exactly on רע, however it is translated). Also, the conjunction "because" actually is a more logical break because it begins the full statement explaining why the psalmist does not fear: "because you [God] are with me, your rod-staff comforts me." The phrase "you are with me" (v. 4bi) is the only one, other than the one that began the first section ("YHWH is my shepherd"; 1bi), that is a verbless clause. So, it can be seen as an opening statement for part two (vv. 4bii–6) as 1bi introduces part one (1bii–4a). Verse 4bii begins the next pattern of verbal stems: *piel-qal-piel-qal-qal* (A-B-A-B-B), which also has a corresponding subject pronoun pattern of [I]-they-you-you-they-I ([A]-B-C-C-B-A). The two *piel* verbs that alternate with *qal* do not conform to the chiastic pattern as the stems did in Section I. These two verbs have either no uses in the *qal* or only one. Therefore, *piel* is functionally like a *qal*, but still, the pattern of *piel-qal-piel-qal* (B-C-C'-B) is formally present. In this section the direct mention of the name YHWH ends rather than begins the strophe. The constant refrain is not he and me but you and me (I and Thou). In the first section, God is consistently "he" but now is addressed as "you" (cf. Tables on pp. 83–84, 86 above).

	Stem	Verb	Subject	Object	Translation	State	Verse
A	[*qal*]	[היה]	You	me	You [*are*] with me	———	4bi
B	*piel*	ינחמני	They	me	They comfort me	*yiqtol*	4bii
C	*qal*	תערך	You	me	You prepare (for me)	*yiqtol*	5a
C'	*piel*	דשנת	You	me	You refresh (my head)	*qatal*	5bi
B'	*qal*	ירדפוני	They	me	They follow after me	*yiqtol*	6a'
A'	*qal*	ושבתי	I	You	I will return to You	*weqatal*	6b

This present analysis proposes a major break not supported by the MT disjunctive accents. The second strophe or section, this new analysis suggests, begins with the statement "for you [are] with me." The Hebrew text makes this clause the conclusion of 4a, but the suggestion here is that it be understood as the beginning of 4b. The first reason for this is its nature as a verbless clause. Since a (and the only other) verbless clause begins strophe I, perhaps this one begins strophe II. Additionally, this prepositional phrase is only the first part of the explanation given for why the psalmist is not afraid. Therefore, it has to be grouped with 4b and following as a section that explicates the basis for the psalmist's confidence (cf. Tables on pp. 83–84, 86, 89 above):

I will fear no adversity/danger: 4aii
   A   Because You [will be] with me   4bi

  B   Your rod and staff // they will comfort me   4bii
    C   You will prepare a table for me // in the presence of enemies   5a
    C'   You will refresh me with oil // My cup [of wine will be] full   5b
  B' [Your] goodness and grace // they will stay with me all of my life 6a
A'   Thus I will return to YHWH's house all [my] days.   6b

All the verbs in this chart on verses 4aii–6b are future tense, while the first section (1b–4ai) revolves around present realities (based on past experience with future implications). This second section of the psalm presents the psalmist's reasons as to why he had no fear and would not fear. This attitude was established by the fact that he posed a hypothetical situation at the end of part one (1b–4a): if I ever wander off the right path and down a path that is dark and/or deadly, then I will not be afraid (v. 4a). So now with verse 4b and following he told his readers why he would not fear: because YHWH would be with him (4bi). Then he delineated three basic features that characterize YHWH's presence when he needs protection (vv. 4bii–6a, B-C-C'-B'). Being in YHWH's presence frames this strophe (A–A', YHWH will be with him … so he will be with YHWH). The futuristic sense is strengthened by the introduction of the *w^{e}qatal* verb in 6b, that mirrors 4bi. The "they" elements of B and B' (4bii and 6a) are functionally "you" elements because they describe things that YHWH possesses and prescribes for the psalmist when he is in need of assistance. But how can he come into a needy situation when he began the psalm by saying that since YHWH is his shepherd he has no needs? The point seems to be that although the psalmist can get into trouble, YHWH is always at hand to provide spiritual resources for rescue and renewal. When people read in verse 1 "shall not be in want" (NIV), or the like, they must wonder, how can someone never want something or have a need, no matter how much they believe in God? When this verse is read in light of the psalm as a whole and its purposeful structures and parallels, it becomes fairly clear that the emphasis is not on the "sheep's" sufficiency but that of the shepherd. YHWH's expected presence when in trouble (in the presence of enemies)[13] is defined as:

---

13. David knew a lot about being in the presence of enemies. In his case, his enemies were former friends. At one point his own son, Absalom, rebelled against his rule, sought to usurp it, and even sought his father's life. Psalm 3 laments this episode in his reign, a good part of which he spent on the run, hiding out in caves. Numerous times in the OT psalms David complained to God that these former friends ("workers of iniquity") ridiculed him for trusting YHWH and were trying to kill him.

B   Rescue and protection creating personal peace   4bii
C/C' Nourishment and refreshment sufficient to face opposition 5
B' Good and merciful treatment by YHWH as long as he lives   6a

The A-levels of this second strophe, both directly or indirectly, refer to the divine name. As already noted, the verbless clause in verse 4bi ("You *are* with me") is one of only two verbless clauses in this psalm. This associates it with the use of the divine name in the verbless clause of verse 1bi and in the special verbal phrase in 6b, which also directly uses YHWH. It is "special" because this is one of only two places in the psalm that a verb other than a *yiqtol* appears and the only place a *w^eqatal* is used. The only other non-*yiqtol* verb is a *qatal* found in 5bi, which continues the force of the preceding *yiqtol*. So, A and A' (opening and closing) stand out uniquely in this strophe as the only non-*yiqtol* dominated expressions. They play off each other by stressing life in YHWH's presence but in opposite ways: You *are* [YHWH *is*] with me (4bi) ... [so] I *will be* with YHWH all my days (6b). Not to be overlooked in verse 6b is the psalmist's repetition of the verb שוב (the only verb used more than once), which he first enlisted in verse 3a ("He restores my life"). That the intention of the poet in 6b was to say, "I will return" (ושבתי from שוב // "he returns" in 3a), rather than the traditional "I will dwell" (from ישב) is supported by the parallel found between 1bi (YHWH constantly shepherds me) and 6b ([so] I will return constantly to YHWH). Additionally, how could David actually live in the temple?[14]

The second level of this chiasm (B–B') is parallel in the use of third masculine plural verbs that tell about two pairs of things (rod and staff, 4b, and goodness and mercy, 6a) that belong to YHWH as the shepherd, which he employs for the spiritual and/or physical benefit of the "sheep." Although the technical subject of the verbs in these lines is "they," the true subject is God because they are his or "Your" weapons and ways. So, like the other lines in this section that speak directly of what "You" do (i.e. he,

---

14. It also makes little or no sense for David to say, "I will dwell in Your house [the temple] all my days [or 'forever']." David could not live in the temple for the rest of his life, much less forever. But he could continually return to the temple—that is, keep seeking to be with YHWH because of his commitment to always be with him (vv. 1 and 4). Neither can "God's house" be interpreted as "Heaven" since the psalm has nothing to do with life after death or with death at all (v. 4a is not about a valley of death but one of darkness or danger [see discussion of צלמות in n. 10 above.]) Both these verses employ one of the only two verbless clauses in the psalm and emphasize YHWH's promised presence with the psalmist. Verse 6b again mentions YHWH and the palmist's promise to practice being with YHWH.

YHWH, does), the B and B' lines also can be said to address the I-Thou relationship. Thematically, each of these stanzas tells about YHWH's nature as a Savior and protector. The expression "your rod and your staff" is likely a hendiadys depicting not two but one tool, the typical shepherd's crook with a curved end for rescue from thorny thickets and a sharp end for protection against predators. YHWH rescues and protects because he is good and merciful. Such knowledge gives the psychological comforts of inner peace and confidence, and this care is available always.

Finally, the inner core and focus of this section (C–C') highlights what "You do for me" (I and Thou). There may be a chiasm here in this verse as well:

A	nourishment (food)	5ai
B	reassurance (with enemies)	5aii
B'	refreshment (with friends)	5bi
A'	nourishment (wine)	5bii

The parallel between the first part of the first line (A) and last part of the second line (A') is obvious (You prepare a table // My cup overflows [by Your doing]). The connection between B and B' is not so obvious on the surface, but one cannot be refreshed or anointed with oil directly by YHWH (literally or figuratively) in most cases. The way that God ministers to us (nourishes, renews, refreshes, restores, etc.) is through people (true friends), and it is people also that negatively impact us and oppose our faith (enemies and, in many cases, former friends, co-workers, or co-worshipers). The psalmist can receive God's bounty, even in the face of opposition, and he does so with the support of his community of believers who have remained faithful.

Summary and Conclusion

The center of each strophe of this psalm is the same thematically: rest, refreshment, and renewal. The psalmist established each strophe with a separate chiasm (cf. Tables above on pp. 84 and 86). The first one aligns with the verbal stems (A-[*qal*], B-*hiphil*, C-*piel*, B'-*hiphil*, A'-*qal*). The second follows subject pronouns and themes (A-You and I, B-they protect, C-You provide, B'-they protect, A'-I and You), which also connect to an alternating verbal stem pattern (A-[*qal*], B-*piel*, C-*qal*, C'-*piel*, B'-*qal*, A'-*qal*). In addition, the entire psalm creates a chiasm (A-YHWH is with me, B-He provides abundant food, C-Direct reference to the name and protection, D-I am not afraid, C'-Indirect reference to the name and protection, B'-You provide abundant wine, A'-I will be with YHWH). The psalm is divided into four sections by direct or indirect references to the divine name. The first and last are direct and the middle two are indirect. The first reference (with a non-verbal clause) and the third (with the only other non-verbal clause) establish the beginning of each major section (vv. 1bi and 4bi). So, the major break between the two strophes comes not at the end of verse 4, as usually thought, but in the middle of it. The fourth and last reference parallels the first as one of the only two direct uses of YHWH and frame the psalm as an inclusio. The second and third indirect references to the name form the C and C' levels of the chiasm. The third is the most indirect since it just says "you are with me" while the second uses the expression "his name," but the third can be seen as such a reference because it parallels the only other non-verbal clause in verse 1, where the name YHWH appears. These C-level references frame the climax of the psalm: I am not afraid. In each of the two strophes, the center point is, first, renewal and rest (vv. 2b–3a), and, second and similarly, refreshment and rest in the face of opposition.

All verbs are *yiqtol* with two exceptions, but the first of these exceptions is where a *qatal* is merely a stylistic change that still continues the mood and tense of the preceding *yiqtol* to which it is subordinate (v. 5). The other is the use of a *weqatal* in verse 6, and it helps us conclude that the *yiqtols* of the second strophe have a future-tense sense. The present tense is carried by the *yiqtols* of the first strophe. The emphasis is on YHWH's current and continuing provision and protection based on past experience. The future is in view, mainly in the second section, indicating what the psalmist believes he can expect YHWH to do in terms of protection and provision based on his present realities. A shift occurs in verse 4 when the psalmist begins to speak hypothetically and says, "if I might wander off the right path onto one that is dark and/or deadly" then "I will not be afraid of any danger." The second strophe is then initiated with "because You are/will be with me! [v. 4bi]" because it begins to enumerate the reasons why the psalmist was not afraid and need not be afraid from that point on: YHWH would protect him (v. 4b), nourish him (v. 5), and be good and loving to him as long as he lives (v. 6); i.e., YHWH is his shepherd. He would have needs, especially spiritual and emotional ones (since David had many enemies wanting his crown and his life), but all his needs would be met. He had this confidence in the future because this had always been true in the past. YHWH had always been with him, so he promised to always return to YHWH's house as a lifelong habit.

6

The Spirit in Psalm 51:10–12[1]

Introduction

The Problem

IF asked to provide a key verse or the first verse that comes to mind about the Holy Spirit in the OT, or that shows how the Holy Spirit's ministry during the old covenant contrasts with the new, most Bible students would cite Ps 51:13 in its popular English version: "Cast me not away from thy presence; and take not thy Holy Spirit from me" (KJV).[2] Traditional use of this verse among some evangelicals has provided a proof text for the doctrine that the Holy Spirit did not permanently indwell believers prior to his coming at Pentecost. Commentators differ over whether or not this verse directly supports this idea. If it were not about the person of the Holy Spirit, it would have no bearing whatsoever on this belief about the non-permanent influence of the Spirit in OT times. The problem is that the usual translation of this verse may present an erroneous exegesis—especially

---

1. Originally published as "'Spirit of Your Holiness' in Psalm 51:13," 29–49. Stylistic and corrective but no substantive changes have been made. Tables (originally appendices in the published article) are placed at the end of this chapter to conform to the current required book style and to allow maximum conformity to the article as first published in *Trinity Journal*.

2. The versification of Psalm 51 differs in the Hebrew of the Masoretic Text (hereafter MT) and English Bibles (hereafter EBs or EB). Throughout this paper the Hebrew versification will be given (sometimes followed parenthetically with the corresponding English versification).

when "holy" and "spirit" are capitalized, which freezes the interpretational options. For example, for St. Basil the Great all the descriptions of the "spirit" in Psalm 51 are titles for the Holy Spirit: "For He is called the Spirit of God, and the Spirit of Truth . . . the Upright Spirit, the Princely Spirit."[3] The editor's footnote to this statement connects it to Psalm 51 and, at least in the editor's opinion, corrects it by saying:

> Psa. Li.10, 12. Sept. Heb. A steadfast spirit, *i.e.*, "a spirit steadfastly purposed to lead a new life," cf. lxxviii. 37, cxii. 7, and a free, *i.e.*, willing spirit. Whether the latter does not refer to the Holy Spirit (in this case, "Thy freely-bestowed Spirit") is disputed. It must be noted, however, that "the Holy Spirit" is not spoken of in the Hebrew Scriptures as a Person, but as an influence.[4]

This verse may not be about the person of the Holy Spirit. A closer look at the grammar and context allows for an alternative understanding, and if this proposal is accepted, then Psalm 51:13 should not be used doctrinally regarding the nature of the Spirit's indwelling performance in OT times.

The Proposal

Scripture versions, sermons, sober commentaries, and songs have long stated and studied the significance of the person of the Holy Spirit in Psalm 51:13(11; EB). This paper will re-examine the suitability of this interpretation and suggest alternatively that it is a spiritual attribute of holiness that David prays will not leave him rather than the actual presence of the Holy Spirit. In other words, ורוח קדשך, which literally rendered is "spirit of your holiness," refers to personal spirituality, not the person of the Spirit. In English translation, consequently, "spirit" should not be capitalized and "holy" should be "holiness" or at least understood that way. But this "human" explanation and exegesis of "spirit" in the OT canonical context does not eliminate the spiritual and theological significance of ורוח קדשך for the NT believer as regards the Holy Spirit. Any spiritual fruit of holiness on the part of David or any human member of his spiritual lineage is the result of the influence of the Spirit. The question is: what is it that David fears he might have taken from him—the indwelling presence of the Holy Spirit per se or

---

3. Lewis, *St. Basil the Great*, 52.
4. Lewis, *St. Basil the Great*, 52.

the inner presence of a spiritual power provided by God's Spirit? This paper will suggest the latter was the key issue for David in Psalm 51. His intended meaning was a request to maintain a holy life, separated from the folly of sin but not from fellowship with his Savior (v. 13a[11a]). This is a prayer for Christians as well, who—having extended revelation—know more fully than David the requirement and role of the Holy Spirit in spiritual rebirth and renewal unto holiness.[5]

Two Interpretive Problems

Two particular problems emerge in dealing with the translations and commentaries on Psalm 51. The first problem is that the choice to use lower- or upper-case letters in the phrase "your [i.e., God's] spirit of holiness"[6] without commentary may imply something not intended by the translator. Lower-case letters, for example, may be employed for stylistic reasons while the understanding of the translator or interpreter is the meaning indicated by upper-case letters. While somewhat inherently and inescapably interpretive, even if very literal, a translation—especially a literal one—may or may not clearly reflect a specific interpretation. For example, the capitalization of "spirit" in Luther's *Die Heilige Schrift* is due to the nature of German nouns. Luther's commentary on Psalm 51 will have to be consulted to find out if he interprets the three uses of "spirit" in verses 12–14 as human or divine in each case. On the other hand, Brenton's use of capital letters in his English version of the Septuagint clearly indicates his understanding of the Holy Spirit of God in verses 13 and 14.[7] The MT and versions like the LXX, Vulgate, and NEB that do not employ upper-case letters leave the reader in doubt about the exact meaning of "your spirit of holiness" or "your holy spirit." The second-person possessive pronoun ("Y/your; T/thy") in Psalm 51:13b is clearly God. But that still leaves the question whether "spirit of

---

5. A related issue that muddies the water is the question whether an OT believer could experience the temporary and occasional indwelling of the Holy Spirit, usually in relation to obedience or repentance (which most believe is impossible for a Christian, who is permanently indwelt).

6. A mechanically literal rendering of the Hebrew ורוח קדשך, which is open to several interpretations syntactically and a number of translations theoretically, especially out of context: Your holy Spirit, Your Holy Spirit, Your holy spirit, etc. "Your" capitalized or not, has to refer to God.

7. The corresponding passage in the LXX is Psalm 50:10–12. Cf. AV, ASV, RSV, NASB, NIV, NKJV.

holiness" is the Spirit of the triune God or David's desire for holiness that is sourced in or sent by God.

The second problem is that commentaries are not always clear as to whether God's "holy spirit" in Psalm 51:13 is directly the person of the Holy Spirit present in David or indirectly a Holy Spirit-produced spiritual disposition in David. In the first instance, David would have the Holy Spirit in mind as he wrote what modern editors would eventually name in verse 13, but in the second case he would only be thinking of his own desire for holiness, which of course would be related to the work of the Holy Spirit of God in his life, theologically, but would not be the point he was making. If so, then the person of the Holy Spirit is not the issue at stake in verse 13, although by implication the Spirit might be mentioned in the larger context of OT or biblical pneumatology.

Exegesis of the Hebrew Text of Psalm 51:12-14

The Understanding of רוח in Psalm 51 in the Versions and Commentaries

Due to these two interpretive complications, this section will combine a summary of the translational and interpretational problems in versions and commentaries and give emphasis to commentaries with translation.[8]

In Translations

In the twenty English translations or versions compared from 1611–1989,[9] five variations in regard to capitalization in rendering ורוח קדשך appear:

---

8. See the first two tables at the end of this chapter displaying a historical overview of the translation of Psalm 51:12-14 and a selective interpretational summary. Commentaries that include personal translations are listed in both charts. All translation, naturally, involves some degree of interpretation and the two cannot cleanly and neatly be separated; however, one can distinguish between Bible versions that give only a finished translation with little or no commentary, authors' personal translations provided in interpretive commentaries, and commentaries that provide exegesis and exposition of a Bible book or passages without giving a full, private translation of the texts involved. These latter often include a copy of some standard Bible version, upon which the commentary is based.

9. See the in-text table below (p. 108; and see n. 8). The use of upper-case letters in the non-English versions and commentary translations of Psalm 51 is not as much an issue as with the English renderings since often capital letters are not employed in the

your/thy holy spirit, Thy holy spirit, your/thy holy Spirit, your/thy/ Holy Spirit, and Thy Holy Spirit. The latter three clearly indicate the divine person and presence of the Holy Spirit. When commentary is involved, even the first spelling is found to mean the same. Of these twenty, fourteen are Bible versions per se and the remaining six are commentaries in which the author provides a personal translation. Of the fourteen versions surveyed only four have "thy/your holy spirit": JB (1966), NAB (1969), NEB (1970), and NRSV (1989)—all within the last thirty years. The first two are Catholic, the third Anglican (British), and the fourth American (USA). Of the six commentary translations, three have the lower-case phrase, which is, apart from context or comment, open to interpretation: Cohen in the *Soncino Bible* (1945),[10] Oesterley (1953),[11] and Dahood in the *Anchor Bible* (1968)[12]—respectively, Jewish, Anglican, and Catholic. The fourth, Westermann (1984, German edition), a continental Lutheran uses the German equivalent of "thy holy Spirit" (rendering of his translator in 1989), but in German grammar this noun would normally be capitalized anyway. The meaning he attaches to it, however, is somewhat ambiguous.[13] Leupold, fifth, an American evangelical Lutheran (1959), uniquely uses capital letters for the full phrase and gives a translation of ורוח קדשך which seems unmistakable in its meaning: "Thy Holy Spirit."[14] The sixth, Dickson (1653), offers a third variation with the use of capital letters: "thy Holy Spirit."[15] While he follows the usual understanding of David's own personality as the subject of verse 12 (10), he is the only one of these six to capitalize "spirit" in the translation he gives for both verses 13 (11) and 14 (12), and, as might be guessed, is the only other one to agree with Dahood's interpretation of the "spirit" in verse 14 (12) as God's: "thy free Spirit."[16]

---

same manner as in English. The use of upper-cases is of interest, however, when these non-English versions and commentaries do use capitals in a manner similar to English and as observed in the English versions of these translations and interpretations of the original in languages such as Greek, Latin, French, and German. Neither the Septuagint nor the Vulgate capitalize "spirit" in any of these three verses (cf. n. 45).

10. Cf. Cohen, *Psalms*, 163.

11. Cf. Oesterley, *Psalms*, 273.

12. Cf. Dahood, *Psalms II*, 8.

13. Cf. Westermann, *Living Psalms*, 98; p. 111; and n. 53.

14. Cf. Leupold, *Exposition of Psalms*, 405.

15. Dickson, *A Commentary*, 308.

16. Dickson, *A Commentary*, 308. Cf. the discussion of Dahood's approach below in n. 34 and p. 103.

OTHER VOICES IN OLD TESTAMENT INTERPRETATION

In Commentaries

The survey of commentaries for this study was highly selective[17] but includes works from the fourth to the present centuries. Those that include the author's own translation of Psalm 51 were mentioned above along with various English versions.[18] In this section, the remaining commentaries, which do not have original translations, will be briefly evaluated. Many give a meaning for verse 13 (11) that is not explicitly the removal of the person or indwelling presence of the Holy Spirit (e.g., Aglen who has "Divine favour"[19] and Clarke who has "Divine fellowship"[20]) but, still, what David prays to be maintained is seen as a power or influential presence of the third member of the triune Godhead. Besides these two interpretations just cited, the only others who render or refer to the phrase in a potentially substantive way other than "Y/your H/holy S/spirit" are Calvin and Dalglish, who have, respectively, and probably as a stylistically more literal rendering, "Spirit of thy holiness"[21] and "Thy spirit of holiness."[22] Yet a closer look at their comments reveals that the "spirit" is a divine person not David's personality, however his relationship or role with David is defined. But this does not necessarily mean that David fears that God's Spirit may leave him. Even if the Holy Spirit is intended, David's fear may be for the degeneration of his own heart or spirit, which can only be cured through the Spirit's gracious ministry. Of the more than twenty interpretive works on Psalm 51 consulted, only two have upper-case "right Spirit" in verse 12 (10) or propose that meaning. Three do not use the upper-case "Spirit" or "Holy" in verse 13 (11), but none of these explains the reference as David's desire for God's holiness, although it is not clear exactly how some understand "your holy spirit." In most cases the upper-case "Your" or "Thy" appears; either way, these commentators relate this spirit to God, either as the person of the Holy Spirit or a power that he provides. However translated, the sense is frequently related to divine fellowship (for which Clarke[23] makes reference to 1 Sam 16:13–14 and Hag 2:5), but it is the "spirit of holiness" of or

---

17. See table on pp. 113–14.

18. Related evaluation appears primarily in the footnotes; see nn. 34–53 and pp. 103–111.

19. Aglen, *Book of Psalms*, 10.

20. Clarke, *Analytical Studies*, 143.

21. Calvin, *Calvin's Commentaries*, V:298.

22. Dalglish, *Psalm Fifty-One*, 155–61.

23. Clarke, *Analytical Studies*, 143.

from God that is seen as the focus of verse 13 (11). Four use the lower-case "spirit" or the equivalent in all three verses, but none of them interpret the "spirit" the same way in each verse. Only St. Basil and Luther seem to be consistent in that manner by relating each verse to the person of the Holy Spirit in some way, and in both instances, the translators of their commentaries have the capitalized "Spirit" in each verse.[24]

Eight of the commentaries[25] interpret or capitalize "spirit" in verses 13 (11) and 14 (12) and not in verse 12 (10). Still, when verse 14 (12) is explained as referring to "[Y/your] willing/generous spirit," it is not always clear whether this is a name for the Holy Spirit or a description of God's S/spirit, as opposed to a spiritual quality that comes from YHWH God. We are then left with eleven or twelve (half of the) commentators who interpret verses 12 (10) and 14 (12) as pertaining to David's inner spiritual condition and only verse 13 (11) as God's Holy Spirit. The remainder of this study will examine exegetical aspects of the text of Psalm 51 in light of the previous comments.

The Use of רוח in the Old Testament

The Use of רוח in All Contexts

A look at the use of רוח in the Old Testament may prove helpful for this discussion but only a summary presentation of the data is possible.[26] Leon Wood's *The Holy Spirit in the Old Testament*[27] makes a strong case for some type of reconsideration and redefinition of the absolute assumption made by many that OT believers were not renewed or indwelt by the Holy Spirit, as NT believers were. One should not, consequently, merely cite this assumption—as some do—as a settled and unquestionable evangelical consensus that ought to prevent the interpreter from asking if the "spirit of holiness" in Psalm 51 is God's Spirit or David's spirituality. A desideratum

---

24. Basil is unique among all the commentators surveyed in having both the term "spirit" and its modifier capitalized. Cf. Lewis, *St. Basil the Great*, 52. For Luther, cf. n. 209 below.

25. See tables below (pp. 113-14) on the history of the translation and interpretation of MT Psalm 51:12-14.

26. See table below (p. 115) regarding the OT chronology of *ruach*, and cf. nn. 5 above and 28 below.

27. See Wood, *Holy Spirit*, esp. chapter 6. Cf. n. 29.

for OT "spirit" is a comprehensive presentation of uses of רוח where it signifies an attitude in biblical and extra-biblical literature.[28]

A preliminary chronological study of רוח in the OT reveals that the person of the Holy Spirit is referred to (where "Spirit" versus "spirit" is not debated) as follows:[29] (1) "Spirit of God (*Elohim*)" is used in approximately twelve passages, in all the historical periods except the post-exilic; (2) "Spirit of the LORD (YHWH)"[30] is used in approximately twenty passages from the conquest of Canaan to the exile (but not prior to the conquest or in post-exilic writings); (3) "My Spirit" is used in approximately ten passages, only one of these (Gen 6:3) prior to the divided monarchy; and (4) "The/His/Your Spirit"[31] is used in approximately twenty passages in all periods, but it is the only expression for God's Spirit used in the Psalms, unless Psalm 51:13(11) is the sole exception.[32] The phrase "holy spirit" is used in only two passages and three verses including the passage under discussion in this paper (Ps 51:13[11]; Isa 63:10; 63:11).[33] When these texts

---

28. A personal, unpublished chronological study of the uses of רוח in the OT was instrumental in leading to this paper. This preliminary study found no instance in the OT—other than probably Psalm 51:13 and possibly Isaiah 63:10–11—where רוח is a human attitude when a divine pronoun or proper name is attached or added. That רוח—apart from a direct connection with a divine appellation—often indicates a human attitude or attribute is obvious from Psalm 51:12, 14 and from many other passages from Genesis to Malachi (e.g., Gen 45:27; Num 5:14; Deut 2:30; 1 Sam 1:15; Ezra 1:1; Job 7:11; Ps 32:2; Prov 16:18; Eccl 7:8; Isa 57:15; Ezek 18:31; Mal 2:15–16; et al.). Worthy of special mention is Numbers 27:16, "YHWH, the God of the spirits of all flesh." Cf. nn. 32–33, 40, and 55 below. Of interest is Curtis, "'Private Spirits,'" 257–66, in which the interpretation of the phrase "private [human] spirits" as used in the *Westminster Confession of Faith* is discussed.

29. See table below (p. 115) on the OT occurrences of the divine רוח. The OT periods and related observations assume, generally, traditional dates for the biblical books. Phrases like "an evil spirit from the LORD" are not considered here.

30. This category also includes the rare "Spirit of the Lord YHWH."

31. The definite sense, whether or not the definite article appears (i.e., morphologically or syntactically definite), is included here as well as forms that have suffixed pronouns, but only the second- or third-person.

32. There is no reference to God's Spirit in the poetic books of Proverbs, Ecclesiastes, and Song of Solomon. The one exception, according to some translations, is Eccl 11:5, but in light of the immediate context most scholars and modern versions now understand רוח there to refer to the wind and not any "spirit." In the historical books pertaining to David's life, God's Spirit is usually referred to as "the Spirit of YHWH" or "the S/spirit of God," and only a couple times as "the Spirit"—but never as the "Holy Spirit."

33. For now, since this study is only concerned with an exegesis of the use of "holy spirit" in Psalm 51, the Isaiah context may be thought of as the place where "Holy Spirit"

THE SPIRIT IN PSALM 51:10–12

speak of the רוח empowering someone for service it is not usually, if ever, clear if this is being done by a "S/spirit" already and permanently present in the person or by a "S/spirit" that comes upon the person as an external, temporary force.

Most often, the person of the Holy Spirit is referred to as the Spirit of God or Spirit of YHWH (i.e., "the LORD" in most translations). This is also true of the Scriptures composed during or concerning the time of the United Monarchy of Israel (traditionally and roughly ca. 1050–930 BC). Of the poetic and Wisdom books related at least in part or in some way to this period (Psalms, Proverbs, Ecclesiastes, Song of Solomon), רוח appears six times, five of these in the Psalms (Pss 51:11; 104:30; 106:33; 139:7; 143:10; Eccl 11:5). The verse in Ecclesiastes can be set aside for now since its context and parallelism, and therefore numerous commentaries and translations, indicate that "wind" and not "spirit" is the meaning of רוח. Most interesting is that of all five uses of this term in the Psalms, all except Psalm 51—without any doubt—refer to God's Spirit (only Psalm 51 has the word קדש ["holy" or "holiness"]).

It is hard to tell if Dahood means all of these to describe God's Spirit or a godly spirit which can be manifest in a human person.[34] His reference to Psalm 143:10 ("With your good spirit lead me into the level land") clearly identifies the "spirit" as belonging to or coming from God and leads him to posit a human spirit in verse 12 (10) but a S/spirit of or from God in verses 13–14 (11–12). The lack of any capitalization and the sparse nature of the commentary makes Dahood's exact sense hard to nail down, except that these different types of "spirit," in the same way, describe God and may be directed to people in fellowship with God for their good and his glory. Regardless, the fact that Dahood has reasons to place verse 13 and 14 on the same level, along with the fact that most see no reason to connect the "spirit" in verses 12 (10) and 14 (12) with anyone except David (only Dahood limits David to v. 12 [10]), argues for the plausibility that the "spirit" in verse 13 (11) is the same as the other. But this makes it likely that this

---

refers to God's Spirit, limiting this usage to Isaiah. None of the poetical and historical books related to David's life refers to God's Spirit as "Holy" (unless Psalm 51 is the exception); yet even the use of "spirit of holiness" in the Isaiah context may be questioned for similar reasons as in Psalm 51, as noted briefly above.

34. Dahood's full lower-case rendering of רוח קדשך ("your holy spirit") refers (a bit ambiguously) to a spirit of or from God, similar to the others surveyed who do not capitalize "holy spirit," but unlike all others, he interprets the "spirit" in the last two verses (13–14 [11–12]) identically as to source if not substance (Dahood, *Psalms II*, 8).

"spirit" also is not God's (as Dahood suggests). If Dahood is right, then the "spirit" in Psalm 51:13–14 (11–12), if not verse 12 (10), is either God's or David's but not a mixture of the two.[35]

Presumably, the use of lower-case letters in Psalm 51:13 (11) by Oesterley is for consistency with "spirit" in the preceding and following verses, or is due to adoption of a style that does not capitalize "holy spirit";[36] however, Oesterley does capitalize "Lord" and "God." He clearly identifies the "steadfast spirit" as David's but the "holy spirit" as God's (yet he does this implicitly rather than explicitly through a parenthetical listing of cross-references: 2 Kgs 13:23; Pss 102:10; 143:10). His understanding of the "willing spirit" is unclear; he states simply that David "recalls the time long ago when he had not fallen away from God and prays: *Restore unto me the joy of thy help, and,* as of yore, *sustain me with a willing spirit* [italics in the original]."[37] Apparently, the "willing spirit" is David's own attitude since (1) it is poetically parallel with the "joy of thy help," which David asks to be restored, and (2) the Holy Spirit, in Oesterley's thought, still resides with David because he fears it could be removed and, consequently, prays that it not be taken from him.

The Use of רוח *with "Holy"*

In addition to Psalm 51, "holy spirit" (or literally "spirit of holiness") appears just three times in the OT. The remaining two occurrences are in Isaiah 63:10 and 63:11, where God's Spirit is usually assumed to be in view (Psalm 51:13 [11] is the only place in the OT where "holy spirit" is used with the second masc. sing. pronoun).[38] These are the only two contexts in the OT where "H/holy S/spirit" occurs. Isaiah 63:14, interestingly, refers to "the spirit of YHWH," which clearly equals (to many readers) God's (Holy) Spirit. An inspection of the Hebrew of Isaiah 63:10–11 reveals the same genitive, construct form as in Psalm 51:13 (11), the only difference being

---

35. See Dahood, *Psalms II*, 8.

36. In some modern examples, like Oesterley, *Psalms*, 273 (whose opinion of "spirit" in verses 12–14 [10–12] parallels Cohen's), when capitals are optional, the use, or non-use in this instance, of upper-case letters in the author's personal translation may contradict the proposed interpretation. "Holy Spirit" may be meant by "holy spirit." Of course, some translators and commentators are not greatly concerned in such texts with the Trinitarian issues.

37. Oesterley, *Psalms*, 273. Cf. n. 36.

38. See n. 5.

the number of the pronoun suffix used in each case. Could it be that the phrase "holy spirit" is reserved for situations when a godly attitude of separation from sin is in view? In this case, of course, the reference will not be to the Holy Spirit per se, although such a human spirit can only result from the influence of God's Spirit. Also curious in this light, and perhaps compelling for Isaiah 63, if not Psalm 51, is the fact that the terminology "Holy Spirit" did become—contra the OT pattern—the principal nomenclature for reference to the Spirit of God as a member of the triune Godhead. This is especially noteworthy if, in fact, "holy spirit" in the OT perhaps never or only once or twice means God's Spirit per se. Isaiah 63:11 (but less likely 63:10) could be a reference to "a spirit (attitude) of holiness" for a number of the same reasons posited for Psalm 51:13 (11). It is striking that when Isaiah wanted to speak of God's Spirit (63:14) he chose the phrase "[the] S/spirit of YHWH." Additionally, one wonders why the OT authors did not use the absolute form for an attributive or predicate adjective construction instead of the construct genitive to indicate that "your/his holy spirit" (literally, "your/his spirit of holiness") refer to "the Holy Spirit" in Psalm 51 and Isaiah 63. H. C. Leupold notes, "One can scarcely escape the conclusion that this passage comes close to Is. 63:10, 11, where not a principle but a personal divine Spirit is under consideration. But in the mind of the writer the loss of the Spirit means the total loss of God's grace."[39] According to Leupold, David fears that his sin will incur the wrath of God, as happened with Saul, from whom the Spirit was withdrawn (cf. 1 Sam 16:1, 7).[40] Leupold equivocates a bit because he equates the presence of God's grace, a principle, with the Holy Spirit, a person. He says the motivation for the petition of verse 13 (11) was David's concern over exclusion from the

---

39. Leupold, *Exposition of Psalms*, 405.

40. But this may beg the question. Was Saul deprived of the person or rather the power of the Spirit, as when a believer today sins intentionally and unrepentantly and loses communion with and control from the Spirit but not complete connection? To be sure, we must be careful not to introduce nuanced notions like the interplay between the Spirit's presence, power, and person that might be foreign to the OT. Individual OT authors usually look at matters more generally and simply. Consequently, taking isolated statements about the removal of the Holy Spirit at face value may lead to overly literal or too simplistic conclusions theologically. But even if an OT saint was not permanently indwelt by the Spirit, that does not necessarily mean that is what David had in mind in Psalm 51:13 (11). If not, the wording should not be used as a proof-text for this theory of OT pneumatology. Neither should this passage be interpreted primarily through this theological presupposition, even if correct. Cf. Leupold, *Exposition of Psalms*, 405, and n. 55.

presence of God and from free access to his throne. Seemingly in contrast with his translation and conclusion, Leupold here sounds like it is not the person or presence of the Holy Spirit in David's life that is in jeopardy, but his interpersonal participation with God's Spirit on a regular basis regarding repentance. The "spirit" in verses 12 (10) and 14 (12) is clearly presented as a disposition of resoluteness and willingness that David desires from God's grace. The immediate context is the key.

A possible significant consideration in this regard would be a comparative/contrastive study of the functions of terms in the OT, which have both construct and absolute forms used with an adjective. "Holy spirit" in the OT is always used as an object, whereas the other formulae, which by contrast are undoubtedly and principally used to refer to the person of the Holy Spirit (i.e., "spirit of *Elohim*/YHWH), are usually the subject grammatically, and definite morphologically or syntactically. These latter expressions are of course genitive constructs because their function is not attributive but possessive or appositional. In the case of attributive adjectives, Hebrew can use either an absolute (free) or construct (bound) form, so the latter is certainly a possible way to express the meaning "your Holy Spirit"; but the construct, unlike the absolute form, leaves more open the question of what kind of construct genitive the syntax intends (appositional, attributive, possessive, or result)? The absolute construction would narrow the choice to an attributive ("your Holy Spirit") or predicate ("Your Spirit is holy"). Furthermore, in Psalm 51:13 (11) only the attributive absolute would be contextually possible, so the writer could have used the absolute construction to make "your Holy Spirit" more apparent.

The Setting and Structure of Psalm 51

The historical context of Psalm 51 in general, and verses 12–14 (10–12) in particular, is David's prayer and plea for mercy and forgiveness as he repents of his sin of adultery with Bathsheba following a rebuke from the prophet Nathan.[41] The immediate living and literary context of these three verses is 51:1–9 and 13–19. The first nine verses establish the main theme of David's longing to be cleansed from his sin and include statements like "cleanse me from my sin" (v. 2); "You desire truth in the inward parts" (v. 6a); "teach me wisdom in my secret heart" (v. 6b); "purge me" and "wash me" (v. 7); and "hide your face from my sins" (v. 9). David was fiercely

41. Cf. 2 Sam 11:1—12:15, esp. 12:13.

focused on the restoration of his inner being, that is his spiritual state or soul. His confession of sin and general pleas for cleansing and change in verses 1–9 give way to the more specific requests of verses 10–11, where he asks for restoration of his former state of fellowship with God and for renewal of spiritual vitality. His sin has already blocked fellowship with God, and thus with the Holy Spirit, so David should not be expected in these verses to be fearful at the prospect of losing contact with God or having the indwelling person or power of the Spirit removed. If David means anything like this, it would be that God not keep his presence and Spirit at a distance, but David, not God, is the one that has moved. The need is not for the person or presence of the Holy Spirit to be maintained or reclaimed but for David to be spiritually revitalized and his sins removed.

R. Cohen's decision to capitalize "Thy" only is crucial for his Jewish audience because it makes clear that this spirit is divine but keeps the reader from thinking it is a separate member of the Godhead.[42] Only YHWH is God. So, for Cohen, the "holy spirit of God" is synonymous with God's presence, from which a sinner can be excluded. But once more, the fearful prospect of having "Your holy spirit" taken from David is not a matter of a person being removed from David's life but of the privileged position of prayer and personal interaction with God being disrupted. The רוח קדשך is not someone who can be lifted on or off David but a relationship that can be lost. Furthermore, from this perspective, even if this presence or person is seen as the Holy Spirit or God's holy spirit (as divine or a spiritual dimension of the psalmist), David's point is the paralyzing prospect that God's holy will and work in his life will be wanting.[43]

---

42. Rabbi Cohen's "Thy holy spirit" (*Psalms*, 163) represents a conservative Jewish perspective and also seems to contrast with his interpretation of this "spirit" as the "spirit of the LORD" (which Cohen as well compares to the spirit that departed from Saul) and the "Presence of God," since words like "God" are capitalized. It may be, however, that upper-case letters are reserved for names of God and "holy spirit" is not used or understood that way. Still, Cohen sees this spirit in verse 13 (11) as God's, while the "stedfast [sic] spirit" in verse 12 (10) and the "willing spirit" in verse 14 (12) belong to David as human, emotional, and attitudinal qualities. For Jewish theology this "holy spirit" can be called a "Presence of God" in the commentary but not the "Holy Spirit" in the translation because of a strict monotheistic and non- (or anti-) Trinitarian doctrine.

43. Cohen, *Psalms*, 163, and cf. the previous note (42).

The Significance and Structure of Psalm 51:12–14

This section will examine the effect that literary and linguistic mechanics of Psalm 51:12–14 have on the meaning of these verses, especially verse 13. If the Hebrew text of these verses is literally displayed in English translation, the analysis as shown in the following chart results:[44]

Cola	Literal English Translation	Pattern	Word Pairs
10a	*a heart pure* /create/in me/O God	A-B-C-D	a pure heart
10b	and a *spirit of steadfastness*/renew/in me	A'-B'-C'-[D']	a right *spirit* (רוח)
11a	do not cast me/from *your* presence	A-B	*your* presence
11b	and [the] *spirit of your holiness*/ do not take from me	B'-A'	*your* holy *spirit* (רוח)
12a	restore to me/[the] joy of *your salvation*	A-B	*your* joyous salvation
12b	and [with] *a spirit of willingness*/ you uphold me	B'-A'	a willing *spirit* (רוח)

If this "human" interpretation of רוח in verse 13 (11) is accepted (as it usually is in vv. 12 and 14), then only indirectly in the larger theological context of the analogy of faith is there any allusion to the person of the Holy Spirit. With this approach, the parallelism between verses 13a (11a) and 13b (11b) would be synthetic rather than "synonymous" (or "static"). This is more pleasing stylistically because it is consistent with the fact that, of the three verses concerned, only verses 13 (11) and 14 (12) share the chiastic A-B//B'-A' pattern and it would place both verses 13 (11) and 14 (12) in synthetic parallelism (which v. 14 [12] is with most renderings), in contrast to verse 12 (10), which is clearly a "synonymous" restatement of sorts and set apart with its A-B-C-D//A'-B'-C'-[D'] structure. Verse 13 parallels, "do not cast me away from your [i.e., God's] presence" with "do not take your [i.e., God's] holy spirit from me," but in light of the clear concerns of the immediate context, this could be seen as David's continued cry for cleansing and re-creation, as specifically begun in the preceding and continued in the following verse. David is saying, it seems, as most consistent with his flow of thought, that he desires the restoration of fellowship with God, which is based on his return and not God's. He wants to return to a lifestyle of holiness inwardly, and as a result outwardly, which will please God and enhance communion with God. David knows this is only possible with God's

---

44. Verses 12a–14b in the Hebrew MT equal verses 10a–12b in the English versions.

enablement. Therefore, he does not vow to do better in his own strength but throughout the Psalm hungers for, and in fact almost demands, God's help. Grammatically, either morphologically or syntactically (by form or function), David's requests are imperatives and forceful. Consequently, if verse 13 (11) is meant to be a consistent or synonymous, rather than complimentary, parallel with the surrounding two verses, then David, having asked earlier to be forgiven and thus positionally holy before God, is now, as in verses 12 (10) and 14 (12), asking God to strengthen him spiritually so that he might become more practically holy and then be able to enjoy God's presence.

How do Luther and Calvin[45] explain the "spirit" in Psalm 51:12–14 (10–12), especially "the holy spirit" in verse 13 (11)? Luther sees all three of these verses as pertaining to gifts of the Holy Spirit because the name of God's Spirit is repeated in each.[46] For some reason, "spirit" is not capitalized in verse 12 as in verses 13–14. Interestingly, Luther, in commenting on verse 12 (10), expresses his uneasiness with disputes "as to whether he [David] is speaking about the 'efficient' Spirit, or divine person, or about the gift of the Spirit" [asking], How do precise disputes about such things edify?"[47] He seems to support the idea that whatever the "spirit" is in these verses, it is the same kind of spirit, and for Luther it is God's Holy Spirit characterized with appellations that allude to inner qualities this Spirit gives as gracious gifts to believers. If Luther is right to claim that consistency and context demand that the "spirit" be the same in each verse and that each relate the Holy Spirit to a gift of grace for sinful humans like David, then perhaps it is the gift itself that David requests in each case. Calvin, as translated by

---

45. Luther (*Die Bibel*, 546) has "Geist" for all three appearances of רוח in verses 12–14 (10–12). But in German this term would be usually capitalized regardless of context (cf. Pelikan's note on Luther's interpretation of Psalm 51:12 [10]: "The translation to which Luther came in his revision of the Psalms in 1531 was: '*Und gib mir ein newen gewissen geist*'"; Pelikan, *Luther's Works*, 12:379). However, it is clear from his commentary he understands the "spirit" in verse 13 (11) to be the Holy Spirit of God. Only the English edition of Calvin's commentary was consulted, and the translator capitalized "spirit" in verse 13 (11)—"Spirit of thy holiness"—but not in either of the surrounding verses (cf. Calvin, *Calvin's Commentaries*, V:298). The translation "holy spirit" is used by Luther (German), the Vulgate (Latin), and the LXX (Greek) but not Calvin (cf. n. 9 and p. 110 and the table below about the history of translating Psalm 51:12–14 (p. 113).

46. Sometimes Pelikan translates Luther with "holy spirit" and at other times with "Holy Spirit."

47. Pelikan, *Luther's Works*, 12:377.

Anderson, capitalizes "spirit" only in verse 13 (11).[48] Having already been endued with the Holy Spirit, he argues, David asks in verse 12 (10) that God would renew his human spirit by making it right or righteous. He then interprets verse 13 (11) as a presentation of "the same petition" as in verse 12 (10) "in language which implies the connection of pardon with the enjoyment of the leading of the Holy Spirit."[49] In other words, Calvin seems to suggest that while God's Spirit is mentioned in verse 13 (11), "take not the Spirit of thy holiness from me" expresses David's need for a new heart or spirit. If this is the real issue at stake, and Calvin is right that David already viewed himself as having God or God's Spirit at work in his life, then perhaps it is the spiritual quality of personal holiness that David desires in verse 13 (11) along with steadfastness 12 (10) and willingness 14 (12), which all come through God's help.

The Significance of "Spirit of Your Holiness" in Psalm 51:13

The interpretation of Psalm 51:13 being proposed by this study may be further supported by noting that the statements "Do not cast" and "Do not take" in verse 13 (11) involve the use of imperfect verbs of a precative mood with the negative אל of subjective denial rather than the negative לא of objective and strong denial or prohibition. The result is a tone that should be translated something like "may I not be cut off from Your presence // may Your spirit of holiness not be taken from me." This enhances the synthetic relationship between the two lines, whereas the connection between the two lines in the traditional reading—"Do not cast me // Do not take your Spirit—is somewhat ambiguous, especially if one assumes David is preoccupied with the possibility of the indwelling Spirit being removed. The interplay intended between the lines is curious unless the second line is seen as the continuation or re-creation of what God or his Spirit can accomplish in David's life, because otherwise the parallel is "Do not take me away from" versus "Do not take away from me." But if verse 13b (11b) is David's plea for personal, God-like holiness as this study suggests,[50] then

---

48. Cf. Calvin, *Calvin's Commentaries*, V:298.

49. Cf. Calvin, *Calvin's Commentaries*, V:299; and see n. 9.

50. This is true even if David's request is for an empowered but assumed presence of the Holy Spirit, because either way the interpretation has to do with power in David's life spiritually. The issue is not whether the person of the Holy Spirit is a presence permanently or temporarily, or with the fear that David's sin will ultimately lead to the Spirit

the interplay between the lines is more logical and meaningful in light of the context. The sense would be: "Let me not be cut off from your presence [i.e., fellowship] // May Your holiness not be removed from me [i.e., so that I will not sin and consequently contaminate my communion with You]."

If "your holy spirit" in Psalm 51 refers directly to a quality of God-produced holiness in David's life and not to God's Spirit (at least not directly), then the best rendering is "Your holy spirit,"[51] or more interpretively: "Do not repel me from your presence // Do not remove my desire for your holiness" (i.e., otherwise sin that will block access and fellowship will result). This understanding is consistent with the ancient Near Eastern court, where one who displeases the king is banished from his presence. Claus Westermann writes: "'Cast me not away from thy presence' is a reminiscence of the liturgical blessing 'The Lord make his face to shine upon you'. [sic] The shining face of God means His benevolent, shielding protection."[52]

According to Westermann,[53] the "right spirit" and "willing spirit" in the verses surrounding verse 13 are David's. Both result from divine renewal. Verse 13 (11), where he employs "Spirit," explains the desire expressed in verse 12 (10) for a clean heart and a right or "firmly fixed spirit." These are endangered when fellowship with God is broken (cf. 51:4); so apparently Westermann understands the "taking" of "thy holy Spirit" (his rendering) in verse 13b (11b) as equivalent to being "cast from thy presence" (v. 13a [11a]) to signify the potential of violating (v. 13b [11b]), and thus damaging (v. 13a [11a]), the divine-human relationship. David fears not the loss of the person of the Holy Spirit but of interpersonal communication with God, who is Holy and Spirit. David "knows that only through uninterrupted communion with the gracious and holy God is true renewal possible. Verse twelve describes a life so renewed."[54]

---

being withdrawn.

51. Cohen (*Psalms*, 163), the conservative Jewish commentator, has the same conclusion but for different reasons. Cf. n. 42.

52. Westermann, *Living Psalms*, 98. This blessing among Israel also was connected to the ancient court culture.

53. Westermann's ambiguous explanation (see p. 111) is that the request by David to not have this taken away "points to the danger of violating the Holy" (*Living Psalms*, 98). This sounds more like the fear of David's own spirit of holiness failing, i.e., the loss of holy power due to the Spirit's influence, rather than the fracture of his union with the presence of God's Spirit.

54. Westermann, *Living Psalms*, 98; cf. nn. 52-53.

The indwelling nature of God's Holy Spirit, consequently, is not the direction of David's thoughts. His direct intention is related to the "spirit [inner quality] of holiness," which he desires to deepen, and to the fact that it is "your [i.e., God's] holiness"; that is, he recognizes and remarks that behind the attainment of holy attitudes and actions is the necessary inward work of God himself; but David is not here naming the one to whom he looks for help, i.e., the Holy Spirit.

Conclusion

Psalm 51:13 (11) does not deal with the issue of the Holy Spirit in the lives of OT saints. If "holy spirit" in 51:13 (11) means God's Spirit, then David fears not that a "person" will leave him but that he might lose some things that can affect and enable the spiritual life or inner renewal of godliness that David desires. Yet it is just as possible that this person is not named in verse 13 (11) but that the "holy spirit"—better rendered "spirit of [i.e., characterized by] your holiness"—is a power, the spiritual quality of holiness, which is shown in other Scriptures to be a by-product of walking in the Spirit.[55] The structure of the Hebrew text does not suggest that the "spirit" in any of these verses is a kind of spirit different from that in the adjoining verses or in verse 19 (17)—spiritual and sinless (cf. v. 11[9]) attitudes or activities which David prays to attain out of gratitude for forgiveness and in order to maintain fellowship with God and minister (cf. v. 15[13]) to other sinners. These desires require one to have a holy spirit (or inner holiness), which of course is only possible—and David assumes this—through the power of YHWH's *ruach*.

---

55. By comparison and contrast cf. 1 Samuel 18:10, where "an evil spirit from God rushed upon Saul, and he raved within his house" (NRSV), or "an evil [or injurious] spirit from God came forcefully upon Saul" (NIV). "Evil (i.e., bad) spirit from God" in the MT is רוח אלהים רעה. Regarding "God's presence" as the meaning of 51:13, cf. n. 42 and 1 Samuel 16:14, where the "spirit of [*ruach*] the LORD [YHWH] departed from Saul." Was it the person, the power, or both that departed, or was it merely that Saul lost his own spiritual power by no longer living a holy life and depending on God's Spirit? See comments on p. 105 and n. 40 and nn. 5, 40, 42, and note that Psalm 143:10 is about the Spirit's guidance of believers. Consider also Acts 2:14–21 in this discussion and passages in the Bible about the power of the Lord, such as Numbers 14:17; 2 Kings 3:15; and Luke 5:17.

TABLES

History of the Translation of MT Psalm 51:12–14 (10–12 EBs)[56]

OT Version	Date	51:12(10)	51:13(11)	51:14(12)
LXX [Ps 50] Arndt/Gingrich Brenton NETS	250 BC 1957 1851 2014	πνεῦμα εὐθὲς "right spirit" "right spirit" "upright spirit"	πνεῦμα τὸ ἅγιόν "holy spirit" "holy Spirit" "holy spirit"	πνεύματί ἡγεμονικῷ "guiding spirit" "directing Spirit" "leading spirit"
Vulgate (Ps 50) (Jerome)	400 AD	*spiritum rectum*	*spiritum sanctum*	*spiritu principali*
Biblia Sacra Iuxtum Vulgatum	2015, tagged	*spiritum stabilem*	*spiritum sanctum*	*spiritu potenti*
Douay (Psa 50)	1609	right spirit	holy spirit	perfect spirit
Luther's Bible	1532	*beständigen Geist*	*heiligen Geist*	*willigen Geist*
AV (1st ed.)	1611	right spirit	holy Spirit	free Spirit
AV (rev. ed.)	1632	right spirit	Holy Spirit	free Spirit
Dickson	1653	right spirit	thy Holy Spirit	thy free Spirit
ASV	1901	right spirit	holy Spirit	willing spirit
Soncino Bible (Cohen)	1945	stedfast spirit [*sic*]	Thy holy spirit	a willing spirit
RSV	1952	right spirit	Holy spirit	willing spirit
Oesterley	1953	steadfast spirit	holy spirit	willing spirit
Peshitta/Lamsa	1957	right spirit	holy spirit	glorious spirit
Leupold	1959	steadfast spirit	Holy Spirit	willing spirit
NASB	1960	steadfast spirit	Holy Spirit	willing spirit
JB	1966	constant spirit	holy spirit	spirit . . . willing
Anchor Bible	1968	resolute spirit	holy spirit	generous spirit
NAB	1969	steadfast spirit	holy spirit	willing spirit
NEB	1970	steadfast spirit	holy spirit	willing spirit
LB	1971	right desires	Holy Spirit	willing to obey
NIV	1978	steadfast spirit	Holy Spirit	willing spirit

56. NETS' translation has been added since the original publication as a new option for comparison.

| NKJV | 1982 | steadfast spirit | Holy Spirit | generous Spirit |
| NRSV | 1989 | right spirit | holy spirit | willing spirit |

History of the Interpretation of MT Psalm 51:12–14 (10–12 EBs)

Author	Date	51:12(10)	51:13(11)	51:14(12)
St. Basil the Great (trans. G. Lewis)	ca. 375 (n.d.)	Upright Spirit	Holy Spirit	Princely Spirit
Luther (trans. Pelikan)	1538 (1955)	right spirit	Thy Holy Spirit	a princely Spirit
Calvin (trans. Anderson)	1560? (1846)	right or steady spirit	Spirit of thy holiness	Free spirit
Dickson	1653	right spirit	Holy Spirit	free Spirit
Watts, Isaac	ca. 1719	my soul averse from sin	Thy good Spirit	That I fall no more
Plumer	1867	right/ready spirit	Holy Spirit	free Spirit
F. Delitzsch (trans. Bolton)	1867 (1949)	steadfast spirit	Holy Spirit	willing/free spirit
Alexander	1873	fixed spirit	Holy Spirit	spontaneous spirit
Perowne	1878	steadfast spirit	Holy Spirit	willing/free spirit
Kirkpatrick	1902	steadfast spirit	Holy Spirit	willing/free spirit
Briggs	1907	spirit . . . steadfast	holy Spirit	princely Spirit
Soncino	1945	firmness in temptation	Presence of God	willingness to do right
Oesterley	1953	steadfast spirit	Holy Spirit	willing spirit
Leupold	1959	steadfast spirit	Holy Spirit	willing spirit
Weiser	1959	steadfast spirit	Holy Spirit	willing spirit
Aglen	1960 edition	constant spirit	Divine favour [sic]	Thy willing spirit
Dalglish	1962	spirit . . . steadfast	Thy spirit of holiness	willing spirit
Dahood	1968	a resolute spirit	Your holy spirit	your generous spirit
Kidner	1973	right/steadfast spirit	Holy Spirit	willing spirit
Clarke	1979	[no comment]	Divine fellowship (1 Sam 16:13–14)	spirit of prompt obedience
Westermann (trans. Porter)	1989	firmly fixed spirit	Holy Spirit	ready/willing spirit

The Chronological Use of רוח in the OT:

OT Period—Chronological	Names of The Spirit Used in Each Period	# of Passages Where Name Occurs
Creation to Conquest	Spirit of God (*Elohim*)	6
	My Spirit	1
	The Spirit (definite; with or with-out a definite article and with or without a pronominal suffix)*	3
Conquest to Captivity (Pre-Exilic)	Spirit of the LORD (*YHWH*)	7
Period of Judges	Spirit of the LORD (*YHWH*)	4
United Monarchy	Spirit of God (*Elohim*)	3
	The Spirit* (counting all Psalms and poetic books except Job)	6–7
	(Holy Spirit [Psalm 51])?	(1)
Divided Monarchy	Spirit of the LORD (*YHWH*)	7–8
	Spirit of God (*Elohim*)	2
	The Spirit*	4
	My Spirit	5
	Spirit of the Lord *YHWH*	1
	(Holy Spirit [Isaiah 63])?	(2)
Captivity to Close of OT Era Exilic Period	The Spirit*	7
	My Spirit	3
	Spirit of the LORD (*YHWH*)	2
	Spirit of God (*Elohim*)	1
Post-Exilic Period	My Spirit	1–2
	The Spirit*	1

PART III

Exegetical & Contextual
Insights in Isaiah

7

The Spirit in Isaiah 11:1–3[1]

Introduction

THE word "spirit" (רוח) is used four times in Isaiah 11:2 and the same root is used in verse 3a in the verb והריחו. The multiple mentions of this construct noun (bound to three modifiers and their parallel expressions, in addition to the name יהוה) begs the question if the "spirit" the author has in mind is the "[H/holy] Spirit" as sometimes translated (e.g., NIV) but not always (e.g., NRSV). Does this verse never, always, or ever speak of the Spirit? If not, is "S/spirit" even the best translation? Another question that is usually not raised is if verses 2–3a might be a chiasm, or at least 2b. Bartelt noted a chiasm in 11:1.[2] Watts observes a chiastic structure for verses 1–10.[3] Of nine major commentaries consulted, none mentions a chiasmus in verses 2–3.[4] The closest is Bartelt's recognition of an inclusio

---

1. Originally published as Marlowe, "A Spirit Chiasm," 44–57. Stylistic and corrective but no substantive changes have been made.
2. See Bartelt, *The Book*, 170.
3. See Watts, *Isaiah 1–33*, 169.
4. See Wildberger, *Isaiah 1–12*, 460–74; Bartelt, *The Book*, 162–63, 166, 169–70; Watts, *Isaiah 1–33*, 169–70; Kaiser, *Isaiah 1–12*, 252–53; Motyer, *Prophecy of Isaiah*, 120–23; Oswalt, *Book of Isaiah*, 276–80; Sweeney, *Isaiah 1–39*, 198–201; Blenkinsopp, *Isaiah 1–39*, 262–64; and Gray, *Critical and Exegetical*, 214–17. No peer review articles were found on Isaiah 11:2–3.

created by רוח in 2a and 3a, surrounding three pairs. He makes a reference to Isaiah 6:2, with its three uses of a pair of wings.[5]

The following will examine the poetics and metrics of verses 2a–3a in order to make some proposals about these questions. Also, the presence of *athnach* after 3a suggests a major break (for a conclusion about YHWH's "fear"), not only because it is a strong disjunctive accent but also because *athnach* is used after 2a, separating the introduction of GOD's רוח from the rest of 2b, where the characteristics of Jesse's (King David's father) "shoot" (as one having a godly desire or YHWH's S/spirit) are delineated.[6] The NRSV already is suggestive by making a clear break between 3a and 3b and connecting the former to verse 2:

NRSV		Versification	
Verses	Translation	Verses	Chiasm?
2 The spirit of the LORD shall rest on him,		2a	A
the spirit of wisdom and understanding,		2bi	B
the spirit of counsel and might,		2bii	C
the spirit of knowledge and the fear of the LORD.		2biii	B'
3 His delight shall be in the fear of the LORD.		3a	A'

In this paper the versification will be per the numbers and letters in the box above. There may be more symmetry between 2a and 3a than previously recognized. Additionally, or alternatively, 2a–2biii or just 2bi–iii may present chiastic structures. The use of רוח "spirit" and יהוה "YHWH" in 2a and 2biii, and 2a and 3a (where the root רוח is "spirit" then "delight"), are highly suggestive, as is the strong parallel between 2bi and 2biii, leaving 2bii as a fulcrum without a parallel.

The Use of רוח in the Old Testament

The subject of Isaiah 11:2a–3a is the one called a "stump/shoot" (חטר) and "branch" (נצר) in 11:1; i.e., a descendant of the lineage or "stump" (גזע) of Jesse.[7] In 11:2a the רוח יהוה "spirit from/of YHWH" will characterize him.

---

5. Bartelt, *The Book*, 166, n. 11:3a.

6. This break is recognized by Wildberger, *Isaiah 1–12*, 473.

7. Isaiah 10 ends with the demise of Judah by an Assyrian army invading from the north through Lebanon. From just a "stump" of a nation, however, God would raise up a fruitful "branch" (= a king in the Davidic line) to bring renewal and restoration (Isa 11:1).

Since YHWH is the God of Israel, henceforth "GOD" will represent YHWH and/or "God." LXX uses πνεῦμα τοῦ θεοῦ as if the Hebrew text it used had אלהים instead of the MT's יהוה. Although "spirit" is a standard gloss for רוח, and "Spirit" a frequent traditional rendering, the word can be used of a human attitude ("spirit") or for a spirit-being or the D/divine S/spirit. In the Old Testament the expression "spirit of holiness" (sometimes rendered "Holy S/spirit") appears only three times in two passages (Ps 51:11; Isa 63:10, 11). Expressions like "the S/spirit" or "YHWH's/God's S/spirit" are typical and frequent (unlike in the New Testament, where "Holy S/spirit" is the norm). A good argument has been made that the "spirit of your holiness" (רוח קדשך) in Psalm 51:11b (13b MT) is not the "Holy Spirit" but the attitude of the author's desire for God's holiness (in parallel with a desire for God's presence in verse 11a [13a], and in context with his desire for steadfastness [// "clean heart"] in verse 10 [12] and generosity [// "joy"] of service in verse 12 [14]).[8] The construct expression, naturally in all such cases, can be either "x of" or "x from" God or YHWH or adjectival, "godly spirit," "holy spirit," etc., where "spirit" may mean a human attitude or desire rather than God himself (Spirit) or a spiritual emissary from heaven. With this in mind, we can look at the poetics of Isaiah 11:2a–3a.

The Parallels and Poetics of Isaiah 11:2a–3a

Isaiah 11:2a (the first four words of the MT) is separated from the rest of the verse (ten words) by the strong disjunctive accent, *athnach*. This presents 2a as an introduction to what follows in the verse. It also suggests a parallel between 2a and 3a (three words, also separated from the rest of v. 3 by *athnach*). Isaiah 11:2a as a mono-colon prelude to the rest of the verse may be poetically portrayed as follows:

metrics	d	c	b	a
words	יהוה	רוח	עליו	ונחה
translation	YHWH	"spirit"-of	upon-him	And-it-will-rest

This descendant of a devastated Judah will be characterized by YHWH's "spirit" or his zeal (if not "Spirit [sent] from"). In Psalm 69:9, a Davidic psalm, zeal for the temple consumed the psalmist (and if David is a

---

8. See Marlowe, "'Spirit of Your Holiness,'" 29–49.

type of the Messiah in later Jewish and Christian thinking, Psalm 69:9 is remembered by the disciples of Jesus after he raged against those who turned the temple square into a flea market [John 2:13–17]). This mono-colon has the metric pattern 3:2:2:3 (or ten total syllabic beats).

The rest of verse 2 is composed of three bi-cola, separated respectively by the punctuation marks *rebia*, then *zaqeph qaton*, with a–b // [a]–b' pattern (before the verse-ending *soph pasuq*):

Metrics	[e]	d'	[c]	d	c
Words	[יהוה]	ובינה	[רוח]	חכמה	רוח
Translation		and-insight	[a-"spirit"-of]	// wisdom	a-"spirit"-of
Metrics	[e]	d'''	[c]	d''	c
Words	[יהוה]	וגבורה	[רוח]	עצה	רוח
Translation		power	[a-"spirit"-of]	// counsel	a-"spirit"-of
Metrics	e	d''2a	[c]	d'1	c
Words	יהוה	ויראת	[רוח]	דעת	רוח
Translation	YHWH	and-fear-of	[a-"spirit"-of]	// knowledge	a-"spirit"-of

One is tempted to understand reverse parallelism at work, requiring the substitution of "of YHWH" at the end of 2i and 2ii, as clarified on 2iii.[9] But the "fear of YHWH" could not stand as "fear" alone because this Davidic descendant's zeal is not for "fear [of men]" (a negative characteristic) but "fear of" or "reverence for" God. Qualities like power and insight do not need to be clarified as YHWH's, but contextually it still seems implied that the desire is for godly abilities. It would not do to have mere "fear" as the parallel with knowledge, because even though the reader understands God as the source of each ability, "fear of YHWH" is a technical re-statement for "knowledge."[10] Before each of these bi-cola the reader can also understand

---

9. Bartelt (*The Book*, 163) makes a similar proposal when he translates 11:2bi and bii (what he calls 2b and 2c) by adding "of *Yahweh*" parenthetically to each line. See table on pp. 129–30 regarding Bartelt's metrics.

10. This is seen in Psalm 19:9, where "the fear of YHWH" is the first-line counterpart to "the ordinances of YHWH." "Fearing" God is tantamount to obedience to his laws. In Proverbs 2:5 understanding this fear leads to knowledge about God. In Proverbs 16:6 it helps one avoid "evil" (better "rebellion" [the parallel is "sin"]). In Job 28:28 shunning evil is understanding, and fearing YHWH is wisdom. In Proverbs 10:27 fearing God leads to a long life. But some suggest the repeated "fear" in verses 2biii to 3a is a dittography and an original "second line" following "spirit of knowledge" is missing (see Wildberger, *Isaiah 1–12*, 461, n. 3a-a, who finds no help in the versions [LXX, Targums, Syriac, or

"and it will rest upon him." In 2bi–iii the words used for each bi-colon is 3, 3, then 4. The syllabic count for each bi-colon is: 2:2 // 3; 2:2 // 4; and 2:2 // 3:3.

This leaves the mono-colon 3a to complete the unit, since 3b is a bi-colon and change of emphasis. Like its possible counterpart in 2a, the strong disjunctive accent *athnach* separates it from the rest of the verse. It contains three words compared to four in 2a. Its syllabic pattern is 4, 3, and 3 per word, a total of ten syllables as before. Also, like 2a it includes the root רוח, but this time as a verbal noun (*hiphil* infinitive construct) instead of construct noun. However, LXX does not reflect this verb in 3a. It understands the recurrence of the noun "spirit" as before: πνεῦμα φόβου θεοῦ ("spirit of the fear of God"), and includes, as does Vulgate with the comparable Latin verb, ἐμπλήσει "it will fill" rather than "it will delight."[11] While "fear" (יראה) is not mentioned per se in 2a, it is understood from the fact that 2bi–iii describes the godly attitude and disposition or desire that will "rest" on this Davidic descendant as Torah informed obedience, wisdom, insight, knowledge, counsel, and power. Both 2a and 3a indicate and involve רוח, יהוה, and יראה;[12] so, the possibility of an A and A' chiastic function of 2a and 3a, respectively, has some merit (see below). Each mono-colon has ten syllabic beats and shares a similar lexical stock:

Metrics	d	c	b	a
Words	יהוה	רוח	עליו	ונחה
Translation	YHWH	(the) "spirit"-of	upon-him	And-it-will-rest
Metrics	d	c'	b–a'	
Words	יהוה	ביראת	והריחו	
Translation	YHWH	(the) "fear"-of	And-to-relieve-him	

In 2a the Davidic descendant is characterized by possession of GOD's perspective or a desire for divine duty, and in 3a he is driven by possession or profession of GOD's precepts. In his study of style and structure in Isaiah

---

Latin]). Watts calls the repetition a "choral refrain" (*Isaiah 1–33*, 168, n. 3a-a).

11. See table on p. 131 regarding LXX and MT for a diagram of the Greek OT text compared to the Masoretic Text.

12. The use of רוח in Isaiah 11:3a is debated. Some suggest a different root for the *qal* (I רוח, "be wide; relieve") and *hiphil* (II רוח "to smell," therefore "be attracted to" or "enjoy," hence "delight" in English versions); while others think we have two different uses of the same root. Syrian *rāḥ* means "to breathe, be refreshed [in the spirit or heart]." The Arabic cognate (*rwḥ*) can mean to "revive, rest, relieve" (*HALOT*, s.v. רוח).

2–12, Bartelt concluded that Isaiah 11:2–3a is a verse of five lines, consisting of a split bi-colon (2a and 3a) framing a tri-colon[13] (2bcd or what I call 2bi, ii, iii; since I see all of v. 2 after 2a as a unit, as does Bartelt). He says further:

> The three middle lines are held together by repetition of the initial word, each followed by parallel pairs as compound *nomina recta*. The final pair is expanded by the further bound form יראת, and it culminates in the divine name יהוה, which thus becomes the final *nomen rectum* for all the pairs in 2bcd.[14]

The Meaning of רוח in Isaiah 11:2a–3a

Does רוח mean divine "Spirit" or human "spirit" in these verses? Does "spirit of YHWH," as well as "spirit of wisdom, power, etc.," indicate a desire for godliness or a godly (YHWH-like) attitude, as "spirit of holiness" in Psalm 51:11[13] may mean not "Holy Spirit" but "desire for holiness"? Does this text in Isaiah 11 allow for an exegesis that the third person of the Trinity empowered this flowering branch of the Davidic lineage? Is every רוח in this passage the Holy Spirit, or only one, some, or none? Does the uppercase "Spirit" in English do justice to Isaiah's intentions? Is there more than one intention simultaneously? Or is there a human intention separate from a divine intention? Walter Kaiser's proposal of *theoria* based on Psalm 72, where an author can give a double meaning, is dependent on the presence of hyperbolic language as the textual clue for this kind of exegesis (taught in early church times by the Antioch school, in opposition to the allegorical Alexandrian school).[15] Hyperbolic language is abundant in this passage. Consider verses 6–9:

13. Bartelt, *The Book*, 170.
14. Bartelt, *The Book*, 170.
15. See Kaiser, "Psalm 72," 257–70. Regarding Psalm 72, Wildberger comments that verses 3–5 in Isaiah 11 present an ideal "Messiah" the same as Psalm 72:2, 4, 13, which is much older than Isaiah. Gunkel, he says, places it in the kingship era. Its Sitz im Leben is a Jerusalem kingship festival at the time of a king's enthronement. Yet there are striking differences between Psalm 72 and Isaiah 11. The former presents a petition on behalf of the king while the latter has a prediction about a future ruler. Israel's neighboring nations also had prophecies about a future king bringing salvation (e.g., those of the Egyptian priest Nefer-rohu and several Akkadian prophecies or apocalypses). See Wildbereger, *Isaiah 1–12*, 463–64, citing *ANET* 444, n. 1; Hallo, "Akkadian Apocalypses," 231–42; Grayson, "Akkadian Prophecies," 7–30; Gressmann, *Altorientalische Texte*, 283–end; and *ANET* 451–end (1969).

> The wolf will live with the lamb, the leopard will lie down with the goat, the calf and the lion and the yearling together; and a little child will lead them. The cow will feed with the bear, their young will lie down together, and the lion will eat straw like the ox. The infant will play near the hole of the cobra, and the young child put his hand into the viper's nest. They will neither harm nor destroy on all my holy mountain, for the earth will be full of the knowledge of the LORD as the waters cover the sea. (NIV)

So, if Kaiser is correct, then the exegete can propose that Isaiah understands that this shoot from Judah's reduced kingdom will both desire GOD's power and be empowered by GOD's Spirit. Even this approach, however, admits the former is in the text as the historical sense and the latter as the messianic. That still supports an exegesis that finds the primary textual meaning as a godly attitude on the part of this "shoot from a root." Or perhaps GOD's Spirit is in verses 2a and 3a, framing this text, and the desire is in between and comprising the center of the core or chiasm between these two parallel parts of an inclusio. רוח appears to signify an attitude or desire in most, if not all, of these verses from 2a–3a.

Arthrous and Anarthrous רוח

רוח in Isaiah 11:2 is written without the definite article in Hebrew (anarthrous), but in English translation is, e.g., in the NIV, translated as "the Spirit." The fact that NIV uses upper-case "s" for "Spirit" shows that the translators interpret it as the Holy Spirit or third member of the Godhead in Trinitarian theology. Hence the rendering "*the* Spirit" instead of "*a* spirit." Naturally, the author of a Hebrew document can write a noun without the article yet still contextually indicate definiteness. The presence of the article (arthrous) just makes definiteness certain and objective. When "the Spirit" appears in many English versions, normally it is anarthrous, but the translators understand the Holy Spirit of GOD to be the subject. A look at such passages will raise the question if this is what was intended by the author of the Hebrew text in many cases. One case where רוח is arthrous is in Numbers 11:16–26. In that passage GOD tells Moses to bring seventy elders to the meeting tent and then he will take "the spirit" (הרוח) that is on Moses and place it on these men. Technically the text has GOD saying, "I will take from the spirit that is upon you and I will place [it] upon them." The NIV reads as if the entire spirit is removed from Moses, but again that is because the translators/interpreters assume this is the Holy Spirit and, therefore, cannot be moved in part. Again, "s" is upper-case, proving the Holy Spirit or at least GOD's Spirit is in view. The Hebrew text, however, allows for the interpretation that YHWH will give these elders some of what Moses possesses emotionally. In that case, "the spirit" is not a person but a power and is also a specific kind of emotion that GOD wants the elders to have. So arthrous רוח is not necessarily GOD's Spirit any more than anarthrous רוח. Whether anarthrous רוח in Isaiah 11 is the Spirit of GOD or a godly or other kind of inclination (e.g., for wisdom or counsel, etc.) is a function of the context, wherein a possible poetic chiasmus parallels a "spirit" of wisdom with a "spirit" of knowledge, surrounding a "spirit" of power" and framed by either a (H/holy) S/spirit from YHWH or a desire for his revelation and relevance.

The Chiastic Structures in Isaiah 11:2a–3a

A/A' Inclusio Levels: Desire for GOD

Framing this chiasm is an emphasis on YHWH's desire and deposit. The divine name appears only in 2a, 2biii, and 3a, linking to his "spirit" (רוח) once and "fear" (יראה) twice, respectively. Perfect symmetry is broken by the introduction of this "fear" in the body of the chiasm, but it provides a transition to "fear" in 3a as a parallel to "spirit" in 2a. As alluded to already, YHWH's "fear" is a way of speaking about his verbal revelation. The only other use of this expression in Isaiah and in the prophetic books of the OT is in Isaiah 33:6. There as well, the focus is on this "fear" as a source of divine information: "He will be the sure foundation for your times, a rich store of salvation and wisdom and knowledge; the fear of the LORD is the key to this treasure" (NIV). As already shown, this expression parallels "the ordinances [or judgments] of YHWH" (משפטי יהוה) in Psalm 19:9. In this psalm, general (vv. 1–6) or natural and specific (vv. 7–11) or verbal divine revelation are highlighted. GOD's fear comes in this second section along with comments on the values of GOD's laws, statutes, precepts, and commands. These all have the effect of helping a servant of GOD know what GOD desires via his decrees. The transition to "GOD's fear" or wisdom in Isaiah 11:2biii to 3a is a restatement of 2a, where the branch from Judah's stump is defined by GOD's "S/spirit" or a "desire for godliness." If, alternatively, "fear of GOD" is taken as "reverence for GOD," there is still the parallel framework or inclusio emphasis on seeking GOD's ways as opposed to GOD's desire ("spirit") or his directives ("fear"). A and A' characterize the subject as devoted to YHWH. Uniquely common to these two bi-cola (11:2a and 3a) in this context (11:2a–3a) is the combination of the roots יהוה and רוח.

B/B' Intermediate Levels: Desire for Apprehension of Godly Wisdom

The next level of emphasis falls on this servant's devotion to and desire for GOD's revealed will, i.e., his wisdom, understanding, knowledge, and "fear." All these terms are typically interchangeable and parallel in other OT texts. The use of "fear" to restate "[divine] ordinances" has been explained. The word "understanding" (בין) is restated just in Isaiah as "knowing" (ידע) in 6:9 and 40:14, 19, "wisdom" (חכמה) in 10:13, and "instruction" (לקח) in 29:24. The words "wisdom" (חכמה) and "understanding" (בינה) as in 11:2bi are parallel terms outside Isaiah in Job 38:36, Psalm 49:3, 111:10, Proverbs 1:2, 7, 2:2, 6, 3:13, 19, 4:5, 7:4, just to name some. These parallel bi-cola share words or expressions related to divinely revealed information: wisdom (חכמה) // understanding (בין) in 11:2bi; knowledge (ידע) // "fear" of GOD (יראה יהוה) in 11:2biii. The emphasis thematically is on the subject's possession of, or desire to possess, GOD's or godly perception. In fact, the LXX translates "fear of YHWH" (or "fear of *Elohim*," if that was the reading it used) as εὐσεβείς ("godliness" or "piety").

C Climax Level: Desire for Application of Godly Wisdom

Central to the surrounding levels (A-B-B'-A') is the climax or fulcrum of this passage. This is the main point being highlighted: the "branch's" propagation of or desire to promote GOD's, or godly, knowledge and wisdom. His divine desires are not just to *want* to be godly or just *obtain* godly instruction but to actually *perform godliness* by using the godly knowledge he has. This bi-colon stands alone and central since no other bi-colon makes this same or a similar statement. The words used here are עצה ("counsel" in the NIV; root יעץ) and גבורה ("power" in NIV; root גבר). *HALOT* explains the former as "advice of which God is in charge" and the latter as "God's strength."[16] In Isaiah 16:3, this "counsel" or "advice" is requested so a proper decision may be made. In 28:29 it is parallel with GOD's wonderful wisdom. But in 11:2bii it is not just wise advice per se but powerful advice, i.e., the activity of rendering good counsel to others. In 41:28 Isaiah laments the continuing lack of anyone to "give advice" (יועץ) as an answer to a question. Here, the verbal noun or participle form is used as "counselor," although as the NIV shows it can be translated in terms of what a counselor does frequently: give counsel. In Isaiah 33:13 this "power" is a quality of GOD, related to his judgment on idolatry, that he calls on the far-off nations to acknowledge or "make known." Here again we see the tension between knowing something, like GOD's power, and making it known. Isaiah 28:6 predicts a coming age when GOD Almighty will be a "spirit of justice" (רוח משפט) for judges // "[a source of] strength [גבורה]" for warriors defending the city gate. This wording evokes images of the military "judges" like Samson during the time of the conquest of Canaan. At any rate, here, the "spirit" or רוח is clearly not the Holy Spirit but describes GOD as one who will enable judges to be just in their attitudes and actions. The words used for "justice" and "judges" are the same as in Psalm 19:9, where the "fear of GOD" is parallel with the "judgments" or "ordinances" of GOD. Dispensing justice demands divine laws as directives for what is just. In Isaiah 30:15, GOD tells Israel that her salvation is to be found in "repentance" (שובה) and "rest" (נחת). This "rest" is from the same root as the "rest" in 11:2a, "the spirit of YHWH will rest on him," or "a godly desire will characterize him," we might say. This is parallel, as mentioned, with the statement in 11:3a, based on the verb רוח, which has the meaning at times of getting relief or being at rest. It pictures a wide place removed from the anxiety of crowded conditions. Being able to breathe easily (cf. the noun רוח meaning "breath; wind; spirit"). The way we expel air can indicate how we feel. Some attitudes that ought to be followed by actions are not, and some that should not be acted upon are. A wind or breath from *Elohim* (or for some, God's S/spirit) blew over the surface of the initial and incomplete creation in Genesis 1:1–2, followed by the creation week. The "shoot from Judah's root" in Isaiah 11:2a–3a will dispense GOD's strong counsel or powerful advice because he has sought GOD's wisdom. Together, these verses seem to suggest the power of preaching the good news.

---

16. *HALOT*, s.v. עצב and גבורה.

With all this in mind, we can propose one or more chiastic structures for Isaiah 11:2a–3a. From verses 2a to 3a one can find the thematic parallels and chiasm:

A A desire for GOD ['s knowledge] will rest on him   2a
  B [an appetite for] wisdom and understanding   2bi
    C [an appetite for] counsel and power   2bii
  B' [an appetite for] knowledge and "fear" [i.e., divine revelation] 2biii
A' He will be restless for the knowledge of GOD   3a

Or if "spirit of YHWH" = GOD's Spirit

  A   GOD's Spirit [the source of his revelation or "fear"]   desired
    B   Spirit of Wisdom and insight [through revelation]   possessed
      C   Spirit of strong [divine] advice   proclaimed
    B'   Spirit of knowledge through revelation ("fear")   possessed
  A'   GOD's revelation ("fear") [by God's Spirit]   desired

The metrical parallel and chiasm is: (a) 10 (b) 7 (c) 8 (b') 10 (a') 10. Or

X	Vv.	Beats per Word				Words	Syllables
A	2a	3	2	2	3	4	10
B	2bi		2	2	3	3	7
C	2bii		2	2	4	3	8
B'	2biii	2	2	3	3	4	10
A'	3a		4	3	3	3	10

Cf. Bartelt's analysis:

Bartelt's Metrical Analysis of Isaiah 11:2a–3a[17]

Isaiah 11:	TEXT MT	Syllable Count		Stress Count	
			MT		MT
2a	ונחה עליו רוח יהוה	8	9	3/(4)	4

[17]. Bartelt, *The Book*, 162. I assume the numbers other than MT are Bartelt's. I do not include the MT vowels as he does. Cf. also Wildberger's metrics (*Isaiah 1–12*, 465). He says the most important ideas are found in the eight-stress cola, emphasizing predictions.

2b	רוח חכמה ובינה	6	7	3	3
2c	רוח עצה וגבורה	(6)/7	8	3	3
2d	רוח דעת ויראת יהוה	7	9	3	4
3a	והריחו ביראת יהוה	(8)/9	9	3	3

In terms of Hebrew lexica, the chiasm is:

X	Verses	רוח desire	יהוה God	יראה fear	נחה/רוח rest/relieve	Words for "knowing"	Words for "doing"
A	2a	X	X		X		
B	2bi	X				X	
C	2bii	X					X
B'	2biii	X	X	X		X	
A'	3a	X	X	X	X		

The climax (C) uses words that have no parallels in the passage. They depict knowledge culminating in action. The words found in B and B' all have to do with revelatory information or divine knowledge: wisdom, understanding, knowledge, and GOD's "fear," which reappears in the first part of the next verse and final line of the chiasm (3a or A'). The key movement of ideas is that of desiring and delighting in GOD's wisdom with the central focus on doing GOD's ways. The shoot from Judah's root will use divine revelation and perceptions to carry out divine restoration and establish peace through "powerful persuasion." Just a few verses later in 11:9b we read, "for the earth will be full of the knowledge of the LORD as the waters cover the sea" (NIV).[18] In 9:6 there is the promise of a "wonderful counselor" (NIV).[19] Many years ago Gray commented that, "the king receives power not only

---

18. Motyer notes that in its fullest sense, knowledge is truth applied, and that the words translated *counsel and power* are "strategy and military strength" in Isaiah 36:5 (Motyer, *Prophecy of Isaiah*, 122). He mentions 11:9 on p. 120. For Watts, *Isaiah 1–33*, 172, the "knowledge of YHWH" has a special place in Isaiah's vision. In the charismatic kingship of the OT, God's Spirit speaks and acts through his anointed. Anointing imparted the spirit (see Watts, *Isaiah 1–33*, 171).

19. Oswalt suggests the hendiadys "mighty counselor" by comparison to Isaiah 9:5, and says a king was ineffective if he could not both gather the data needed for a decision and carry the power to make it (*Isaiah, Chapters 1–39*, 276, n. 4). Watts translates these terms as "counsel and heroism" and compares the throne names in 9:5 (6) as "Wonder Counselor, God-Hero" (Watts, *Isaiah 1–33*, 172). The adjective *gibbor*, "mighty," is used in Isaiah 9:6 (MT 5) and the noun *gebûrah*, "might, strength," in Isaiah 11:2. NIV in 9:6 has "Wonderful Counselor, Mighty God [*ēl*]."

to discern the right, but to execute it."[20] Even more straightforward is the Greek version (cf. table below):

A   He will be characterized by a spirit of/for God   [desired]
    B   [by a] spirit of/for wisdom and insight   [possessed]
        C   [by a] spirit of/for mighty counsel   [proclaimed]
    B'   [by a] spirit of/for knowledge and godliness   [possessed]
A'   He will be filled with a spirit of fear of/for God   [desired]

The possibility of a hendiadys with "counsel" and "power" as "powerful advice" in verse 2bii suggests the possibility of a hendiadys in each of the three, central bi-cola:

    B by an affection for *insightful wisdom*
        C by an aptitude for *mighty counsel*
    B' by and affection for *godly knowledge*

LXX and MT Texts of Isaiah 11:2–3a Compared

Verse	MT and Translation	LXX and Translation
11:2a	ונחה עליו רוח יהוה	καὶ ἀναπαύσεται ἐπ' αὐτὸν πνεῦμα τοῦ θεοῦ
	And the spirit of YHWH will rest upon him	And the spirit of God will rest on him
11:2bi	רוח חכמה ובינה	πνεῦμα σοφίας καὶ συνέσεως
	A spirit of wisdom and of insight	A spirit of wisdom and of understanding
11:2bii	רוח עצה וגבורה	πνεῦμα βουλῆς καὶ ἰσχύος
	A spirit of counsel and of might	A spirit of counsel and of strength
11:2biii	רוח דעת ויראת יהוה	πνεῦμα γνώσεως καὶ εὐσεβείας
	A spirit of knowledge and of fear of YHWH	A spirit of knowledge and of godliness
11:3a	והריחו ביראת יהוה	ἐμπλήσει αὐτὸν πνεῦμα φόβου θεοῦ
	And in the fear of YHWH he will find room	And the spirit of the fear of God will fill him

20. Gray, *Isaiah I–XXVII*, 216. Wildberger notes that "the king needs wisdom in order to discharge the obligations of his royal rule" (Wildberger, *Isaiah 1–12*, 472). The king is a hero (cf. 9:5 throne names, but not deriving "counsel" from יעץ) because he makes war plans and decisions; see 7:5; yet Isaiah 11 is not about military but civil planning. See Proverbs 8:14, which combines עצה and גבורה (see Wildberger, *Isaiah 1–12*, 472).

Conclusion

To summarize and surmise, this study has revealed a probable chiasmus in Isaiah 11:2a–3a. A key lexical feature of this pattern is the use of the nominal root רוח throughout and the same verbal root once. The presence in Isaiah 11:3a of the verb רוח (meaning "delight" in the NIV) suggests a parallel with the רוח of YHWH in 11:2a, together with 3a making a frame or inclusio for a chiastic structure. The similarity of "spirit" and "delight" becomes clearer when one understands that this noun, usually translated "spirit" and thought to mean "[Holy] Spirit," can also be used of a human "spirit," "desire," "attitude," or "affection." The construct or bound genitive expression רוח יהוה has to be interpreted syntactically as possessive (YHWH's S/spirit"), attributive ("a YHWH-like spirit or desire"), or appositional ("Spirit, that is YHWH"). The same is true of the other expressions using the bound form of רוח in this passage (appearing seven times): of wisdom, understanding, counsel, power, knowledge, and fear (two times). Additionally, construct "fear" is used twice with YHWH and also has to be interpreted syntactically in context. YHWH appears in the inclusio verses 2a and 3a, and just once more immediately at the end of the line before 3a. Only 2a and 3a have the combination of יהוה and רוח. Psalm 51:10–12 has the expression "spirit of your holiness" (רוח קדשך), which in context there is most likely "a desire for holiness" since the "spirit" in the verses surrounding it is a human affection or attitude. Therefore, Psalm 51:11 is not about the Holy Spirit or YHWH's Spirit, especially in Trinitarian terms. This suggests the same is possible for Isaiah 11:2a–3a, where "spirit of YHWH" is connected to a "spirit of wisdom, power, and knowledge." If these latter three "spirits" are the subject's personal passions and powers (rather than the Holy Spirit) then the "spirit of YHWH" in verse 2a may also be a characteristic of the "shoot from Jesse's root." Further, the expression "fear of YHWH" as a word pair with "knowledge" and in parallel with "wisdom and understanding" suggests it has the meaning found in Psalm 19:9, where this "fear" is semantically parallel with GOD's ordinances. In verse 3a this is repeated instead of "spirit of YHWH" because the climax of the chiasmus in verse 2bii is this predicted one's ability to use divine knowledge as counsel and with power. His zeal for being like God means that he passionately and powerfully understands and uses divine revelation, i.e., the "fear [instruction or information] that comes from YHWH" (objective or source genitive). The Bible emphasizes the necessary relation between information and inspiration. Proverbs 19:2

reminds the reader that zeal without knowledge is a problem. The apostle Paul grieved over the same problem when he wrote about his Jewish contemporaries: "For I can testify about them that they are zealous for God, but their zeal is not based on knowledge" (Rom 10:2; NIV). And later he told the believers in Rome to "Never be lacking in zeal, but keep your spiritual fervor, serving the Lord" (Rom 12:11; NIV). Such zeal for YHWH's words and ways is typical of texts that have messianic types: Psalm 69:9, "for zeal for your house consumes me, and the insults of those who insult you fall on me" (NIV). Jesus' disciples recalled this verse after Jesus furiously engaged those who used the temple grounds for commercial rather than spiritual business (John 2:13–17).

Isaiah 9:7, "Of the increase of his government and peace there will be no end. He will reign on David's throne and over his kingdom, establishing and upholding it with justice and righteousness from that time on and forever. The zeal of the LORD Almighty will accomplish this" (NIV).

Isaiah 11:2a–3a tells the reader that a descendant of Judah will come who will powerfully, passionately, and persuasively preach or proclaim, as well as produce, the "fear" of GOD which, according to the verses that follow (3b–9), will principally and eventually bring about judgment on the wicked, justice for the poor, and perfect peace because GOD's knowledge will be universal.

8

The "Messianic" Prophecy of Isaiah 53:9[1]

Introduction

THE meaning and pointing of עשיר in Isaiah 53:9 (usually rendered "rich") remains a controversial subject and needs resolution because of the importance of this verse and chapter in the history of Old Testament (OT) messianic interpretation.[2] One approach has been to emend it to "evil-doers" (עשי רע).[3] Others leave the text as it stands in the MT, believing the text anticipates or predicts the burial of Jesus in the tomb of the rich Joseph of Arimathea.[4] The fact that "rich" is a tri-consonantal reversal of its parallel term "wicked" (רשעים //עשיר) has been noticed by a few

---

1. Originally published as Marlowe, "Wicked Wealthy," 68–81. Stylistic and corrective but no substantive changes have been made.

2. *TDOT* recognizes this verse as "the most disputed text" (as regards this term in the OT) which many and especially older scholars consider corrupt. See Botterweck, *Theological Dictionary* [*TDOT*], XI:419, s.v. עשר by Sæbø.

3. See Koehler-Baumgartner, *Lexicon*, 1958, s.v. עשיר; Blenkinsopp, *Isaiah 40–55*, 348; North, *Second Isaiah*, 231; Schoors, *Jesaja II*, 326; Torrey, *Second Isaiah*, 420; Westermann, *Das Buch Jesaja*, 205, n. 6; and Delitzsch, *Isaiah*, II:327. The use of "evil" today is questionable since the way the term is used in general is not compatible with the contextual usages of its counterpart Hebrew terms (mainly רע) in the OT.

4. See, as representative of much Evangelical popular scholarship, the *Moody Monthly* article by Allan A. Macrae, which argues that the *waw* connecting each parallel line must be adversative ("but") and that the singular "rich" must mean "a rich man" (Macrae, "With Rich," 70). For a defense of the messianic prophecy position, see Young, *Book of Isaiah*, 353, n. 34.

commentators. But since "rich" is not a normal parallel for "wicked," they conclude emendation is the best solution. Most, however, do not mention this literary feature or see it as exegetically significant. This article will argue that emendation is not required because "rich" can provide a proper "synonymous" and semantic parallel to "wicked" in this text and within its OT context.[5] These "rich" are the "wicked rich." While rejecting the MT reading as the Hebrew word for "rich," some in principle have agreed by proposing a sense like "rabble" based on an Arabic cognate. What follows will establish that Isaiah 53:9 is not a prophecy applicable to the wealthy Joseph in whose tomb Jesus was buried. A contribution to scholarly debate on this matter is made, not by discovery of the interplay of common letters for "wicked" and "rich," but by demonstrating that this play on words is an intentional use of the word "rich" because it offers this pun and provides a suitable synonymous parallel to the "wicked ones" of the preceding poetic line. These "rich ones" in the OT cultural climate also would have been considered disreputable people. This study hopes to answer the challenge posed by Watts in his commentary on Isaiah: "With a rich one remains unexplained. The phrase has been applied to Jesus ... but it is difficult to find the meaning in its original setting."[6] Further it will challenge the answer given by Young's commentary: "There is no need to assume that עשיר necessarily connotes rich men who are evil."[7] Isaiah 53:9a (the first of two bi-cola in v. 9) will be shown to be a "synonymous" and symmetric

---

5. In this article, parallelism of the verses concerned will be described in traditional terms as synonymous, synthetic, or antithetic for convenience sake. That such a bi-colon may be read in these three ways may offer some support to the insight of Lowth's three basic categories of *parallelismus membrorum* (see Lowth, *De Sacra Poesi*, in toto). While the author is very aware of the modern trends and theories regarding the nature of parallelism, these do not prove that the categories of synonymy or antithesis are not valid in many cases. "Synthetic" masks the great variety, complexity, and mystery of bi-cola that are not strictly "synonymous" or antithetical, but time and space do not allow me to discuss these matters here. "Synonymous" may be otherwise understood as restatement or static lines. Suffice it to say that the following essay is an argument for the recognition of synonymy in these verses, regardless of the fact that many OT poetic passages or verses are mono-cola, tri-cola, or simple statements of "A, also B." It is well recognized that the OT poets could work apart from parallelism when desired or required, and that debate continues over the precise nature of meter and parallel thought, as well as the concept and character of Hebrew poetry. See, e.g., publications by A. Berlin, J. Kugel, R. Alter, J. P. Fokkelman, A. Schökel, A. Cooper, M. O'Connor, F. Landy, W. Watson, and D. Clines, inter alia, listed in the Bibliography.

6. Watts, *Isaiah 34–66*, 231.

7. Young, *Book of Isaiah*, 353, n. 34.

parallelism: a-b-c // [a']-b'-c' with a 3:2 word-count meter. The translation of this text that will be defended is:

A	B	C
And-it-was-assigned	with-the-wicked	his-grave //
[A']	B'	C'
[And-it-was-allocated]	with-the-wealthy [oppressors]	his-death.

Survey of Modern Interpretations/Translations of Isaiah 53:9a

The issues that divide interpreters and translators of Isaiah 53:9a are evident when versions and commentaries are compared. Many leave interpretation open to the reader while others are minimally or highly interpretive, but rarely is עשיר rendered other than "rich."[8] Others also have accepted that "[the] rich [ones]" is a repetition of "[the] wicked ones" in Isaiah 53:9a. While concluding that "'rich' is not a natural [parallel] to 'wicked,'" North refers to Nyberg's work in 1942, which insists that these terms are synonymous and uses the OT prophets' denunciations of the rich as proof.[9] What follows will pick up where Nyberg left off and provide similar and additional, yet hopefully more convincing, support for the "synonymous" parallel of "rich" and "wicked" in Isaiah 53:9a. What is new is the conviction that the author purposefully employed עשיר to symbolize the "wicked" (רשע), using this reversal of letters as a literary device to enable his readers to make the interchangeable connection between the wicked and the "wicked wealthy." Childs rejects this approach by saying that a link between

---

8. Among more recent and popular English versions, the NIV has "He was assigned a grave with the wicked [plural], and with the rich [singular] in his death," while NRSV has "tomb" instead of "death." If this is a "synonymous" bi-colon then the singular "rich" would have to be taken as a collective singular (singular in form but plural in function). NASB interprets the text as an intentional messianic prediction: "His grave was assigned with wicked men, Yet He was with a rich man in His death." But Blenkinsopp translates: "His grave was located with the wicked, his sepulcher with reprobates" (Blenkinsopp, *Isaiah 40–55*, 345). Along similar lines North offered: "And they gave him burial among felons, And with the dregs of men when he died" (North, *Second Isaiah*, 65). To move away from just English texts, and more traditional by contrast, Baltzer has "*Und Er gab ihm bei Verbrechern sein Grab und bei einem Reichen seine Stätte*" (Baltzer, *Deutero-Jesaja*, 494). Luther's text reads: "*Und man gab ihm sein Grab bei Gottlosen und bei Übeltätern, als er gestorben war*" (*Die Heilige Schrift*, 669).

9. North, *Second Isaiah*, 231, citing Nyberg, "Smärtornas man," 5–82.

the burial of the rich and wicked "hardly offers a natural parallel within Israel."[10] This is true in terms of the burial customs for each class of citizens, but the concern of the text of Isaiah 53:9 is with the fact that the servant undeservedly was treated like a criminal (which concept is identified as those who are "wicked" // "rich"). Even Childs helps on this point by noting that this juxtaposition (wicked // rich) continues the typology of the servant as the righteous and innocent sufferer of the Psalter.[11] Others, in line with Nyberg, as Childs points out, allow for "rich" to have, within its semantic range, the sense "rich through extortion."[12]

Exegesis of "Rich" in Isaiah 53:9a

The main controversy that surrounds Isaiah 53:9ai (ויתן את־רשעים קברו) is the meaning of the opening verb based on the root נתן ("give"; "place"). Regardless of how this is resolved, it has little or no bearing on whether עשיר in 9aii means "a rich one" or "the rich ([oppressive] ones)."[13]

The phrase ואת־עשיר במתיו (53:9aii) is the great challenge for the exegete of this verse. Who is this rich one or rich ones? Why the plural

10. Childs, Isaiah, 417.

11. Childs, Isaiah, 417.

12. Childs, Isaiah, 417. But no footnote is offered to tell who these are.

13. KJV has the strange but literal "he made his grave," which represents the kind of translation that led to the desire for emendation. Cf. Baltzer, Deutero-Jesaja, 494; Childs, Isaiah, 408; Torrey, Second Isaiah, 253; North, Second Isaiah, 65; North, Suffering Servant, 122; Westermann, Das Buch Jesaja, 205; Schoors, Jesaja II, 326; Koehler-Baumgartner, Lexicon, s.v. נתן. The verb as it stands has an indefinite subject, which apparently led Torrey to translate it "appoint" (Torrey, Second Isaiah, 253, 420). Exegetes face the urge to re-point the verb as passive ("he/it was assigned") or use a third plural subject ("they appointed"). Change *wayyittēn* either to *wayyuttan* (Qal passive third sing.) or *wayyittenû* (Qal active third pl.). This latter option follows 1QIsa^a *wytnw* (ויתנו). Blenkinsopp renders it "located" (Blenkinsopp, Isaiah 40–55, 345, 348). The LXX, interestingly, has the equivalent word but uses a future tense and first-person pronoun ("and I will give"), whereas the MT is unmistakably past tense and third-person. Similarly, the Vulgate employs the future tense but stays with the third-person subject ("and he shall give"). Sapp has suggested that the consonantal text of MT or Qumran represents a present tense imperfect (ויתן *wytn* "he gives" or ויתנו *wytnw* "they give"). Sapp takes the Qumran text as a corrective on the MT (Sapp, "LXX, 1QIsa, and MT," 190). With simple *waw* these could be interpreted, alternatively, as future tense, since the morphology would be the same—context making the difference. Some argue for an active form with passive function (e.g., Macrae alludes to examples in Gen 11:9; 48:1; Amos 6:12; and Mic 2:4; see "With Rich," 70). But none of these examples uses נתן.

expression "in his deaths"? Is the initial *waw* antithetical? Since the verse begins with a *wayyiqtol* (preterite, past tense) verb, and not a *we-qatal* (so-called prophetic perfect), why do some say this text prophesies the death and/or burial of this servant with a rich man?[14] Is he Israel or an individual? Was he associated in death with the wealthy and wicked (synthetic parallel), just the wicked ("synonymous" parallel), or, contrary to expectation, with the rich (antithetic parallelism)? Our concern is with the meaning of this clause in its immediate literary, linguistic, and living contexts. Notably, the NT does not use this text (Isa 53:9a) as one fulfilled by Jesus.[15] The term עָשִׁיר ("rich") is singular but is it a collective (plural) or numerical (singular) single form in function?[16] The LXX uses plural forms for both "wicked" and "wealthy."

The poetics of Isaiah 53:9a are arguably those of a so-called "synonymous" parallelism (see n. 5). The verb of 53:9ai must be supplied for 53:9aii and the final terms mirror each other ("his grave" and "in his deaths," which latter is often emended to "in his tomb"). All this warrants that the remaining and medial terms (adjectives) of 53:9ai and aii be viewed as mirror

---

14. Of interest is the fact that only Matthew finds it necessary to speak of Joseph's wealth (Matt 27:57-61; Mark 15:42-47; Luke 23:50-56; and John 19:38-42).

15. However, Peter does utilize Isaiah 53:9b (the second of the two bi-cola in v. 9; 1 Pet 2:22), which suggests a mindset among the apostles that the entire verse and perhaps chapter are christological, at least by application. Peter calls Christian slaves to follow Christ's example of not retaliating against those who mistreat them but rather fully trust in God (1 Pet 2:18-24). Isaiah 53:9b is quoted as a prooftext that Christ did not retaliate verbally when insulted on the cross, what Peter calls "the tree" (1 Pet 2:21-24). The text, if messianic, only foreshadows or foretells that the S/servant will be treated in purpose, if not in practice, as a criminal when dead and buried, although he committed no crime.

16. This is handled in one of two ways by the versions. NRSV, KJV, NKJV, NIV, and JB (to name a few) all read "with the rich," while the ASV and NASB, for example, have "with a rich man." The former versions take this word as a collective singular while the latter ones as a numerical singular. LXX and Vulgate have "and the rich" (respectively, καὶ τοὺς πλουσίους and *et divitem*) as well as Syriac (*'tyr'*) and Targum (*'attîrê*). Macrae's argument that something must be added after "rich" is insightful, but this does not mean that "man" must be added. It is just as reasonable to add "ones." His point that languages like German and Hebrew often use a singular adjective like rich to mean "rich man" applies equally to "rich men" (Macrae, "With Rich," 70-71). The definite use of anarthrous nouns in Greek or Hebrew is well documented. In OT poetry many nouns are definite without the definite article prefixed. Nothing in the Hebrew language indicates clearly that an anarthrous noun (as "wicked ones" in Isa 53:9ai) applies to a small number of people while if definite it would mean "a large group." The surrounding context defines this wicked group as more than a few.

images.[17] Since "[the] wicked [ones]" is plural, "rich" can be interpreted as a collective singular, i.e., "[the] rich [ones]." Further, since the context is about the intentional and/or actual mistreatment of a righteous one as if unrighteous, the mention of the "shearers" in 53:7 shows that the author is focused on the oppressors (vv. 7a and 8a) of this "lamb" (vv. 6–7). Such undeserved association with evil oppressors is the concern of Isaiah 53:9. As a result, the initial *waw* of 53:9aii may be taken as pleonastic (stylistic and un-translated) or explicative ("even") rather than adversative ("but"; e.g., NASB uses "yet").

The Poetry and Poetics of Isaiah 53:9a

The Hebrew consonantal text of Isaiah 53:9a may be schematized as follows (note the MT's major disjunctive accents):

Metrics	C'	B'	[A]	9aii	C	B	A	9ai
MT vocalized and accented	בְּמֹתָיו	וְאֶת־עָשִׁיר	[יתן]	9aii	קִבְרוֹ	אֶת־רְשָׁעִים	וַיִּתֵּן	9ai

---

17. See Oswalt, *Book of Isaiah*, 397. Oswalt urges that the text must not be made to say more than it does by forcing an antithetical parallelism onto a text that structurally is clearly synonymous. Delitzsch (*Isaiah*, II:326–29) argues in much linguistic detail for the traditional "rich," also compelled by the presupposition of Jesus' fulfillment of the verse. Disagreement with Delitzsch is not on a linguistic and lexical basis but a poetical and hermeneutical one. Delitzsch is bothered by Luther's marginal gloss "a rich man who sets all his heart upon riches, i.e. a wicked man" (Delitzsch, *Isaiah*, II:327), the very view this article supports. He wrote when conservative scholars had fewer hermeneutical options than today, especially with our expanded understanding of how the NT uses the OT in light of first-century Jewish exegesis. But as will be shown, the understanding of "rich" as synonymous with "wicked" does not remove a valid messianic application to Jesus, it just restricts the fulfillment to his being treated like a criminal rather than that plus being buried in a rich man's tomb. The translation of עָשִׁיר in Isaiah 53:9aii is properly "rich" as Delitzsch and others demonstrate. Its interpretation or application in the context of Isaiah 53, the poetry of v. 9, and biblical prophecy is that of "[the wicked] wealthy." "Rich" here parallels "wicked ones" so is a figurative way to restate the latter (which is the first group named in Isaiah 53:9ai, followed by its counterpart "rich [ones]" in 53:9aii). Word meanings (usages) are principally governed by context and in poetry in relation to parallelism. Authors are not restricted to common lexical options especially when writing poetically.

It forms one line of a "synonymous", incomplete bi-colon with a 3:2 word-stress meter.[18] As the mechanical layout of 53:9a above shows, 9aii is a mirror image of 9ai. Most telling is the fact that the words for "wicked" and "rich" share the same basic consonants but in reverse order, producing a kind of alliteration and assonance: ם+י+ע+ש+ר // ר+י+ש+ע ($r\check{e}$ $š\bar{a}^{c}\hat{\imath}m$ // $^{c}\bar{a}š\hat{\imath}r$). This has been recognized previously by scholars.[19] But the main contention here is that this phonetic and morphological similarity was a pun intended to clarify that these "rich ones" are related to the "wicked ones." These are the wicked rich or wealthy oppressors. For those who interpret this oppressed servant messianically and individually, he would be treated like a criminal in his death and burial. He would be "assigned" by wicked design to a place with the dregs of society, although he did not deserve it. This was the intention of the oppressors, regardless of what kind of tomb he actually received. For those who interpret this suffering servant as Israel (typologically messianic to some), the nation was unjustly treated as one deserving a dishonorable death or burial. This suffering servant, though not guilty of violence or verbal abuse (v. 9b, or if restated, only verbal violence), has a criminal's tribute and tomb planned for him. This proposed synonymy of "wicked" and "wealthy oppressors" is further strengthened by the fact that other approaches to explain contextually this term (עשיר) are: (1) to emend to עשי רע "doers of evil"; (2) to defer to an Arabic cognate (thus Hebrew homograph) meaning "refuse [noun]" or "rabble"; or (3) to

---

18. The word order (explicit or implicit) for each member of the parallel line is verb + indirect, adjectival object + direct object (V/S + IO + DO). Poetic analysis of OT Hebrew continues to be controversial and subject to various systems and nomenclature. Whatever scheme or terminology is employed, the "synonymous" nature of this passage (Isa 53:9a and/or 9b) is made plausible, if not probable, by issues of context and structural and literary features that do not change regardless of how the poetics are labeled or counted. For Isaiah in particular, see O'Connell, *Concentricity and Continuity*, in toto. For surveys of theories of OT poetic techniques see, among many other valuable or classic books and articles: Watson, *Classical Hebrew Poetry*, in toto; Kugel, *Idea of Biblical Poetry*, in toto; Alter, *Art of Biblical Poetry*, in toto; Lowth, *Lectures on Sacred Poetry*, in toto; and Schökel, *A Manual*, in toto.

19. See, e.g., North, *Second Isaiah*, 231, who notes the alliteration; Baltzer, *Deutero-Jesaja*, 527, who points out the reversal of the consonants רשע r-š-^{c} and עשר ^{c}-š-r, as previously observed by Gesenius. North makes no more out of this than to defer to an emendation to עשי רע "those doing evil." Baltzer only comments on this word-play in passing and agrees that the "rich" is somehow related to an "evil doer" ("Frevler"), then moves on to what he considers the most pressing exegetical matter for this verse, the plurality of "death" in 9aii.

emend to "demons" (שֵׂעִרִים).²⁰ It should be noted that no textual data exist to support these or any other proposed emendations. We are left, therefore, to do the best we can exegetically with the text as it stands.

A major exegetical issue for many commentators is the plural form of the final term of 9aii "in his deaths" (בְּמֹתָיו).²¹ The point of the various proposals is that this may have referred to a burial place or tomb built at a religious site.²² An argument, that tries to support the plural MT form "deaths" as original, says that it refers to the nation of Israel rather than an individual, or it is a plural collective to parallel the singular collective in the synonymous colon.²³ "Tomb" is a more exact parallel with "grave," but

---

20. The Arabic cognate *šr* ("wicked") could suggest a Hebrew consonantal homograph (עשׂר) that is used just this one time in the OT literary corpus. In transmission it could have been corrupted to עשׁיר (and this form is a *hapax* in Isaiah). Of course, this is highly conjectural. See Alexander, *Prophecies of Isaiah*, II:301-2; and Delitzsch, *Isaiah*, II:327. North, *Second Isaiah*, 231 cites A. Guillaume's reference to Arabic *ġuṯrun* "rabble" or "refuse of mankind" (Guillaume, "A Contribution," 10). For the "demons" hypothesis, see Thomas, "A Consideration," 79–86.

21. The entire phrase "and with a wealthy one [or 'the wealthy'] in his deaths" is usually deemed unintelligible, so re-punctuation is resorted to automatically (בָּמָתוֹ *bāmātô* instead of בְּמֹתָיו *bĕmōtāw*), since the change affects only the removal of one letter, the *yod* from the MT. This changes the meaning to "his burial mound" or "his sepulcher" (following Albright's proposal; see also Blenkinsopp, *Isaiah 40-55*, 348; and Whybray, *Isaiah 40-66*, 178, both who cite Albright, "High Place," 242–58, and note that this option may also be supported by 1QIsaᵃ). Since this approach preserves the consonantal text, with the minor exception of the removal of a vowel letter which may have been inserted later by the Naqdanim, it is arguable and plausible that here we are dealing with a lexical rather than transcriptional error (although accepting that the vowel points were applied to the wrong word, the authoritative consonantal text remains unchanged). Rather than reading preposition ב + "death/s" (מות) + possessive pronominal suffix 3ms (*waw*), the root is במה "back, hill, ridge, high place" > במות "high place(s)" or "great high place(s)." The ות suffix may be interpreted otherwise as feminine or abstract (Ugaritic cognate is *bmt*, "back"). One wonders why not just suggest בְּמֹתוֹ; "in his death" as a better alternative, since "[the] rich [one]" is singular morphologically if not functionally.

22. *BDB* wonders if "funeral mound" is the meaning in Ezekiel 43:7, a passage among a few others that Albright considered to validate במות as "funeral mounds" or "tombs" (cf. Koehler-Baumgartner, *HALOT*, s.v. במה, where one meaning given is "Canaanite grave"; cf. Ezek 43:7; and Job 27:15 as a conjecture). Still, this view is currently thought unlikely by some authorities (see VanGemeren, *NIDOTTE*, s.v. במה by Martin J. Selman, where only Isa 6:13; 53:9; and Ezek 43:7 are possible supports).

23. See "Isaiah 53." *Sacred Scripture* (blog), *Catholic Answer Forums*, January 2009, https://forums.catholic.com/t/isaiah-53/138654. The source mentioned originally is no longer accessible ("Is Isaiah 53:9 referring [sic] to Jesus?" www.geocities.com/Athens/Agora/4229/isaiah.htm). But even if a collective plural or not, if the text is about the nation, the nation may be typological of and, therefore, applicable to the Messiah as a

"death" does not remove the "synonymous"-like nature of these two parallel lines in Isaiah 53:9a. Whatever the conclusion ("death" or "tomb"), the evidence for the meaning of "rich" (עשיר) presented so far is not affected one way or the other.

Some suggest that the interpretation of the preposition (על) that begins the bi-colon immediately following (Isa 53:9b) does tip the scales one way or the other as regards the subject of Isaiah 53:9a. Oswalt, for example, notes that antithetical parallelism (thus adversative *waw*) for Isa 53:9a could be supported by a causal use of על in 53:9b; that is, that the original plans were thwarted due to the servant's righteousness.[24] But since "synonymous"-like parallelism is so likely in 53:9a, the preposition beginning the bi-colon of 53:9b must be taken as concessive "although," which is a rare but possible use of על.[25] However, regardless of whether one says "because he did no violence" or "although he did no violence," the arguments for the "synonymous" nature of Isaiah 53:9a stand.

The Wicked and Wealthy in the OT

The author of Isaiah 53 could expect his audience to relate to his parallel of "rich" and "wicked" and play on the shared root consonants because in their world of religious thought the "rich" were often considered disreputable. A number of OT passages support this,[26] as well as the collective use

---

retrospective historical parallel (picture or anticipation or foreshadowing). Plural collectives are known in the Hebrew OT, e.g., the well-known אֱלֹהִים "gods" used as the proper name of the one true God. Other uses are for intensity or abstraction. Plural collectives also are common in Arabic (see Joüon, *A Grammar*, II:497–502). NRSV renders במתיו as "tomb" following the proposal of the editors of *BHS* and *BHS-T*. Qumran reads בומתו (see Watts, *Isaiah 34–66*, 226; North, *Second Isaiah*, 231; and Sapp, "LXX, 1QIsa, and MT," 178, n. 10). Singular "death" is found in Greek, Syriac, and Latin OT versions, as well as by Qumran and Targums.

24. Isaiah 53:9 (a or b) is not mentioned in Krašovec, *Antithetic Structure*, in toto.

25. E.g., see Oswalt, *Isaiah 40–66*, 397–98. In support of the concessive use of the preposition על, Oswalt cites Job 10:7; 16:17; and 34:6. The point of Isaiah 53:9, for Oswalt, is to highlight the final irony of this servant's life. He was not buried with the poor, who had been his faithful companions in life but was surrounded in death (not burial) with those who oppressed him and whose sins he carried (Oswalt, *Isaiah 40–66*, 398). In this way, Oswalt tries to make sense of the use of "grave" in 53:9ai and "death" in 53:9aii.

26. See 2 Samuel 12:1–4; Job 27:13, esp. verse 19 (and note the word-play between ʿšyr "rich" [עשיר] and ʿryṣ "ruthless" [עריץ]); 31:24; Psalm 49:5 (6 MT); 52:9; Proverbs 11:28; 18:23; 22:7, 16; 28:6, 11; Ecclesiastes 4:8; Micah 6:12 (using the same word for "violence" as in Isa 53:9b); and Amos 4:1; inter alia. See Schoors, *Jesaja II*, 326, who also

of singulars like "rich."²⁷ In the book of Isaiah, עָשִׁיר is a *hapax legomenon*.²⁸ It is found twenty-two other times in the OT.²⁹ Little is said of riches in Isaiah when other words rendered "rich" are investigated. Mainly, riches are the spoils of the nations and salvation that God's people will receive eschatologically (Isa 25:6; 30:23; 33:6; 45:3; 60:5, 11; 61:6; 66:12). In Isaiah 10:3, wealth is left behind when disaster strikes. North notes that Nyberg insists the words "rich" and "wicked" in Isaiah 53:9a are synonymous and quotes the prophets' denunciations of the wealthy. In addition, he quotes a Targum as identifying these "rich" as "rich in possessions they have obtained by violence."³⁰ The translation "a rich man" is viewed as pedantic since the singular Hebrew form (עָשִׁיר) is a collective (plural) in function.³¹

"Synonymous" Parallelism of Isaiah 53:9b

The bi-colon in 53:9b does not have to be "synonymous" in order for the one in 53:9a to be "synonymous," but then the likelihood that 53:9a is a restatement is strengthened. Most have taken 53:9b as synthetic, but an argument can and will be made that it is "synonymous"-like. The following will confirm this for the second bi-colon of 53:9: he did no violence [with his mouth] // that is, no deceit [was] in his speech. The structure and poetry of this verse is suggestive of its nature as static or restatement:

---

recognizes promised riches for those who fear YHWH (Ps 112:3; Prov 22:4). In the NT see Matthew 19:23–24; Luke 6:24 (which proves the "poor" of v. 20 are the economically poor); 16:19–25; 1 Timothy 6:17; and James 1:9–11; 2:5-7; 5:1–6.

27. Exodus 30:15; Jeremiah 9:23 (22 MT); Ruth 3:10; Job 27:13 ("wicked man" parallels "ruthless ones"); Psalm 37:16 ("righteous" // plural "wicked"); 49:2 (3 MT); Proverbs 22:2; 28:11; Ecclesiastes 5:12 (11 MT); and possibly Ecclesiastes 10:20. See esp. Ecclesiastes 10:6, where collective singular "fool" parallels plural "rich."

28. Gesenius (*Hebrew-Chaldee Lexicon*, s.v. עָשִׁיר) speaks of both "good" and "bad" wealth as options of meanings for עָשִׁיר. The latter is the sense of "haughty" or "impious" given that riches are a source of pride and pride in the OT is impiety. In relation to Isaiah 53:9 he cites Job 27:19, "They go to bed with wealth, but will do so no more; they open their eyes, and it is gone" (NRSV; and cf. Clines, *DCH*, s.v. עשׁר).

29. Exodus 30:15 (where the arthrous and collective singular form appears for "rich" and "poor"); 2 Samuel 12:1–2, 4; Jeremiah 9:23 (22 MT); Micah 6:12; Psalm 45:12 (13 MT); 49:3; Job 27:19; Proverbs 10:15; 14:20; 18:11, 23; 22:2, 7, 16; 28:6, 11; Ruth 3:10; Ecclesiastes 5:11; 10:6, 20.

30. North, *Second Isaiah*, 231.

31. North, *Second Isaiah*, 231.

A	B	C	[D]
Although	no-wrong	he-did	[with-his-mouth]
עַל	לֹא-חָמָס	עָשָׂה	[בְּפִיו]
[A]	B'2 B'1	[C]	D
[Although]	and-no deceit	[he-did]	with-his-mouth
[עַל]	וְלֹא מִרְמָה	[עָשָׂה]	בְּפִיו

This results in a line of "synonymous" bi-colon, with the pattern a-b-c-[d] // [a]-b1-b2-[c]-d, and a 3:3 word-stress meter. The waw beginning the second half of this parallelism is to be understood not as coordinative ("also") but as pleonastic (stylistic), explicative ("even"), or emphatic ("especially").[32] Reverse parallelism is perhaps less rare than often imagined.[33] The second member of the parallelism may contribute to the first, whereas most often it happens the other way around. Not only poetically is synonymy supported but also lexically and contextually. The word often rendered "violence" (חָמָס) can just mean "wrong" (especially "as a false witness").[34] In context 53:9b is a flashback to verse 7, where the servant's mouth is first mentioned for its virtue: "He was oppressed, and he was afflicted, yet he did not open his mouth; like a lamb that is led to slaughter, and like a sheep that before its shearers is silent, so he did not open his mouth" (NRSV). The emphasis in context is on the lack of speech-related sins. He refused to be abusively defensive or to lash out verbally in revenge or anger at those who abused him. Isaiah 53:9b, then, may be read not as

---

32. NRSV, JB, and NEB have "and"; ASV, NASB, KJV, NKJV, NIV, NAB, Vulgate, and LXX have "nor" or "neither."

33. See Freedman, "Ass and Ox," 42–43.

34. See Genesis 16:5, where NIV has "wrong" (also Job 19:7; 21:27; Prov 8:36). In several passages this term is used in a context of false speech (e.g., Exod 23:1; Deut 19:16; Jer 51:46; Mic 6:12; Pss 27:12; 35:11). See Koehler-Baumgartner (1958), Lexicon, s.v. חָמָס, where the following verses are given for this term meaning a witness who does wrong or false witness: Exodus 23:1; Deuteronomy 19:16; and Psalm 35:11. There is a homograph (II חמס) that means "devise," and this fits the context better, although this is speculative and not firmly fixed in Hebrew lexicography. It can be considered, however, as a possible solution (see Koehler-Baumgartner, Lexicon s.v. II חמס, which compares Syriac ḥmas "to devise"; and Arabic hamasa "to mumble"). Job 21:27 has "the schemes by which you would wrong [חמס] me." See also VanGemeren, NIDOTTE, s.v. II חמס, by John E. Hartley, which word is said to mean "think, invent" (Syriac "meditate, muse, study"). The verb in Job 21:27 is said to be related to this Syriac cognate. Clines mentions this verse and others in Job in relation to II חמס, but in line with its lexical philosophy gives no etymological data (DCH, s.v. חמס).

the servant's avoidance of physical and verbal retaliation but as only the latter, restated as reverse parallelism. The "violence" of Isaiah 53:9bi is the verbal violence of a false or hostile witness.[35] A key OT theme is the importance of knowing how and when to speak. OT Wisdom literature abounds in advice about speaking seldom, sensibly, and sanely.[36] The apostle Peter (1 Pet 2:21-24) may have reflected upon this OT spirituality in the light of Jesus' teachings,[37] when he recalled the words of Isaiah 53:9b to illustrate the sinless life of Christ, who stood silent before his accusers and went willingly and quietly to his undeserved crucifixion.

New Testament Use of Isaiah 53:9b

The NT does make messianic use of Isaiah 53:9b (1 Pet 2:22) while it nowhere employs 53:9a. Such an argument from silence does not prove the interpretation of "rich" as "[wicked] rich" as opposed to "rich [man]," but why the apostles would have bypassed such a precise proof-text if they saw a parallel between it and the rich Joseph of Arimathea is very curious. Peter, apparently, was more impressed with the typology of the parallel between the Isaiah 53 servant's silence than his burial, for whatever reasons. The interpretation being proposed merely clarifies that 53:9aii is a restatement of what is said about him in 53:ai (that he was treated like a criminal at the time of his death). Isaiah 53:9b adds that he was not deserving of such abuse, although (or "because") he had committed no violence or spoken deceitfully (as most versions have it). But as shown above this second bicolon of 53:9 is likely "synonymous," as is the previous one.

Immediately before Peter cites Isaiah 53:9b, he says that the way Jesus suffered is an example to believers (2:21) and, immediately following, he explains how this example is primarily in how he managed his mouth (2:23). Part of Matthew's account of Jesus' trial explains that he gave no answer to his accusers and refused to reply to a single charge from Pilate, to his amazement (Matt 27:12-14). Peter does not introduce this quotation with a formula of fulfillment or as being a pronouncement of Scripture and makes no reference to the OT author or book. He does employ it contextually,

---

35. For 53:9bii NAB has "spoken any falsehood"; NEB "spoken no word of treachery"; JB "no perjury in his mouth."

36. See Job 2:9—3:1; Proverbs 4:24; 6:12; 13:3; 17:27; 18:7; Ecclesiastes 5:2, 6; 6:11; 9:17; 10:12, 13; 12:10, inter alia.

37. See Matthew 6:7; 12:34, 37;

however, in a manner that indicates he understood Isaiah 53:9b (and presumably 9a) as suitable for application to Jesus. But Peter's version of Isaiah 53:9b is more reflective of the Greek than Hebrew OT. Instead of "he did no violence [or 'devised no scheme']" of the MT, 1 Peter 2:22 has "who committed no sin" (cf. NETS, "because he committed no lawlessness").[38] Apparently, Peter wanted to emphasize that the Messiah (Jesus) was sinless not just innocent of particular types of wrongdoing or harm (physical or verbal). While the LXX uses "because," Peter chooses to focus on this sinless character, and is not concerned with the connection to 53:9a.

Conclusion

Challenging the consensus of opinion that "rich" (עָשִׁיר) in Isaiah 53:9aii is either synthetically or antithetically related to "wicked ones" (רְשָׁעִים) in 53:9ai, this examination of Isaiah 53:9 has determined that the relationship is most likely "synonymous" (see n. 5), and that the best translation of עָשִׁיר is as a collective singular adjective functioning as a plural indirect object (the same as "wicked ones" in the previous colon): "rich [ones]." Further, the common association of wealth and wickedness in the OT world suggests that within this parallel restatement, the full sense is "[the] wealthy [wicked]." The author's intention in verse 9 was to tell about the servant's undeserved suffering (v. 9b), wherein he was portrayed and processed as a criminal in his death and burial by his persecutors and prosecutors (v. 9a). The plan of these wicked people (rich and reprobate) was to place him among the refuse of mankind (v. 9a), even though he had committed no violent and verbal crimes (v. 9b). The overlap of "wicked" and "wealthy" is strengthened by the fact that these two Hebrew words share the same basic consonants, but in reverse order. The author intended his readers to take this as a sign that "wicked" of the preceding parallel line is intertwined with the "wealthy" of verse 9aii. Therefore, emendation of עָשִׁיר to "workers of iniquity" (עֹשֵׂי רַע) as often resorted to, in spite of no textual evidence, is unnecessary. The content, construction, and context of Isaiah 53:9 argue for a "synonymous" parallelism not only in verse 9a but also in 9b. This depends on accepting the presence of reverse parallelism in both cases, in addition to observing how other structures and statements in the immediate and more distant contexts support the "synonymous" nature of these two

---

38. NETS rendering of LXX ὅτι ἀνομίαν οὐκ ἐποίησεν. This influenced the Vulgate, "he had done no iniquity" (*imquitatem non fecerit*). Cf. Peter's, ὃς ἁμαρτίαν οὐκ ἐποίησεν.

bi-cola. Consequently, the proposal being made is that "violent" of verse 9bi be understood as a counterpart to "no deceit was in his mouth" of 9bii. The restatement of Isaiah 53:9a is not dependent on this but is strengthened by it. It was demonstrated that OT thought is replete with concepts about the frequent wickedness that comes from wealthy and powerful people, the servant's (or for some the Messiah's) verbal virtue, and the righteousness of speaking the right words at the right time. Silence or economy of words is highly praised. The S/servant especially is praised for being quiet before his enemies and not sinning verbally. A case has been made for the understanding of Isaiah 53:9 as a text that reveals that (1) the suffering servant would be handled by his opponents as a criminal in regard to his death and burial (53:9a); and (2) this treatment would be unfair and unjust because this servant had never sinned verbally or had never acted violently or retaliated verbally (53:9b).

PART IV

Lexical and Contextual Insights in the Old Testament about *Sheol* and Hell

9

"Hell" as a Translation of *Sheol*[1]

Introduction

HELL is no longer a hot issue for many theologians and Christians. Some evangelicals, however, are fired up over its traditional understanding being replaced by the theory of annihilation in some (even evangelical) quarters and being removed as a doctrine, or seldom, if ever, remarked upon within the church as a whole in recent history. Liberal theology long ago dispensed with any need for such a negative and non-universalistic notion. Evangelical theologians maintain a belief in an eschatological and eternal punishment of the unrepentant, but are accepting that the way in which the Bible—especially the Old Testament—has been interpreted (usually proof-texted) and translated, in relation to hell, is ripe for review and reassessment, even reversal of some classic commentaries and conceptions.

A quick look at the major English versions since the KJV or AV (*King James* or *Authorized Version*), based on revisions since the original version of 1611, to the present will demonstrate a remarkable change in the frequency of "hell/Hell" in the Old Testament. "Hell" occurs thirty-one times in the current editions of the KJV and nineteen times in the *New King James Version* (NKJV, 1982).[2] It does not occur in modern, major English

---

1. Originally published as Marlowe, "'Hell' as Translation," 5–24. Stylistic and corrective but no substantive changes have been made (Cf. Tables A and B at the end of this essay, as you read).

2. However, the NKJV uses "hell" for שְׁאוֹל in one extra verse where KJV does not (Ezek 31:15). KJV renders it "hell" thirty-one times. *TWOT* says thirty times, but I count

versions; e.g., in the USA, the *New International Version* (NIV, 1978), *New American Standard Version* (NASB, 1960), *New Revised Standard Version* (NRSV, 1989), or *New American Bible* (NAB, 1970). In twenty-nine of the thirty-one instances of "hell" in the KJV, the LXX has "*Hades*" (ᾅδης) and in all thirty-one the Vulgate has some variant of the root *infer-* ("lower-world/-place").[3] This demonstrates the KJV's dependence, at least in this instance, on these traditional and classic works as much as, or more than, on the exegesis of the "original" Hebrew texts.

The topic of the concept of the earthly or eternal punishment of the wicked in the Old Testament is too large for the nature of this presentation, as is also an evaluation of every occurrence of שְׁאוֹל, even of just the thirty-one verses where KJV translates it as "hell."[4] The purpose and scope of this paper, therefore, are limited to only a summary examination of those eighteen verses where the NKJV preserves this KJV understanding and the one passage where "hell" for שְׁאוֹל is used by the NKJV alone, of these two versions. Obviously, if the NKJV has eliminated thirteen of the thirty-one times "hell" appears in the KJV, then it is clear that scholars who are sympathetic to the KJV find that meaning inappropriate in those cases and, consequently, this study can treat those instances as secondary and supplemental to this discussion and focus on those places where the NKJV maintains the meaning of "hell" for שְׁאוֹל in the Hebrew Bible. It will be demonstrated exegetically that none of these contexts calls for this

---

thirty-one as does the *OED*.

3. Plus, the extra passage where the NKJV uses "hell" (Ezek 31:15), in relation to the KJV and LXX. For the Latin Vulgate: *infer- i, os, ni, no, num, nus*. It should be recognized that the theology or interpretation of some or all of these verses may or may not be the same among these translators. The KJV translators may have read their theology into the Vulgate or based their approach—regardless of Jerome's doctrinal beliefs—on the fact the Vulgate consistently employed the root *infer-* and chose to interpret and translate שְׁאוֹל as "underworld" (realm of the dead; hell?) rather than merely transliterate it, as now is often favored by modern translation committees.

4. This term appears in the Hebrew OT over sixty times and only appears in other Semitic languages as a loan-word from Hebrew (see Gaster, "Abode of Dead," 787 [cf. Smith, *Old Testament Theology*, 382], and Harris, "Sh°ol," II: 892–93. This last work is a very recent evangelical contribution to OT lexicography and theology. The KJV is described as having the two-meaning theory of "grave" in general for שְׁאוֹל but later specialized as "hell"; however, KJV has "hell" very early in the OT. Harris believes that "hell" is probably, at times, the point in passages later than the Pentateuch; but KJV has "hell" as early as Deuteronomy 32:22, and Harris later in the article is quite attracted to the meaning of "grave" or "tomb" for שְׁאוֹל in most if not all places. Harris mentions the royal tombs of Ur which were thirty-feet deep.

translation or are concerned at all with the forever fate of the unfaithful. In that sense, the KJV and NKJV will be de-*hell*enized (especially when one remembers that much of what moderns assume about hell or what the Bible says about it comes from the influence of Greek mythology).

An Evaluation of the Eighteen Times the KJV/NKJV Render שְׁאוֹל "Hell"

Deuteronomy 32:22

This verse is part of a song which recites the past idolatry of the Israelites not long saved from Egypt (vv. 16–18, 21a) and reveals God's plan to judge them through the means of a "foolish nation" (v. 21b). Then in verse 22, which begins with "because," God gives a reason why and further explains how this chastisement will take place *on these chosen people* who acted unfaithfully: i.e., because God's anger is red hot, hot enough to burn throughout the earth's surface and through its crust into the realm of the dead (which was believed to be subterranean).[5] This realm is translated as "Sheol" in the NRSV and "nether world" in the NAB. The former is less of a translation than a transliteration of the Hebrew term, except for the fact that the English rendering is capitalized, which style Hebrew does not employ.[6] The upper- case use of the term does provide some meaning since this

---

5. While God would know the truth that people do not go to a place under the earth after death (except for the grave—which is why the connection to subterranean worlds along with the influence of other ancient mythologies of that time and Greek mythology on later times—the writer only knew what had been revealed up to that point in history and could only use שְׁאוֹל according to its then current Hebrew meanings, apart from strict copying of Egyptian mythology, which in light of the other usages in the Pentateuch suggests "grave" or "death" or "realm of the dead" (grave world). The writer has to use and mean the term in a way that communicates to his audience. So, the best explanation is an allusion to the grave or subterranean death world as people perceived it then. "Hell," as we know the term from progressive revelation, would not be understood or assumed by anyone reading שְׁאוֹל then. God makes the point by using images and language with which the audience is familiar. This does not mean their perception of reality is correct or sanctioned by God as real and true, just how thought and good communication have to start with where people are at using language they understand. "Hell" as we know it had not been revealed in Scripture yet, so it cannot be the intended meaning here, or the verse has no validity in its historical and literary context.

6. "Sheol," of course, is in a way unfair to the reader because it is a non-translation. It tells the reader what Hebrew word is used but not what it means. At least the KJV made a stab at a meaning the reader could understand, even if misleading. The same problem

tends to personify or institutionalize the term and consequently connect it with ideas like the underworld/netherworld or realm of the dead. "Hell" is a true translation albeit inaccurate and anachronistic.[7] Why? Because what is meant by "hell" today is not consistent with the immediate historical and linguistical contexts of this passage. The verses that follow (vv. 23–52) confirm that the judgment concerned is earthly and temporal, not spiritual and eternal, involving arrows, hunger, plague, wild animals, the sword, etc.

Psalm 9:17

The main idea here is that the wicked gentile nations (i.e., those who forget God by ignoring that he is the God that chose Israel and thus mistreat his people) will be destroyed, as YHWH (יהוה) promised Abraham (Gen 12:3). Consequently, the psalmist concludes with, "Rise up, O LORD! Do not let mortals prevail; let the nations be judged before you. Put them in fear, O LORD; let the nations know that they are only human" (vv. 19–20). In verse 18 (19 in the MT)—which immediately follows the use of שאול and the statement about the nations that "forget God"—this psalmist offers a reason why God will punish them, i.e., because God will remember the promise to Abraham regarding those in need of rescue from persecution:

occurs with a number of biblical words. Various factors and forces make individual translators or translation committees merely transliterate a difficult or controversial word (e.g., Greek *baptizo* becomes English "baptize"). This allows the reader to give the word whatever meaning desired in line with one's tradition and allows the translation to escape from forcing a meaning on readers and being charged with sectarianism or bias of some sort. Thus, the translation is neutral on such an issue and stays out of trouble with the majority of readers.

7. Especially for the NKJV because the modern sense of "hell" is clear, and for the KJV if their sense of "hell" was the same as today. The *OED*, s.v. "hell," shows that "hell" in English has the usage of a place of torment and the abode of devils in literary works dated at 1522 (citing Skelton, *Why Come Ye?*, 590: "as ferce [sic] and as cruell [sic] as the fynd of hell") and 1667 (Milton, *Paradise Lost*, n.p., 230 times; e.g., "Within the Gates of Hell sate Sin and Death"). Naturally, the question arises as to what people in 1611 meant when they used the word "hell." Did they mean what we mean or something like Hades or underworld? If the latter, then they cannot be accused of reading NT theology anachronistically back into the OT. But if they meant something akin to "eternal, conscious retributive punishment of the unbelieving sinners after death," then their rendering becomes hermeneutically and exegetically and translationally open to great doubt in terms of accuracy. Only if the Bible is lifted out of history and spiritualized can such an approach—where the same meanings can apply to OT and NT regardless of progress of revelation and historical, cultural, and grammatical contexts—be possible and defended with consistency (yet with any credibility, is doubtful).

"For the needy shall not always be forgotten, nor the hope of the poor perish forever" (NRSV). "Needy" and "poor" refer to those who are experiencing defeat at the hands of ungodly nations.

Psalm 55:15

This is a lament psalm of twenty-three verses. Psalm 55 is about David's fear of death at the hands of an enemy who seems to be on the verge of victory over God's anointed unless a divine rescue occurs (vv. 2–7). The verse with which this debate is concerned (v. 15) must be read in context along with the three verses immediately following (vv. 16–18). That שׁאול in verse 15 is the grave or realm of death is obvious from the preceding colon, which calls for the physical "death" (מות; v. 16 in MT) of David's enemies. מות may be pointed as either *māwet* "death" or *môt* "one dying; to die." This verse is a combination of a "synonymous" parallel bi-colon (v. 15ai–ii) and a "synthetic," explanatory mono-colon (v. 15b), with the major disjunctive punctuation (*athnach*) coming after the bi-colon (cf. NIV and NRSV):

A	B	C	[D']
Let-it-come	death	upon them	[by surprise] /
A'–C'	B'	[C']	D
Let-them-go-down	[to] שׁאול	[them]	alive (*athnach*); //
E	F	G	
for-trouble [is]	in-their-homes [and]	in-their-midsts.	

Consequently, שׁאול and "death" have to be similar ideas, the parallel lines working together like the two speakers of a stereo to produce a blended, harmonious sound. These stereophonics, in linguistic terms, mean that verse 15a has one idea: "May they [= my enemies] be slain!" Perhaps David says "go down alive" because he hopes God will create an earthquake so the ground will open and swallow them alive, as God had done in the past with wicked Israelite rebels and traitors (Num 16:3–35).[8] Line 15b then adds the reason: they are bad in actions and attitudes.

---

8. Interestingly, these Koraites who were swallowed alive in the earth for their rebellion had relatives who were not killed at that time and whose descendants included the

Psalm 139:8

Psalm 139 is one of the best known and loved Davidic psalms of the OT. Verse 8 is where שׁאול is used. The issue of whether to render what in Hebrew is literally "heavens" as "heavens" (the celestial sky) or "H/heaven" (where God "lives") is a crucial matter for understanding the author's intention. Is he really reflecting on the theoretical potential of hiding from God in heaven or in hell? God is so obviously unavoidable in heaven that the writer would seem silly to make such an unnecessary observation. And one of the standard understandings of hell is that, whatever it is, it is the absence of God's personal presence. The verse under question is brought about by the poet's rhetorical question in verse 7, where can I go where you are not present?—to which the obvious answer is "nowhere." Since God is also obviously in heaven and the psalmist is clearly concentrating on the hypothetical idea of a location where one could hide from God, then the concern of 139:8a cannot be with heaven, but only the seemingly limitless sky above, which means the synonymous and alternative parallelism in 8b has to be earthly in orientation. Also, the larger and immediate context of verses 7–12 is earthly in focus. The text of verse 8 is structured literally as follows:

A	B
If-I-ascend	to-the-[heights of the]-heavens (שׁמים) [above],
C	
there-are-You! //	
A'	B'
Or-if-I-descend	to-the-depths (שׁאול) [of the earth below],
C'	
behold,—You [are there also]!	

For David, שׁאול is only the grave, the tomb, the realm of death. He uses it again in Psalm 141, which even the KJV renders "grave" as well as NIV and NKJV. In Psalm 6:5 also, the KJV accepts with NIV "grave" as the necessary

---

sons (= children, not just males, most likely) of Korah known for their musical abilities and, hence, became responsible for many psalms for generations, along with David as the "sweet singer of Israel," the author ostensibly of Psalm 55, et al.

sense, while NKJV uses "death." Assonance is also a reason for the employment of *shemayim* ("heights above") and *sheol* ("depths below").

Proverbs 5:5

Often individual proverbs stand alone without a context, but this verse is one of the exceptions. Proverbs 5:1–6 is an extended set of maxims about the wisdom of avoiding a prostitute or, as the Hebrew puts it, "strange" woman. The text of 5:5 is easily spotted as a "synonymous" parallelism with שְׁאוֹל and "death" as a standard, stock-in-trade, poetic word pair.[9]

The contextual argument flows like this: my child, listen to my wisdom (v. 1) so that you will obtain prudent and practical understanding (v. 2). This is important because the prostitute can have persuasively sweet words (v. 3), but when all is said and done, her advice is extremely bitter and dangerously sharp (v. 4). The path upon which she will lead you is deadly and dark (v. 5) because in her ignorance she wanders off the path that enhances life (v. 6).

It may be true that many people who visit prostitutes are also people that are unbelievers and unrepentant and in the next world will be eternally cast away from God's presence. But one can hardly imagine that the point of the proverbial perspective in verse 5 is that all prostitutes and those who visit them will go to "hell." This is not consistent with the nature of wisdom literature in particular or Scripture in general. Structurally, the verse makes it clear that שְׁאוֹל is the counterpart to "death"; so as a re-stated or static parallel, it has to mean the equivalent of "death," i.e., the grave or tomb. The opposite idea is then presented in verse 6: sexual activity like this is anti-(abundant) life. The point must be that prostitution is foolish because there is the real and present danger of physical disease and emotional distress, which diminish life. The end may well be disease, depression, or even

---

9. As in other articles in this volume (see nn. 4:51; 5:11; 8:5; 8:8; 8:17–18), terms like "synonymous" (for Hebrew poetic lines; reflecting the early and now-dated work of Lowth [*De Sacra Poesi*, in toto]) are used for convenience, while recognizing the advanced research that opposes the idea of specific and distinct kinds of parallelism at work in the ancient context. The last word has not yet been said on OT poetry, and some cola do appear "synonymous" in that they engage in re-statement or are static. Others are clearly antithetical, but "synthetic" as a category is obviously too broad to be useful. What kind of synthesis is employed must be investigated. J. Kugel notwithstanding, to say only "there is line A, then B" is too reductionistic or minimalist. Many past and present publications still speak of parallelism in traditional terms. The tradition needs reassessment but is still useful and describes parallelism in a way most current readers expect.

death, i.e., a sooner-than-necessary progression towards or entrance into the tomb or grave world.

Proverbs 7:27

The same is basically true of this passage as the foregoing one. Again, the context is an extended discussion of the attractions and distractions but also potential and probable problems with adultery and/or prostitution (sexual license outside marriage). The entire chapter of twenty-seven verses (of which the one with שׁאוֹל is the concluding verse) concerns this topic. That the issue is not the possible (especially certain) loss of eternal life but physical life is seen in verses 21–23. The similarities with Proverbs 5:1–6 can be seen with the final verses (24–27) of chapter 7. שׁאוֹל is again a synonym with "death."

Proverbs 9:18

In this verse prostitution ("foolish" woman; v. 13) is in view once more, so most or all of what has been said about שׁאוֹל in OT Wisdom and Proverbs so far is applicable. The parallelism is the same, although the word used for "the dead" is different than the normal one, which, unfortunately, is not apparent in many versions. The word rendered "dead" in both NRSV and KJV is not the usual מות but רפאים (*rᵉphāʾiym*), which some render "shades," or "spirits of the dead (ghosts)," but the basic idea is "dead ones." Only the assumption that OT authors shared certain views with the Egyptians or Canaanites about the netherworld can lead to ideas like "disembodied spirits or souls in *Sheol*." Another use of the same term or a homograph was as the name (*Rephaim*) of some of the pre-Israelite dwellers of Canaan.[10] In this latter capacity the questionable translation "giants" is sometimes given. When the same triconsonantal root is used for a verb it means "to heal," and the feminine noun form means "medicine." But this masculine form, when not used of the *Rephaim*, has to do, seemingly, with "the dead." It functions as an alternative term for מות. The immediate and larger contexts give unambiguous evidence that the liabilities of illicit lust lie intrinsically in this world and not the next (cf. 8:33–36; 9:1–5; 9:10–18).

---

10. See Koehler-Baumgartner, *Lexicon*, 904.

Proverbs 15:11; 27:20

These proverbs have no essential or necessary connection to the surrounding verses. In both cases the parallelism is "synthetic" (see n. 9), so no synonym for שְׁאוֹל is used but it is paired with אֲבַדּוֹן ("destruction") as a closely related idea; and this same term is elsewhere used as a structural synonym for שְׁאוֹל or other terms for "grave." For example, in the similar and coordinate "synonymous" (see n. 9) parallelism of Psalm 88:11 [88:12 MT], literally portrayed as:

A	B	C
Will-it-be-declared?	in-the-grave [קבר]	your-lovingkindness //
[A]	C'	B'
[Will-it-be-declared?]	your-faithfulness	in-destruction [אבדון].

Another example is Job 26:6, literally rendered as:

A	[B']	C	D
Naked	[is]	שְׁאוֹל	before-him //
B	A'	C'	[D']
And-there-is-no	covering	for- אבדון	[before-God].

However, קבר (*qeḇer*, "grave") in the OT never seems to be used in parallel with שְׁאוֹל ("death; grave," etc.) or מות ("death; one dying"), but often is found with "pit" (בוֹר) since it represents the "grave" per se. שְׁאוֹל is, however, often paired with "death" (usually מות). When "death" and "grave" or "pit" are paired in OT poetry, the terms are usually and respectively, שְׁאוֹל, מות, and בוֹר. In Job 21:32, קברות ("graves") is parallel with גדיש "tomb" (KJV = NRSV). In one instance (Ps 49:14) in the OT, שְׁאוֹל ("realm of death"), מות ("death"), and קבר ("grave") may all be used interchangeably in the same verse (see, e.g., NRSV; KJV; LXX; and Vulgate).

As for Proverbs 15:11, שְׁאוֹל and אֲבַדּוֹן are both described as things about which God has complete understanding (v. 11a). The sage then makes the comparative statement that, if this is true, then God certainly and even more so knows about all human thoughts and schemes (v. 11b). While the surrounding verses of 15:11 do not help, שְׁאוֹל does appear again thirteen verses later, which is the next verse to occupy the concerns of this study. No particular topic (other than assorted aphorisms of wise advice) or logical procedure, though, seems to guide the poet's development of his advice from 15:11 to 15:24. A number of exegetes see a change from "death" to "grave" with שׁאוֹל (see 15:11 and 27:20 in NRSV, KJV, LXX, and Vulgate).

As for Proverbs 27:20, most of the same arguments apply. In this case a different observation is being made: i.e., just as human desire seems endless so do the appetites of death (שׁאוֹל) and destruction (אֲבַדּוֹן). One additional point, showing how "H/hell" is improbable in such a verse, that can be made for Proverbs 15:11 as well is that since the terms are used coordinately in the same colon and not the same or similarly in parallel cola, then they cannot be different words for the same idea (i.e., hell) as thought by some who translate שׁאוֹל "hell" and אֲבַדּוֹן "the pit." They are different words for a similar or overlapping semantic category (i.e., the end of life); so they can be used in "synonymous" parallelism, where similar ideas are stated and restated with different words. But if they are seen as strict synonyms for an idea like hell, then in verses like these two in Proverbs, the logical outcome would be absurdly redundant: "*Sheol* ('Hell') and *Abaddon* ('Hell') are never filled." Even if these are taken as strict synonyms, this would work in parallel structure but not in a coordinated sequence.

Proverbs 15:24

This is a case where the phrase "upward" (v. 24a) paired with "downward" (v. 24b) seems to be a major if not the major factor in explaining why some see "Hell" as the meaning of שׁאוֹל. But this wording cannot prove "Hell" is intended in such a verse, because one could just as easily and sensibly speak of going down into the grave or to the realm of death and contrast it with the upward path of life itself. It is mainly our preconceived notions about the afterlife that makes us immediately think of heaven and hell when we read expressions like these, but not the actual verses or contexts themselves.

Furthermore, in relation to Proverbs 15:24, the expressions "down" and "up" as physical directions are not as clear in the text as some versions suggest (cf., e.g., NRSV, NASB, KJV, and NIV). Even the KJV and NKJV avoid the wording that contrasts "going up" with "going down," while translating שׁאוֹל as "H/hell." But the NIV's "going down to the grave" makes perfect sense; so without any other clues in the immediate context (unless "above" in the previous parallel line can be proven to mean heaven) "H/

hell" is not warranted as a possible or probable meaning. The point is simple and perfectly in line with what would be expected of Wisdom literature: i.e., making wise choices in life leads one in a direction up and away from the grave below.[11] A major theme of OT Wisdom is the idea that the wise

> 11. E.g., many of those that contrast the righteous and the wicked, such as Proverbs 10:1–32. The non-absolute nature of proverbial truth must be kept in mind and accepted to avoid misunderstandings and misapplications (which may be very harmful at times) of these scriptures in day-to-day life. This does not mean that truth is relative because absolute truth, like "You must not commit murder," cannot ever be relativized; however, another type of truth—wisdom, experiential, horizontal—is relative and conditional. This is why one proverb can tell us to "answer a fool" (26:5) and another command just the opposite "answer not a fool" (26:4), without being a contradiction. Both are true although opposites because the truth involved is that of practical, earthly advice (not direct, propositional, and heavenly affirmations like the Ten Commandments). OT Wisdom truth usually (though not always) deals with the circumstances of life, which means the guidance can be different in various situations. Sometimes foolish people need to be corrected with information, so it is right to confront them, but at other times a foolish person is best handled with silence. It would be a waste of time and energy (and thus wrong) to seek to convince him or her. The danger of making OT proverbs into inflexible promises rather than flexible principles is that of absolutizing a relative, which is just as problematic as the reverse, relativizing and absolute. The fact that this latter must be carefully avoided with the Bible is no reason to go to the other extreme. Both abuses will cause much damage and division in the body of Christ. Many have been discouraged by thinking a certain verse offered them, in theory, an iron-clad promise only to find out, in practice, that the expected guaranteed outcome did not materialize as other Christians had sworn it would. The result has been often to make the person feel as if their faith was the problem, when all along the problem was a faulty interpretation of Scripture. God's promises are absolute; but we must not mistake a principle for a promise or we can hurt people. We need to be very sure about what we claim is absolutely true. God's Word is true, but it includes absolute commands (law; vertical and propositional) and relative guidance (wisdom; horizontal and experiential). The former is direct revelation from God; the latter is indirect revelation that comes from life (but the life which God created with certain physical and moral laws humans can observe through common sense and rationality apart from God's voice through a prophet). This is why one of the themes of wisdom is the question "why do the righteous suffer?" or "why do the wicked prosper?" Since it seems God promises success for good people and poverty and peril for bad people, the fact that experience teaches that the opposite happens frequently leads to questions about God's fairness, consistency, and faithfulness. The Bible shows wise people wrestling with such issues, but overall the testimony and teaching of Scripture is that no such absolute promises have been made. Wisdom does not say that good people are absolutely guaranteed riches, long lives, godly offspring, etc. What is says is that doing what is right is the best pathway in life even though pain, perplexity, poverty, and problems may plague the faithful believer and even though health and wealth may be had by someone very disobedient or rebellious and unfaithful. The point is that experience teaches, and God's Word supports, that "crime does not pay" often enough to make the risks of disobedience and depravity not worth taking. In the end, the wise life is the

life is usually a long life because the wise person avoids the type of attitudes and activities that often lead others (foolish people) to an early or untimely death. This verse in its full sense and literal structure as a synthetic (reason-based) parallelism is as follows:

A	B	C	[D']	E		
(The)-path-of	life	[is]	upward	[from שְׁאוֹל]	for-the-wise; //	
F	G	[E]	D	C'		
In-order	to-keep	[the wise]	from- שְׁאוֹל	below.		

Proverbs 23:14

That anyone would think שְׁאוֹל in this verse means "Hell" is utterly amazing and inexplicable. In this case, a small context is formed by vv. 12–14. The main theme is that of a parent's discipline of a child.[12] Some important interpretive differences are found when various versions are compared, but the most significant is the meaning given to שְׁאוֹל. The value of beating a child dramatically—actually infinitely—increases when the result moves from deliverance from mere physical (an early grave) to eternal death (hell). In literary terms this is a simple proverb making a simple, practical (but true and trustworthy) observation about a reality of life. It would be an abnormal assessment of this genre of revelation and Scripture to see it as a philosophical puzzle which assumes the following logic: a child must be beaten with a stick because that will cause the child to fear doing evil and in turn make him fear God and the prospects of eternal judgment so he will naturally believe and behave properly and thus be saved from hell in the end. Proverbs are pithy principles based on experiential patterns. The obvious fact being observed here is the value of discipline. It normally works in bringing about wise behavior (yet through fear), which in turn usually prolongs life, quantitatively and qualitatively. Biblical theology and logic

---

righteous life and the foolish life is the wicked one. Exceptions only prove this rule.

12. Literally, a father is indicated by the use of "my son" in the surrounding context, and a son is described by the use of the term for "young man" (נַעַר) and the third masc. sing. pronoun; but the overall sense must relate to all children, male or female, and must be applicable to whomever dispenses the punishment in a given case, father or mother, although the ancient, cultural context would emphasize the father's responsibility.

both argue strongly and conclusively against the idea that this verse says physical punishment normally nets a heavenly reward. Spanked children and unspanked children will populate both heaven and hell in the end (no pun intended). On the other hand, many more disciplined (not a synomym for "spanked") children than undisciplined will make the kind of decisions that increase life; and many more undisciplined children than disciplined will make bad decisions that lessen or lose life.

נפש (*nephesh*) in verse 14 should be translated "life" or "him" and not "soul." It seldom, if ever, means in the OT what the word "soul" does in current, popular usage, especially when, as here, a possessive pronoun is attached. The context shows that discipline saves from physical death, so the emphasis is on the prolongation of the child's physical and earthly health and holiness. The phrase "he will not die" (v. 13) is not an attempt to console the parent with the opinion that "a spanking or beating will not kill someone" (obviously a beating might), but it means "discipline can keep him from an early grave." This argues that the same sense is intended in verse 14. Punishment does not "save an eternal soul from hell" but "can help preserve a life from an untimely death."

Also most, if not all, who would want to translate שׁאוֹל here as "hell"—or who accept the KJV as the preferred or "perfect" translation—do not believe (or belong to a church tradition that believes) that one's eternal destiny is determined by how often or not one sins. But to have "hell" in this verse seems to teach this: i.e., you must physically and painfully punish them (understood: because you will teach them obedience) and therefore they will be saved from eternal damnation. The chief concern of the wise author of Proverbs 23 is with the value of discipline, whatever kind is used (although it is fair to say that harsh physical punishment was the norm of his time), to achieve behavior patterns that are healthy, as long as not cruel or crippling.[13] Verse 14 should be read with verse 13, which demonstrates that שׁאוֹל in the latter is equivalent to מות ("to die") in the former. Both verses mapped out literally look like this:

A	B	C
Do-not-withhold	from-a-child	discipline [מוּסָר] //

---

13. See Ephesians 6:4, where Paul warns parents to be careful not to "provoke anger" in children but rather "bring them up in the *discipline and instruction of the Lord*" (italics added; NRSV).

D	E	F	G
If-you-punish-him [תכנו]	with-the-rod [בשׁבט]	not	he-will-die.
A	B	C	
You	with-the-rod [בשׁבט]	punish-him [תכנו] //	
D	E	F	
And-his-life [נפשׁ]	from-death [משׁאול]	you-will-save.	

Amos 9:2

The context of this verse is an oracle about the destruction of Israel. It follows the Lord's frightful introductory statement of his intention to bring death on the entire population through collapsed buildings and the sword (v. 1). Most interesting is the fact that the KJV has a colon at the end of this verse, which means the translators understand the following verse or verses to be explanatory or illustrative of what this verse says. And those verses are about anything but hell! Of course the parallel line contains "heaven," which begs the question. The terms are clearly meant to be antithetical linguistically, but these cola are "synonymous" semantically. The same idea being expressed in two different ways is that no one can hide from the death God has declared he will execute on Israel, regardless of which direction one runs, even if one tries to climb into the terrestrial tomb world or into the celestial star world. The directions used are opposites for effect but the intentions of each colon are identical. Verse 2 is meant to reiterate the parallelism at the end of verse 1: "not one of them shall flee away, // not one of them shall escape" (9:1d; see NRSV). Contextually, "them" can only refer to ancient Israelites caught in the catastrophic destruction of their cities and countryside. Furthermore, the rest of the verses (vv. 3–4), which conclude the opening pericope of chapter 9, are structured as similar restatements of the fact that whatever these "Israelites elected for execution" try to do to escape will be hopeless. All the parallel cola have a similar style: the protasis colon beginning with "though they [try such and such]" and the apodasis colon following with "I will [stop them]." All these further explicate verse 2 by giving other earthly and temporal examples of impossible escape plans, be they high or low: hide on Mount Carmel or at the bottom of the sea (v. 3; see Jonah 2:3, 5–6) or into captivity as a political prisoner (v. 4). Verse 2 is composed of two "synthetic" parallelisms (second-line completion type) which are similar and alternative synonymous parallels. "Heavens" again has to be understood as "the skies above us" (not "Heaven"), so the poetically paired term (בשאול) has to be seen as the lower counterpart; i.e., "in the depths [of the land below us]." These may be literally represented as:

A	B	
Though-they-dig-down	into-the-depths [בשאול] /	
C	D	E
from-there	my-hand	it-will-take-them; //
A'	B'	
Or-if-they-climb	the-[heights of the] sky [השמים], /	
C'	[D']	E'
from-there	[I myself]	I-will-bring-them-down.

One other feature of interest in this passage—and one some might try to interpret as another allusion to hell—is the "sea-serpent" in verse 3b (NRSV), just rendered "serpent" in KJV. In context, however, the idea is that individual Israelites cannot escape God's inevitable destructive judgment, no matter where they try to hide on, in, or above the earth. The language is hyperbolic. Even if they flee to the bottom of the sea, God will capture or kill them through the instrumentality of a sea-creature. This "serpent" has no connection with the crafty serpent of temptation at the beginning of human creation. But each serpent episode does reflect the ancient religious mentality that understands seas and sea monsters or serpents as representative of chaos or anti-creation in the cosmos. The same Hebrew word for "serpent" (נחש; *nāḥāš*) is used in Genesis 3:1 and Amos 9:3. The Canaanites viewed the sea and the sea serpent as gods—named, respectively, Yam and Lotan (= Hebrew *Leviathan*).[14] The OT is careful to expose the truth that YHWH the God of Israel is the Creator and controller of all such forceful and fearsome dark features and facts of existence in this fallen and sometimes seemingly undirected and unstable universe.

---

14. These terms are both the Hebrew and Ugaritic words for "sea" and "sea monster." Ugaritic is the language of Canaanite religious poetic texts and is a northwest Semitic dialect like Hebrew. Ugaritic *lôṯan* = OT Hebrew *liwyāṯān* (Leviathan; the Hebrew *waw* can be *w/v* or *o*; in consonants the Hebrew לויתן used for the Ugaritic letters would be לותן.

Isaiah 14:9

This chapter of Isaiah is famous (or infamous) for its traditional and popular interpretation, which identifies the king of Babylon mentioned in verse 12 (if not in vv. 3–11) with Satan—supposedly named "Lucifer" in this passage. In verse 12 the expression "shining one" or "day star" was translated "Lucifer" in the KJV and NKJV, which rendering was a transliteration of the Latin word used in the Vulgate: *lucifer*, which means "light-bearing" or "morning star."[15] The capitalization of the word as a proper noun in such versions is the only time it is used as a name. No such name for Satan is known outside of this verse.

With this in mind, שׁאול in verse 9 could not possibly be about hell unless the author is saying that such would be the eternal destination of this king. And even if verses 12–14 were about Satan, this verse 9 (where NKJV has "hell") is in the section that most do interpret as dealing with the human king of Babylon.[16] The traditional "Satan view" usually begins with verse 12 and is often limited to just verses 12–14. Also interesting is the fact that שׁאול appears again in verse 11 but also in verse 12 in the so-called Satan section. Yet in both instances the NKJV renders it "Sheol" not "hell." The KJV has "grave" in verse 11 and "hell" in verses 9 and 15.

The שׁאול of verse 9 should be the same as in verses 11 and 15 since the destruction and destiny of the same person is in view in each case. But is his eternal destruction in view? None of these contexts supports this idea. Only if Satan is the subject can a case be made for something like "hell" as the meaning of שׁאול in Isaiah 14. In verse 9 it is paired with a synonym רפאים, rendered "spirits of the departed" in the NIV, "shades" in the NRSV, and (ironically, most accurate) "the dead" in both KJV and NKJV. The basic idea should be obvious to an objective reader: the grave, i.e., the realm of the dead, is anxious to receive this one whose wicked pride is so great that the world longs to be rid of him as quickly as possible. Now he is fallen, so

---

15. However, the NKJV adds a footnote that the term literally means "Day Star." In Holland, matches are called "lucifers."

16. The text says "king of Babylon" (see vv. 4, 22 e.g. but cf. v. 25), but the time period concerned (Isaiah's) is Assyrian. It has been demonstrated that Assyrian kings sometimes were called kings of Babylon (before the rise of the neo-Babylonian empire) because Assyria dominated the region that once was the old Babylonian kingdom, centered around the city of Babylon and its glorious history. Therefore, Assyrian kings saw themselves in the grand tradition of being rulers of Babylon or Babylonia, even though their capital was elsewhere. An exact identity of this Assyrian king is difficult, but Sargon II fits the time period and did die a disgraceful death on the battlefield as the text describes (vv. 18–20).

the grave is personified as longing for his presence. This "grave" poetically is first named שׁאוֹל ("the place of the dead") and then רפאים ("those in the grave" or "the dead/departed ones"). Adding to this second idea, notions like "spirits of" or "shades" reads into them a specificity not required. Contextually, these terms just refer to the grave as the place where dead people end up. Even this grave and its inhabitants are poetically and figuratively pictured as being relieved that this king's time has come. This grave imagery is more explicit in verse 11, which is why neither KJV nor NKJV continue with the meaning of "hell" for שׁאוֹל there. In verse 11 worms are said to also inhabit שׁאוֹל; such that they become a bed for the corpse of this king. שׁאוֹל is simply and straightforwardly the pit or hole in the ground where a dead body is laid to rest. However, in this case, this normal grave is only a potential reality. The actual grave is not a stately sarcophagus, befitting a king, but the bare ground itself, where maggots and worms reside. The king described here is killed and, therefore, is a candidate for a royal burial and grave site; but to add insult to injury, so to speak, his shame is intensified, for he is not only defeated in death but fails to receive the expected honor of a king's burial. Instead he is left to rot on the ground for a grave. Beyond the disgrace of dying in battle—which kings almost never did and which great kings were never supposed to do—this king also was shamed by not receiving a royal reception for his body or a rich and stately return of it to the earth (see vv. 18–20). In verse 15 the synonymous poetic parallel is between שׁאוֹל and בוֹר "pit." The one who sought divine heights as a god or demi-god ended up in death like all mortals. Death in this verse is defined as being brought down from pride and power of life to insignificance and indignation (i.e., as existence in the grave, a hole in the ground). But this king ironically and justly does not even get to the grave per se; he is left in his ruin and ridicule (vv. 16–17) to decay among the maggots, without proper burial (vv. 18–20a).

Habakkuk 2:5

The notion that שׁאוֹל means "hell" in this verse can be dispensed with quite readily. The immediate context is God's reply to Habakkuk's question about the propriety of God using the wicked Assyrians to judge the chosen, albeit imperfect, Hebrews. This answer involves verses 2–5 of chapter 2 and contains the somewhat controversial and significant statement quoted in the NT and applied to Christian soteriology, "but the righteous live by their faith" (2:4b; NRSV). The following verse is the one that uses שׁאוֹל and makes the basic point that arrogant nations—i.e., those who abuse others—never stop looking for another victim, but also will not go unpunished. Even verse 4 begins with the subject of proud people ("Look at the proud!" [NRSV]), who are then contrasted with the righteous, who live by faith. They keep trusting God even when they do not understand how the wicked can be allowed to win. In verse 5b the proud powers of earth are described poetically as greedy for the gain of other nations' goods. This verse presents a continued synonymous and somewhat chiastic structure, which parallels "the grave" (שׁאוֹל) with "death." Literally the text reads:

A	B	C	D
Because	it-makes-large	like-שׁאוֹל	his-greed //
D	C'	E	F
And-it [his greed]	like-the-מות	that-never	it-is-satisfied.

The parallel and synonymous word pair is שׁאוֹל and מות, of which the latter means "death," which is the meaning also given in the NKJV. To be more exact and consistent, if שׁאוֹל does mean "hell" here, then מות should have been translated "eternal death." But contextually it should be clear that the author's intention was to portray these vicious nations as death personified (Madam Death). No one is excluded from death's design to devour. So שׁאוֹל is again used in its most common sense of " the realm of death" or the "grave." The verse says nothing about the eternal destiny of these wicked nations, only that they are characterized by an unquenchable thirst for the wealth of the world. That they will be judged is stated but nothing more is said about the nature of that judgment. Their relationship to שׁאוֹל is the same as death: a cavernous capacity. The final "synonymous" colon of the verse repeats this idea (see NRSV):

They-gather	all-nations	for-themselves //
And-[they]-collect	all-peoples	as-their-own.

Hell is also hungry for many inhabitants, one could claim; but while that is also true it is not the focus of this verse, since death itself is the twin term with שׁאוֹל.

Ezekiel 31:16–17

Chapter 31 of Ezekiel continues the pronouncement of judgment against the king of Egypt begun in chapter 30. These chapters sit within and near the end of Ezekiel's proclamations against the gentile nations in chapters 25–32. In 31:1–9 this doomed monarch is asked to remember the fallen fate of the mighty Assyrian nation, which is compared metaphorically and poetically to a lofty cedar tree. Then in verses 10–14, poetic prose is interspersed with poetic verse (vv. 13, 14b), wherein Pharaoh's punishment is predicted due to his pride, just as the ruler of Assyria. In verse 14, just before verses 16–17 (where KJV and NKJV translate שְׁאוֹל as "hell") the statement is made that such godless pride has been and will continue to be answered with "death" (מוּת). In the poetic stanzas which occupy the last half of verse 14, "being given over to death" is parallel with "going to the lower ground/earth [אֶרֶץ]" and with "going down to the pit [בּוֹר]." Then in verses 15–16 God's felling of the lofty cedar tree (i.e., proud Assyria) is again reviewed and restated as going down (v. 15) or being cast down (v. 16) to שְׁאוֹל. In verse 16 שְׁאוֹל is used synonymously with the same "pit [בּוֹר]" of verse 14. The original narrative text of verse 16aii–bi translated literally is:

When-I-brought-down	it [Assyria]	to-[the]-grave [שְׁאוֹל]
with-those-going-down-into		[the]-pit [בּוֹר];
then-they-were-consoled		in-[the]-ground [אֶרֶץ] below.

The שְׁאוֹל of verse 16 is clearly similar to "the pit," which is the same as "death," which is equated in the context with a hole in the ground ("pit") or the lower parts of the earth; i.e., the grave or realm of the dead. Verse 17 continues the flow of thought already established and again uses שְׁאוֹל as "the grave," since going down to it is described in verses 17 and 18 as being in the same place as those "killed by the sword" (what v. 18 also describes as lying "among the uncircumcised"). The שְׁאוֹל of verse 15, logically and contextually, must be the same as that in verses 16–17, but surprisingly (although completely understandably in light of the immediately preceding verse, 14b) KJV renders it "grave," while NKJV (obviously for the sake of consistency with vv. 16–17; see n. 7 and Table A, p. 172) has "hell."

Ezekiel 32:21, 27

Ezekiel 32 continues and concludes God's proclamation of doom and destruction for Egypt (vv. 17–27) and its pharaoh (vv. 2b–16) by shifting to a lament or dirge (קינה, *qiʸnah* v. 2) over their fate and fall. The term שׁאוֹל is not used until Egypt as a whole is addressed, along with its king, in verses 21 and 27. The same or similar contextual and exegetical arguments may be made for the meaning of שׁאוֹל as "grave" in these two verses as has just been said about it in chapter 31 regarding Assyria and Egypt. One merely has to read these two verses within the overall and immediate context of verses 17–28. The same parallel concepts or words are used which depict death or the grave:

> The mighty ... will speak ... from the midst of שׁאוֹל: "They have come down ... the uncircumcised, killed by the sword" [v. 21, cf. v. 28] ... lie with the fallen warriors of long ago who went down to שׁאוֹל with their weapons of war ... whose shields are upon their bones [v. 27] (Cf. NRSV).

An Evaluation of the Verse where the NKJV and Not KJV Renders שׁאוֹל "Hell": Ezekiel 31:15

Curiously the KJV translators resorted to "grave" instead of "hell" in Ezekiel 31:15, although they used "hell" for שׁאוֹל in 31:16 and 17. Contextually, of course, it is clear why they were compelled to use this meaning in verse 15; but this would seem to raise strong doubt about their practice of using "hell" in other similar contexts. The comments made above (regarding Ezek. 31:16–17) are also pertinent to the argument as to why "hell" should not be the translation of שׁאוֹל in 31:15. The descent of Assyria into שׁאוֹל in this verse is described in verse 16 as something that made the surrounding nations shake with fear. This has to refer to the past historical horror and shock of the ancient Near Eastern nations over the surprising downfall of the great Assyrian empire. If so, then Ezekiel has no intention in this passage of saying that the Assyrians went to hell, especially as that expression would have meaning among believers today. Also verse 16 (immediately after describing this historic effect on the nations) repeats the fact of this same descent into שׁאוֹל, which means that if verse 15 is about death, decay, defeat, and destruction, then also is verse 16, not to mention verse 17 for similar reasons. Consistently and correctly, either all three appearances of

שׁאוֹל in verses 15–17 are about the collapse of Assyria or its condemnation, but not both ideas simultaneously or alternately. The logic of Chapter 31:3–17 runs as follows:

> Consider Assyria [v. 3] ... because it ... was proud [v. 10] ... Foreigners ... cut it down [v. 12] ... For all of them are handed over to death, [i.e.] to the world below [v. 14] ... On the day it went down to שׁאוֹל ... I restrained its rivers [v. 15] ... I made the nations quake at the sound of its fall, when I cast it down to שׁאוֹל ... and all ... were consoled in the world below [v. 16]. They also went down to שׁאוֹל with it, to those killed by the sword ... those who lived in its shade among the nations [v. 17] (NRSV).

Verse 14b is particularly important because it prepares the reader for the meaning of verses 15–17 and also is composed in poetic parallelism, which makes it unarguably clear and certain that death is a synonym in this passage with "the world below" or שׁאוֹל. The poetic nature of this verse is seen in the NRSV and NKJV, but not in the NIV or KJV. Here it is displayed literally as to its parallel "re-statements":

A	B	C	D	E
For-all-of-them	they-are-destined	for-the-death, //		
[A]	[B]	C'		
[For-all-of-them	they-are-destined]	for-earth-of below.		
[A]	[B]	C	D	E
[For-all-of-them	they-are]	among	sons-of humaness	
[F]				
[in the grave], //				
[A]	[B]	C'[-D'-E']		
[For-all-of-them	they-are]	with-those-[humans] down-in		
F				
[the] pit.				

Conclusion

None of the nineteen contexts (verses) where שׁאוֹל is translated "hell" by the NKJV (eighteen of which have "hell" in the KJV also) is supportive of that translation. In each case the flow of argumentation and/or the poetic parallels prove(s) that the author uses שׁאוֹל for the concept of the grave or death.

Table A: The Structure of the Verse Where NKJV Renders sheol as "Hell"

REFERENCE	PARALLELISM
Deut 32:22	For a fire is kind led in My anger, // and shall bum to the lowest *sheol*; It shall consume the earth with her increase, // and set on fire the foundations of mountains.
Psalm 9:17	The wicked shall be turned into *sheol*, // and all the nations that forget God.
Psalm 55:15	Let death seize them; // *let* them go down alive into *sheol*, / for wickedness is in their dwellings *and* among them.
Psalm 139:8	If I ascend into heaven, You *are* there; // if I make my bed in *sheol*, behold, You *are there*.
Proverbs 5:5	Her feet go down to death, // her steps lay hold of *sheol*.
Proverbs 7:27	Her house is the way to *sheol*, // descending to the chambers of death.
Proverbs 9:18	But he does not know that the dead *are* there, // that her guests *are* in the depths of *sheol*.
Proverbs 15:11	*Sheol* and Destruction *are* before the LORD; // so how much more the hearts of the sons of men.
Proverbs 27:20	*Sheol* and Destruction are never full; // so the eyes of man are never satisfied.
Proverbs 15:24	The way of life *winds* upward for the wise, // that he may turn away from *sheol* be low.
Proverbs 23:14	You shall beat him with a rod, // and deliver his soul from *sheol*.
Amos 9:2	Though they dig into *sheol*, / from there My hand shall take them; // Though they climb up to heaven, / from there I will bring them down.
Isaiah 14:9	*Sheol* from beneath is excited about you, to meet *you* at your coming; // It stirs up the dead for you, all the chief ones of the earth; / It has raised up from their thrones all the kings of the nations.\
Habakkuk 2:5	Indeed, because he transgresses by wine, he *is* a proud man / and he does not stay at home. // Because he enlarges his desire as *sheol*, / and he *is* like death, and cannot be satisfied, // he gathers to himself all nations / and heaps up for himself all peoples.

"HELL" AS A TRANSLATION OF SHEOL

Ezekiel 31:16-17	I made the nations shake at the sound of its fall, when I cast it down to *sheol* together with those who descend into the Pit; and all the trees of Eden, the choice and best of Lebanon, all that drink water, were comforted in the depths of the earth. They also went down to *sheol* with it, with those *slain* by the sword; and *those who were* its *strong arm* dwelt in its shadows among the nations.
Ezekiel 32:21	The strong among the mighty / shall speak to him out of the midst of *sheol* / with those who help him: // 'They have gone down, / they lie with the uncircumcised, / slain by the sword."
Ezekiel 32:27	They do not lie with the *mighty- who are* fallen of the uncircumcised, / who have gone down to *sheaf* with their weapons of war; // they have laid their swords under their heads, / but their iniquities will be on their bones, because of the terror of the mighty in the land of the living.
Ezekiel 31:1	Thus says the LORD GOD: "In the day when it went down to *sheol*, I caused mourning. I covered the deep because of it. I restrained its rivers, and the great waters were held back. I caused Lebanon to mourn for it, and all the trees of the field wilted because of it."

Table B: The Use of sheol in Ancient and Modern Versions

"hell" in KJV 1611-	NKJV 1982	NIV 1978	NRSV 1989	NASB 1960	NAB* 1970	LXX* 200BC	Vulgate* 400
Deut 32:22	hell	death	Sheol	Sheol	nether world	*hades*	*inferni*
2 Sam 22:6	Sheol	grave	Sheol	Sheol	nether world	"death"	*inferi*
Job 11:8	Sheol	grave	Sheol	Sheol	nether world	*hades*	*inferno*
Job 26:6	Sheol	death	Sheol	Sheol	nether world	*hades*	*inferus*
Psalm 9:17	hell	grave	Sheol	Sheol	nether world	*hades*	*infernum*
Psalm 16:10	Sheol	grave	Sheol	Sheol	nether world	*hades*	*infero*
Psalm 18:5	Sheol	grave	Sheol	Sheol	nether world	*hades*	*inferi*
Psalm 55:15	hell	grave	Sheol	Sheol	nether world	*hades*	*infernam*
Psalm 86:13	Sheol	grave	Sheol	Sheol	nether world	*hades*	*inferno*
Psalm 116:3	Sheol	grave	Sheol	Sheol	nether world	*hades*	*inferni*
Psalm 139:8	hell	depths	Sheol	Sheol	nether world	*hades*	*inferno*
Prov 5:5	hell	grave	Sheol	Sheol	nether world	*hades*	*inferos*
Prov 7:27	hell	grave	Sheol	Sheol	nether world	*hades*	*inferi*
Prov 9:18	hell	grave	Sheol	Sheol	nether world	*hades*	*inferni*
Prov 15:11	hell	death	Sheol	Sheol	nether world	*hades*	*infernus*

Prov 15:24	hell	grave	Sheol	Sheol	nether world	*hades*	*inferno*
Prov 23:14	hell	death	Sheol	Sheol	nether world	"death"	*inferno*
Prov 27:20	hell	death	Sheol	Sheol	nether world	*hades*	*infernus*
Isa 5:14	Sheol	grave	Sheol	Sheol	nether world	*hades*	*infernus*
Isa 14:9	hell	grave	Sheol	Sheol	nether world	*hades*	*infernus*
Isa 14:15	Sheol	grave	Sheol	Sheol	nether world	*hades*	*infernum*
Isa 28:15	Sheol	grave	Sheol	Sheol	nether world	*hades*	*inferno*
Isa 28:18	Sheol	grave	Sheol	Sheol	nether world	*hades*	*inferno*
Isa 57:9	Sheol	grave	Sheol	Sheol	nether world	*hades*	*inferos*
Ezek 31:15 "grave"	hell	grave	Sheol	Sheol	nether world	*hades*	*inferos*
Ezek 31:16	hell	grave	Sheol	Sheol	nether world	*hades*	*infernum*
Ezek 31:17	hell	grave	Sheol	Sheol	nether world	*hades*	*infernum*
Ezek 32:21	hell	grave	Sheol	Sheol	nether world	"pit"	*inferni*
Ezek 32:27	hell	grave	Sheol	Sheol	nether world	*hades*	*infernum*
Amos 9:2	hell	grave	Sheol	Sheol	nether world	*hades*	*infernum*
Jonah 2:2	Sheol	grave	Sheol	Sheol	nether world	*hades*	*inferni*
Hab 2:5	hell	grave	Sheol	Sheol	nether world	*hades*	*infernus*

* versification may differ; usually + or - one verse.

10

"Hell" in English Bible Versions Since the 1611 KJB[1]

Introduction

HELL is under fire. Once a fairly unquestioned doctrine among conservative Christians, recent decades have witnessed even some major evangelical leaders questioning the accuracy of the traditional belief in unending torture of unbelievers. The interpretation of eternal punishment of the wicked as annihilation[2] is increasingly a position held or tolerated by evangelicals.[3] In the debate over the nature and reality of hell as traditionally explained, an interesting issue is an investigation of how English translations have or have not changed on this subject.

"Hell" or "hell" ("helle" in the Wycliffe Bible) appears in the King James Bible (KJB or Authorized Version, AV) fifteen times in fifteen verses

---

1. Originally published as Marlowe, "'Hell' in English Bible," 157–78.

2. A prime example is the late John R. W. Stott, globally influential Anglican clergyman, prolific author, and rector of the All Souls Church in London. He suggested this doctrine in a book co-authored with David L. Edwards, published in 1988 in England and 1989 in the USA. See Stott-Edwards, *Essentials*, in toto.

3. As I wrote this chapter initially, a previously unknown pastor of an independent church in the USA was the target of a storm of controversy and condemnation of his book just released that raised, among other things, a doubt if the Bible actually teaches that people who have never heard the Gospel, and never had a chance, will burn eternally in Hell fire. For pertinent articles see, e.g., Meacham, "Pastor Rob Bell"; Galli, "Q&A"; and Galli, "Heaven, Hell." Cf. Bell, *Love Wins*, in toto.

in the Gospels; two times in two verses in Acts, the same in the Epistles, and four times in four verses in Revelation (in the latter it is spelled once with upper-case *h*; i.e., with H, but only in the modern adaptations of the original KJB); in all other instances in the NT it is lower-case (h) (KJB 1611+).[4] By contrast, the NKJV (New King James Version, 1982) has "hell" thirteen times.[5] So NKJV eliminates hell ten times from the KJV NT.[6] Tyndale's New Testament, published in 1526, has "hell" in the same places as KJB except 1 Corinthians 10:18; 15:55; Philippians 3:5; Hebrews 8:10, and adds it in 9 others.[7] The much earlier Wycliffe Bible (1384) has all those of the KJB plus three others.[8]

Already James Orr recognized that the English term "hell" derived from a Teutonic root meaning "to cover," signifying the world of the dead in Chaucer and others as well as in the Christian creedal statement, "He [Jesus] descended into hell." Eventually the term came almost exclusively to designate a place of punishment for the wicked or the unrepentant. KJB (1611+) uses "hell" for NT *hades* everywhere except 1 Corinthians 15:55, although it has "hell" in a marginal note. According to Orr in the OT (for *sheol*) and in the NT (except for Luke 16:23, where a place of torment is depicted), "hell" was intended in the older sense of "grave" or "realm of death" for the KJB translators. Later, it became fashionable for English versions to use the transliterations *sheol* in the OT and *hades* in the NT (cf. *Revised Standard Version* [RSV], ASV, NRSV), keeping "hell" only in Isaiah 14:9 and 15 in the OT.[9]

The following will compare "hell" in various major English language versions and expose those texts where more recent Bibles have reduced the use of "hell" as a translation or interpretation. Most significant for exegesis

---

4. Matthew 5:22, 29–30; 10:28; 11:23; 16:18; 18:9; 23:15, 33; Mark 9:43, 45, 47; Luke 10:15; 12:5; 16:23; Acts 2:27, 31; James 3:6; 2 Peter 2:4; Revelation 1:18; 6:8; 20:13–14. See *King James (Authorized) Version* and *The Holy Bible 1611 Edition, King James Version*.

5. Matthew 5:22, 29, 30; 10:28; 18:9; 23:15, 33; Mark 9:43, 45, 47; Luke 12:5; James 3:6; 2 Peter 2:4. See *The Holy Bible, New King James Version*.

6. Matthew 11:23; 16:18; Luke 10:15; 16:23; Acts 2:27, 31; Revelation 1:18; 6:8; 20:13–14.

7. Matthew 5:15; Mark 4:21; 11:33; 1 Corinthians 10:18; 15:55; Philippians 3:5; Hebrews 8:10; Revelation 2:14; 7:4. See https://www.biblestudytools.com/tyn/ for access to Tyndale's texts.

8. Luke 8:31; Acts 2:24; Romans 10:7. See tables below (pp. 184–85; 188–89); cf. n. 9:7, p. 154.

9. See Orr, "Hell."

will be those texts that contain "hell" in all the versions consulted. These apparently are the irreducible texts that support some doctrine of hell. The question, then, is what do they tell us? The focus will be on the NT as the primary basis for a doctrine of hell for Christians, since if hell is ever really addressed in the OT is questionable.

Hell in the Old Testament Books

By the time the first mention of hell took place in NT times (according to the NT text; 50–100 AD) the subject of hell had developed noticeably in documents and communities predating the NT and the church. Also, hell is described in other writings of the same time period but not accepted into the canon.

A quick look at the major English versions since the KJB will demonstrate a remarkable change in the frequency of "hell/Hell" in the Old Testament. "Hell" occurs thirty-one times in the current editions of the KJB and nineteen times in the NKJV (1982).[10] It does not occur in modern, major English versions; e.g., in the USA, the *New International Version* (NIV, 1978, 2011), in the *New American Standard Version* (NASB, 1960, 1988), or in the *New Revised Standard Version* (NRSV, 1989). In twenty-nine of the thirty-one instances of "hell" in the KJB, the LXX has "*Hades*" ($ᾅδης$), and in all thirty-one the Vulgate has some variant of the root *infer-* ("lower-world/-place").[11] Wycliffe has "helle" in fifty-four and "Helle" in four OT verses; so the KJV eliminated twenty-seven instances where Wycliffe thought this was the correct meaning.[12] This demonstrates the KJV's dependence, at

---

10. However, the NKJV uses "hell" for Hebrew *sheol* in one extra verse where KJB does not (Ezek 31:15). KJB renders it "hell" thirty-one times. *TWOT* (Harris, "She'ol," 892–93) says thirty times but I count thirty-one as does the *Compact Oxford English Dictionary*, 202. See the NRSV.

11. Plus, the extra passage where the NKJV uses "hell" (Ezek 31:15), in relation to the KJB and LXX. For the Latin Vulgate: *infer- i, os, ni, no, num, nus*. It should be recognized that the theology or interpretation of some or all of these verses may or may not be the same among these translators. The KJB translators may have read their theology into the Vulgate or based their approach—regardless of Jerome's doctrinal beliefs—on the fact the Vulgate consistently employed the root *infer-* and chose to interpret and translate שאול as "underworld" (realm of the dead; hell?) rather than merely transliterate it, as now is often favored by modern translation committees.

12. KJB only in parentheses; brackets where Wycliffe and KJB agree: Gen (32:22) 37:35; Num 16:30, 33; Deut 32:22; Judg 5:15; [2 Sam 22:6]; Job 2:8; 7:9; [11:8]; 14:13; 17:13, 16; 21:33; [26:6]; Pss 6:5; [9:17]; [16:10]; [18:5]; 30:3; 31:17; 49:14–15; [55:15];

least in this instance, on these traditional and classic works as much as, or more than, on the exegesis of the "original" Hebrew texts. None of these KJV or NKJV contexts calls for the translation "H/hell" or are concerned at all with the forever fate of the unfaithful.[13]

Hell in the Intertestamental Books

A survey of texts about H/hell in non-canonical sacred texts composed prior to the NT (OT Apocrypha and Pseudepigrapha) will indicate that the current popular and traditional view of hell is informed by these books as much as, or more than, the NT. These are important as part of the background for the NT understanding and use of the terms translated as "H/hell" in modern versions. While it would be instructive to investigate the use of "hell" in post-NT apocryphal and pseudepigraphal books, space limitations and purpose will dictate that this study conclude with the NT materials.

Apocryphal books are those that attained the status of deuterocanonical biblical writings. They are included in the Septuagint Greek and Latin Bibles and with early English Bibles like the KJB, but not with later Bibles used by Protestants.

The KJV Apocrypha (KJVA) has "hell" ten times in ten verses (KJVA 1611+).[14] By contrast the NRSV apocryphal books (translated centuries later) use "hell" only twice.[15] In 2 Esdras 2:10 the LORD promises Ezra the kingdom of Jerusalem and protection during tribulation. The nations against the Jews will be powerless (v. 28) and they will be guarded so their children will not experience "hell" (v. 29). But it seems fairly obvious that in this verse "hell" means "grave," in light of the context, and since the original Hebrew text would have used שאול, which refers to the realm of death.[16] 2

[86:13]; 88:3; 89:48; 94:17; 115:17; [116:3]; [139:8]; 141:7; Prov 1:12; 2:18; (5:5); [7:27]; [9:18]; [15:11, 24]; [23:14]; [27:20]; 30:16; Song 8:6; [Isa. 5:14]; 7:11; [14:9, 15]; [28:15, 18]; 30:33; 38:10, 18; (57:9); [Ezek 31:16–17]; [32:21, 27]; Hos 13:14; [Amos 9:2]; [Jonah 2:2; Hab 2:5].

13. See Marlowe, "'Hell' as Translation," 5–24.

14. *King James Version Apocrypha*: 2 Esdras 2:29; 4:8; 8:53; Tobit 13:2; Wisdom 16:13; 17:14; Sirach 21:10; 51:5–6; Daniel 3:66 (see KJVA).

15. 2 Esdras 2:29; 7:37 (see NRSV).

16. The earliest complete versions are in Latin. Only the Latin texts of chapters 1–2 are extant, but they would have originally been in Hebrew. The Latin version has *gehennam* [= *gehenna*, based on the valley of Hinnom in the OT, the place where trash was

Esdras 7:36 reads differently in KJVA (1611+) and NRSV Apocrypha (1989; NRSV-A), but the latter speaks of a pit of torment and hell, in opposition to a place of rest and paradise. The pit is often mentioned in the OT but never with the modifier "of torment" and is often parallel with שאול as another word for the grave or symbolic of death. Beginning in verse 32 the dead will arise from their graves, and then the most-high will judge without compassion yet with truth and faithfulness (vv. 33–34). Recompense and reward will be dispensed for both righteous and unrighteous deeds (v. 35). After the fire of hell is disclosed (v. 36), the most-high will prescribe judgment in fire for the disobedient in which weeks will seem like years (vv. 37–44). Here, we have a clear use of "hell" (*gehennae* in Vulgate) in the traditional (but not OT) sense of enduring punishment in fire for wicked people.

In 2 Esdras 4:8 in KJVA (1611+) "hell" (*infernum*) is used opposite "heaven" (*caelis*) but, in the Hebrew, "heaven" (שמים) would have been a word that is always plural and dependent on context as to whether it means "sky" (heavens) or "God's abode" (heaven). So שאול here could just as easily be the "grave [below]" since that would symbolize death as the alternative to the heavens above or life with God. "Hell" is possible if by this time (in apocryphal Hebrew) שאול had taken on the usage of "place of eternal torment for the wicked in fire." In the context, verse 7 contrasts the depths of the sea with the heavenly firmament; so, 4:8 is not an obvious reference to hell as traditionally defined. In 8:53 KJVA again renders Latin *infernum* (8:52) as "hell." In context, Ezra (Esdras) reminds God that paradise is open to him, the future is prepared (v. 52 English), evil is sealed, corruption has fled to [שאול, in Hebrew, "hell" in KJVA], sorrow is gone, and immortality has dawned (vv. 53–54). Here, שאול could be the grave where evil and corrupt people are imprisoned (which could imply hell). This location of death is contrasted to paradise and immortality (or eternal life). In Tobit 13:2 again the sense of "hell" (*infernum* in Latin versions) is obscure. Tobit prays and blesses God as eternal (v. 1). In verse 2 what would have been שאול in the Hebrew text is parallel with scourge and antithetical to mercy and to bringing people back. Israel had been scattered among the nations, scourged for iniquities, but would be gathered again (vv. 3–5). So again, "grave/death" could work as good or better as a translation. A similar text is found in Wisdom 16:13, where life and death are parallel to "hell" (KJVA

---

incinerated] behind the English "hell." This Latin word is used only in the Bible in apocryphal and NT books. In the OT *sheol* is translated incorrectly with inferno. Tradition attributes authorship to Ezra.

1611+) and renewal or resurrection. In fact, in this case the Vulgate uses *mortis* ("death") for what was שאול in Hebrew, yet KJVA was determined to read hell into the verse in spite of the context and the Latin rendering. Verse 11 speaks of God healing people. Likewise, in 17:14 the Vulgate (17:13) has *inferis* ("death" or "lower world") not *infernum*, where KJVA again insists on "hell." Nothing in the context is clearly about the traditional hell in the speaker's mind, although some of the images here that are sometimes used of hell are based on this passage and some others (which are similar), only by the *a priori* assumption, are about hell. So only circular reasoning can use these images as proof the subject matter is hell. The "pit of hell" in KJVA Sirach 21:10 translates a text that the Vulgate (21:11) rendered as *inferi et tenebrae et poena*, "death and darkness and punishment," which could be understood as a description of hell, indicating perhaps a growing use of *sheol* for that concept. In 51:5–6 (51:7–9 in Vulgate) KJVA mentions the "belly of hell" and "hell beneath" in relation to what the Latin texts interpreted exactly the same as *ventris inferi* and *infero deorsum*. If שאול is in the Hebrew original, then its fire is a post-OT development. Finally, in Daniel 3:66 three men praise God for deliverance from flames, fire, death, and the *inferno* ("hell" in KJVA). But these are the three men saved from a fiery furnace when Daniel was in captivity under Nebuchadnezzar (cf. Dan 3:6–19). A certain number of these apocryphal passages is not clearly about hell as per the KJVA and Vulgate renderings, but some do demonstrate a development of the idea of punishment in eternal fire based on texts where שאול is used or likely was used, although in the OT refers only to death or the grave (realm of death).

The OT pseudepigraphal books are writings falsely attributed to certain well-known and past Jewish literary and religious leaders, which books never attained even secondary canonical status. First Enoch 51:1 is significant because it parallels "Sheol" with "hell": "And in those days shall the earth also give back that which has been entrusted to it, And Sheol also shall give back that which it has received, And hell shall give back that which it owes."[17] The context is about an elect one who will choose and save the righteous. *Sheol* in 1 Enoch 56:8 has been compared with 54:12 in another variant text where "hell" is the translation:

1 Enoch 56:8	1 Enoch 54:12

---

17. See Charles, "Fragments," n.p.; Jerome, "Ethiopian Enoch"; and Charlesworth, *Apocalyptic Literature*, 36.

In those days Sheol shall open its jaws,	In those days shall the mouth of hell be opened,
And they shall be swallowed up therein And their destruction shall be at an end;	into which they shall be immerged;
Sheol shall devour the sinners in the presence of the elect.	hell shall destroy and swallow up sinners from the face of the elect.

In 63:10–11 darkness = hell in 62:14,

1 Enoch 63:10-11	1 Enoch 62:13-15
Now they shall say unto themselves:	Then shall they say to themselves:
"Our souls are full of unrighteous gain,	"Our souls are satiated with the instruments of crime; but that prevents us not from descending to the flaming womb of hell."
And after that their faces shall be filled with darkness."	Afterwards, their countenances shall be filled with darkness

In 99:11 *Sheol* = hell in 97:11,

1 Enoch 99:11-12	1 Enoch 97:11-12
Woe to you who spread evil to your neighbours [*sic*]; For you shall be slain in Sheol.	Woe to you who expand the crime of your neighbour [*sic*]; for in hell shall you be slain.
Woe to you who make deceitful and false measures, And (to them) who cause bitterness on the earth;	Woe to you who lay the foundation of sin and deceit, and who are bitter on earth;

These readings[18] show that by this time *sheol* was being equated with the concept of hell in some texts, which is characterized as a place of destruction for sinners, whose torments can be watched by the saints. This punishment involved flames, darkness, and death. In 2 Enoch 40:9 the seventh heaven is contrasted with the lowest hell: "And I measured out the whole earth, its mountains, and all hills, fields, trees, stones, rivers, all existing things I wrote down, the height from earth to the seventh heaven, and downwards to the very lowest hell, and the judgment-place, and the very great, open and weeping hell."[19] The previous verse (8) speaks of key holders whose breath rocked the earth and who weighed spirits in their graves. The following verse (10) described prisoners expecting endless judgment, based on their works (v. 11). 2 Enoch 42:1 reads:

18. See Jerome, "Ethiopian Enoch."
19. See Morfill, "Book of Secrets"; and Charlesworth, *Apocalyptic Literature*, 166.

> I saw the key-holders and guards of the gates of hell standing, like great serpents, and their faces like extinguishing lamps, and their eyes of fire, their sharp teeth, and I saw all the Lord's works, how they are right, while the works of man are some (good), and others bad, and in their works are known those who lie evilly.[20]

The expression "gates of hell" immediately reminds one of Jesus' words in Matthew 16:18, and the word "key" of his words to Peter as the key holder of the church (against which hell would not prevail) in 16:19, as well as the "keys of hell and death" (KJB 1611+) in Revelation 1:18 (but "death and Hades" in NIV 1984). Notably, the value of human works is repeated.

The expression "children of pit" or "pit" (as a place of punishment for the wicked) is found in The Damascus Document (fragments of a Zadokite work). In 8:12–13 the readers are summoned to obey the Law and stay away from the children of the pit, who belong to the wicked age and wield polluted wealth. In 16:7 the covenant children are not to do business with the children of the pit except to fight them in hand to hand combat. And in 16:12 those who live according to the covenant stipulations will be saved from the snares of the pit.[21]

Words for "Hell" in the New Testament

Again, Orr had already recognized that in addition to the KJB's almost exclusive translation of *hades* as "hell" (usually meaning "grave" to the translators),[22] *gehenna* was also translated "hell" more in line with our modern sense of a place of punishment for the unfaithful or wicked. Some English versions placed "Gehenna" in the marginal notes (e.g., RSV). Like KJB, the RSV also used "hell" for *tartarus* (Greek ταρταρόω) in its one appearance in the NT in 2 Peter 2:4. But the use here is perhaps in reference to fallen angels (cf. Jude 1:6 and Matt 25:41), which can be seen in Jewish apocalyptic books such as Enoch, Jubilees, and Baruch, which latter apparently references Genesis 6:1–4.[23] The background for the use of *gehenna* in

---

20. Morfill, "Book of Secrets"; cf. Charlesworth, *Apocalyptic Literature*, 166–67.

21. Charles, "Fragments," 799–834 (also known as "The Damascus Document").

22. However, the practical problem remains that the readers do not make this distinction. For the typical lay reader of the Bible, "hell" means "hell" in its traditional sense. Translators must use "realm of death" if that is what they think *sheol/hades* or even *gehenna* imply.

23. See Orr, "Hell," n.p. But cf. Marlowe, "Gen 6:1–4," in toto (see above in this

the NT, and the literature leading up to the NT, was the expression "Valley of Hinnom" in the OT (*ge-hinnom* > *gehenna*). In and around this valley near Jerusalem, idolatry had been rampant in the days of Ahaz and Manasseh, who sacrificed his children in fire there to Molech (cf. Jer 7:32; 19:6).[24] Eventually it became a place where dead bodies and garbage were thrown (hence perpetual fires), and came to symbolize a place of torment (fiery *gehenna*) among the Jews.[25] Yet they also envisioned this as a place of temporary punishment, except for the most wicked of sinners.[26]

Hell in the NT Synoptics in English Versions

The doctrine of hell in the NT (if there is one as traditionally known) developed in light of the ideas that came about in the intertestamental period as exhibited in the apocryphal and pseudepigraphal texts. As seen, the OT passages translated as speaking about hell in versions like the KJV actually, in context, show little or no understanding of hell as currently dogmatized in conservative and most evangelical circles. *Sheol* simply means the realm of death. And those passages like Ezekiel 28 and Isaiah 14 that are considered to be about Satan and use *sheol* as hell are, in context, very likely not about Satan at all. Now it must be considered what actually is said about H/hell in the NT and determined when these references are an illustrative accommodation to current views rather than intended as literal teachings about an eternal place of torment for unbelievers.

"Hell" (lower-case) occurs in the KJB NT Gospels fifteen times,[27] eleven in NKJV (thirteen in all the NT),[28] and still twelve times in modern NIV Gospels (in one case based on *hades*, in all the other cases on *gehenna*)[29]

---

volume, chapter 2, p. 23).

24. Jeremiah announced this valley would someday be called the Valley of Slaughter rather than "Ben Hinnom" or "Topheth." The meaning of *hinnom* is unknown. See n. 36 below.

25. See Orr, "Hell,"; and Masterman, "Valley of Hinnom," n.p.

26. See Bronner, *Journey to Heaven*, 90.

27. Matt 5:22, 29–30; 10:28; 11:23; 16:18; 18:9; 23:15, 33; Mark 9:43, 45, 47; Luke 10:15; 12:5; 16:23. The Gospel of John does not mention hell.

28. Matt 5:22, 29, 30; 10:28; 18:9; 23:15, 33; Mark 9:43, 45, 47; Luke 12:5 (by Jesus) plus James 3:6; 2 Peter 2:4.

29. Matt 5:22, 29–30; 10:28; 18:9; 23:15, 33; Mark 9:43–47; Luke 12:5; 16:23 (see NIV 1984).

and eleven in NRSV.[30] Remarkably, even the CEV NT has "hell" twenty times (fourteen in Gospels)[31] and the GNT NT twenty-one times (fourteen in Gospels).[32] The texts shared by NKJV and NRSV in the Gospels are Matt 5:22, 29–30; 10:28; 18:9; 23:15, 33; Mark 9:43, 45, 47; Luke 12:5 (see table below). The verses are with words no longer translated as "hell" since KJB have already been interpreted as erroneously using "hell," at least by some scholars.

Hell Translation Texts Shared by Versions Since 1384[33]

Translation Texts ↓	Wycliffe 1384	Tyndale NT 1525	KJV 1611–	NKJV 1982	NRSV 1989–	NIV 1978; 1984–	GNT 2005
# of times "H/hell" occurs in English Bibles							
OT	58	------	31	19	0	0	0
NT	26	24	23	13	13	14	21
Comparison and count of the translation of words as "H/hell" in the NT							
Gospels	11						
Matthew	7						
5:22 gehenna	fier of helle	hell fyre	hell fire	hell fire	hell of fire	fire of hell	fire of hell
5:29 gehenna	in to helle	into hell	into hell	into hell	Into hell	into hell	into hell
5:30 gehenna	in to helle	in to hell	into hell	into hell	Into hell	into hell	off to hell
10:28 gehenna	soule and bodi in to helle	soule and body into hell	soul and body in hell	soul and body in hell	soul and body in hell	soul and body in hell	body and soul in hell

30. Matt 5:22, 29–30; 10:28; 18:9; 23:15, 33; Mark 9:43–47; Luke 12:5 (see NRSV 1989).

31. Matt 5:22, 29, 30; 10:28; 11:23; 18:9; 23:15, 33; Mark 9:43, 45, 47; Luke 10:15; 12:5; 16:23; Acts 8:20; Phil 3:19; James 3:6; 2 Pet 2:4, 17; Jude 1:13 (see CEV 1995).

32. Matt 5:22, 29, 30; 7:13; 10:28; 11:23; 18:9; 23:15, 33; Mark 9:43, 45, 47; Luke 10:15; 12:5; Acts 8:20; Gal 1:8, 9; Phil 3:19; 2 Thess 2:3; James 3:6; 2 Pet 2:4 (see GNT 1992).

33. Adds "where the fire never goes out."

18:9 gehenna	fier of helle	hell fyre	hell fire	hell fire	hell of fire	fire of hell	fire of hell
23:15 gehenna	sone of helle	chylde of hell	child of hell	son of hell	child of hell	son of hell	going to hell
23:33 gehenna	doom of helle	dapnacio of hell	dam-nation of hell	con-dem-nation of hell	sen-tenced to hell	con-demned to hell	con-demned to hell
Mark	3						
9:43* gehenna	go in to helle	goo into hell	go into hell	to go to hell	to go to hell	go into hell	go off to hell
9:45 gehenna	sent in to helle of fier	cast into hell into fyre	cast into hell	cast into hell	thrown into hell	thrown into hell	thrown into hell
9:47 gehenna	sent in to helle of fier	cast into hell fyre	cast into hell fire	cast into hell fire	thrown into hell	thrown into hell	thrown into hell
Luke	1						
12:5 gehenna	sende in to helle	cast into hell	cast into hell	cast into hell	cast into hell	throw you into hell	throw into hell
Epistles	2						
James	1						
3:6 gehenna	enflawm-ned of helle	fyre even of hell	fire of hell	fire by hell	fire by hell	fire by hell	from hell itself
2 Peter	1						
2:4 tartaroo	drawun in to helle	cast into hell	cast down to hell	cast down to hell	cast into hell	sent to hell	threw into hell

Prior to Jesus' ministry, hell as place of eternal torture in fire for the wicked is unknown in the OT and only taught by certain Jewish sects or other religions. There are only three ways in the NT in which Jesus uses a word that has been translated "hell," and the word is always *gehenna*. Only one of these has synoptic parallels, when he speaks about avoiding being thrown into *gehenna* (Matt 10:28).

In Matthew 5:22 Jesus mentions *gehenna* in relation to murderous words. KJB says "hell fire" while NIV says "fire of hell" and NRSV says "hell of fire."[34] The NLT has "fires of hell," while the ESV perhaps promotes a

---

34. Cf. Matt 25:41, 46, where those who neglected the poor are condemned to the "eternal" punishment and fire prepared for the devil and his "angels" (but neither *gehenna* nor *hades* is mentioned). *Gehenna* refers to the valley (*ge-* in Hebrew) of Hinnom

symbolic reading with the use of quote marks around hell/*gehenna*: "to 'the hell' of fire." While TM keeps "hell" here, it softens the threat by saying "on the brink of hell fire." "Hell" is maintained by the GNT and CEV.³⁵

In Matthew 5:29–30 (= Mark 9:43–47) and Matthew 10:28 (= Luke 12:4–5) Jesus speaks of being thrown into *gehenna*,³⁶ which KJB, NIV, and NRSV all render "hell" in Matthew 5:29 and 10:28, and Luke 12:5. In Mark 9:43–47 "hell" also appears in KJB, NIV, and NRSV, but in verse 43 this is described, respectively, as a fire that "never shall be quenched," "never goes out," and is "unquenchable."³⁷ In verse 47 KJB adds the word "fire" to a text that only has *gehenna* unqualified.

In 10:28 he tells his disciples not to fear those who can take their life but only he who can "destroy soul and body in *gehenna*." The Lukan version says: "Fear him who, after the killing of the body, has power to throw you into *gehanna*" (12:5b; cf. NIV). Some English versions (see, e.g., NIV) use upper-case ("the One") to indicate this person is the devil.³⁸ ESV has

---

where the trash was burned outside the walls of Jerusalem. Jesus acknowledges the reality of a concept of a "fiery *gehenna*" (τὴν γέενναν τοῦ πυρός) in Matt 5:22. Nothing in the context makes these words mean an eternal torture in literal fire. He warns people who act in anger *without a good reason* (KJB interpretation) that they are subject to the courts and being thrown out with the garbage. See n. 16.

35. See NLT (1996); ESV (2001); Peterson, *Message*, 20; GNT (1992); and CEV (1995).

36. Later in Matt 5 and in 18:7–9 (where "fire" is added), Jesus mentions *hinnom* again in relation to the advice of getting rid of body parts to keep from sinning (5:29–30; cf. Mark 9:43–47). As a result, he says it is better to cut off a body part than have the whole body cast into the incinerator. Mark uses the eye, hand, and foot as illustrations while Matthew only uses the eye and hand. If Jesus means hell by *gehenna* and is teaching doctrines about the afterlife, then one has to conclude that we can cut off limbs to be saved, and if we do go to hell it can be with only a partial body that is not fully resurrected after death (which seems to directly contradict other passages).

37. See KJB (1611+), NIV (1984), and NRSV (1989). This passage includes the odd-sounding (to modern ears) phrase (v. 48), especially in the KJB: "Where their worm dieth not." NIV (2011) has "where the worms that eat them do not die." Jesus has Isa 66:24b in mind, "for their worm shall not die, neither shall their fire be quenched," speaking of the dead bodies of those who rebelled against YHWH (66:23) at the time of the new heaven and earth (66:22). These bodies lie dead on the surface of the earth, so hell does not seem to be in view in the OT context. In the NT, only Mark 9 has this phrase (three times in KJB but left out as redundant by many modern versions). In verse 49 Jesus says *everyone* will be "salted with fire" (KJB), so the fire in this context seems to be something that purifies (thus the fire of *gehenna* is symbolic).

38. In Luke 12:11 Jesus predicts times when the disciples will be brought up on charges before the civil or religious authorities. So, he seems to be using popular language and current thinking about the afterlife to encourage his followers to be more concerned

"hell," but adds a footnote saying the Greek is *gehenna*. Phillips has "fires of destruction," and *The Message* avoids the term completely. Goodspeed (an American translation) uses "pit."[39] This is typical of these last three, so they will not be cited in every case.

Gehenna comes up again when Jesus criticizes some Jewish scholars (Matt 23:15, 33).[40] In Matthew 23:15 and 23:33 Jesus confronts and corrects (pronounces woe upon) those he names as hypocritical, Pharisaical, and venomous (devilish?) teachers of the Jewish Law (see 23:23, 25, 27, 29; "blind fools" in 23:17), and connects or condemns them to *gehenna*. In 23:15 a convert becomes twice the "child of hell [γεέννης]" as they.[41] In 23:33 he asks them (rhetorically?) how they will avoid the verdict of judgment to *gehenna* ("damnation of hell" in KJB; "condemned to hell" in NIV; and "sentenced to hell" in NRSV). Phillips has "rubbish heap."[42] It has to be kept in mind that *gehenna* is a compound of two words, valley (*ge*) and *Hinnom*. By NT times this valley as a historic place of death, destruction, and fire had come to symbolize a place of suffering for societal outcasts, purification of the unrighteous, and then was used for God's enemies in the last days. If the traditional "Hell" is in view in one or more of these

---

about spiritual than physical damage (rather than making doctrinal statements about punishment in the hereafter and using *gehenna* as an illustration, because it has evolved in some Jewish or sectarian theologies to represent the concept of a place of torment for the wicked after death).

39. See NIV (1984); ESV (2001); ETNT, 73; Peterson, *Message*, 32; and Goodspeed in Vaughan, *New Testament*, 41.

40. An important issue so far is that Jesus' use of *gehenna* is not in contexts where he indicates he will give doctrinal information. He refers to it in light of pre-existing beliefs; yet there is no existing OT doctrine to build upon. So those traditional (non-Catholic, conservative, or evangelical) believers who want to use Jesus' statements for an absolutized biblical theology of hell have the challenge that he has no canonical biblical basis (only apocryphal or pseudepigraphal or a midrash) for his comments and does not present his words as new prescriptive pronouncements, only as references to established first-century Jewish (sectarian or orthodox) beliefs.

41. See KJB (1611+) and NRSV (1989) but "son of hell" in NIV (1984).

42. Vaughan, *New Testament*, 98. See KJB (1611+), NIV (1984), and NRSV (1989). Especially in speaking to these hyper-orthodox Jewish legal and biblical (OT) scholars, the reader could assume Jesus is using their own doctrines against them. So his use of "hell" is not an affirmation of their traditional beliefs but an apologetic argument that employs this popular conception as a threat to their own theology if they continue (as their forefathers) defining and doing righteousness in terms of empty rituals and rules that miss the real meaning of what the OT prophets taught and what he and his disciples are now teaching (23:15–34). He predicts (soon?) coming destruction on Jerusalem if they maintain their murderous methods against God's messengers (23:35–24:2).

passages, this single term does not provide enough flexibility in modern usage (if ever) to be used in every text of an English-version NT with *gehenna* (and more so with *hades*). To conclude this section, Jesus' use of *gehenna* is consistently an accommodation to current beliefs as a point of reference to impact his audience with a strong illustration of the consequences (God's disapproval and discipline) of continual conflagration of God's higher principle of dealing with attitudes that ultimately express themselves in acts of violence, unfaithfulness, and ritualistic religion.

Hell in NT Synoptics Not Shared by Many English Versions

Only Jesus in the Synoptic Gospels makes statements that include words that have been translated as "hell." KJB (1611+) has "H/hell" in several other Gospel texts where many modern versions have different renderings: Matthew 11:23 (= Luke 10:15); 16:18; and Luke 16:23 (where exceptionally NIV also has "hell"). In all these cases the term translated "hell" distinctively by KJB is *hades* not *gehenna*, which NRSV and, surprisingly, NKJV transliterate rather than translate as Hades (see also ASV, and table below).[43]

Hell Translation Texts Not Shared by Versions Since 1384[44]

Translation Texts ↓	Wycliffe 1384	Tyndale NT 1525	KJV 1611	NKJV 1982	NRSV 1989–	NIV 1978; 1984–	GNT 2005
Gospels	5						
Matthew	2						
11:23 *hades*	Helle	hell	hell	*Hades*	*Hades*	Depths	hell
16:18 *hades*	Helle	hell	hell	*Hades*	*Hades*	*Hades*	death
Luke	3						

43. See KJB (1611+), NIV (1984), NRSV (1989), and *The New King James Version* (NKJB 1982/2005).

44. All of these use the expression "death [*thanatos*] and *hades*."

8:31 *Abussos*	Helle	depe	deep	abyss	abyss	Abyss	abyss
10:15 *hades*	Helle	hell	hell	Hades	Hades	Depths	hell
16:23 *hades*	Helle	hell	hell	Hades	Hades	Hell	Hades
Acts	3						
2:24 *thanatos*	Helle	deeth	death	death	death	Death	death
2:27 *hades*	soule in helle	soul in hell	soul in hell	soul in Hades ad	Hades	Grave	in the grave
2:31 *hades*	be left in helle	be left in hell	be left in hell	left in Hades	Hades	Grave	in the grave
Epistles	2						
Romans	1						
10:7 *abussos*	Helle	depe	deep	abyss	abyss	Deep	world below
1 Corinth-ians	1						
15:55 *thanatos*	deth	Hell	grave	Hades	death	Death	Death
Revelation	4*						
1:18 *hades*	helle	Hell	hell	Hades	Hades	Hades	world of the dead
6:8 *hades*	helle	Hell	Hell	Hades	Hades	Hades	Hades
20:13 *hades*	helle	Hell	hell	Hades	Hades	Hades	world of the dead
20:14	helle	Hell	hell	Hades	Hades	Hades	world of the dead

In Matthew 11:23 (= Luke 10:15) the term *hades* is used opposite "skies" (NIV) or "heavens" (but KJV has "heaven" making "hell" the logical contrast).[45] In both texts, NIV has "depths." Goodspeed used "down among

45. The object of Jesus' condemnation here is the population of Capernaum (the city symbolic of its inhabitants). If *hades* means "Hell," then Jesus is predicting that every person in the city will be condemned because they failed to repent even after experiencing miracles (11:23b). Sodom will receive a lighter judgment (Matt 11:24). It seems these

the dead!"[46] In Matthew 16:18 Jesus tells Peter he will construct his church (assembly) and the "gates of *hades*" will not conquer it. The NEB and Goodspeed both have "death."[47] Luke 16:23 has the most promise for a place of torment for the wicked, and it even uses *hades*, which NIV and CEV render "hell" (but NRSV and NASB have "Hades," as does the ASV). But Phillips has "among the dead" (cf. ETNT "place of the dead").[48]

---

words refer to the fact Capernaum will not be honored ("lifted up") but experience death and destruction in judgment, worse than Sodom on a coming day of judgment. Again, Jesus uses the word for "afterlife" or "realm of death" rather than *gehenna*, which symbolized a place of burning refuse. See NIV (1984) and KJB (1611+).

46. See NIV (1984) and Vaughan, *New Testament*, 45.

47. If he meant "Hell," then why not use *gehenna* and why speak of its "gates"? Why not just say "*Hades* will not win!"? He apparently is again using *hades* as the grave or realm of death. The church, as Paul strongly noted, would be characterized in one key manner by its lack of being intimidated by death (see Rom 8:2–6; 1 Cor 15:26; 15:54–56; Heb 2:14). See NEB and Vaughan, *New Testament*, 67.

48. Regardless, this is clearly a place of painful punishment (or torture; ὑπάρχων ἐν βασάνοις, Luke 16:23; even "agony in flames" ὀδυνῶμαι ἐν τῇ φλογί, v. 24b). The context of these words is a parable of Jesus about a rich man who ignored a beggar daily at his door. They both died, and the beggar is carried by heavenly messengers to Abraham's side, while the rich man was buried and then ended up suffering in *Hades*. This rich man clearly "went to hell" for his wicked deeds, his lack of compassion for the poor. The beggar goes to "Heaven" (if that is what is meant) for no reason given, other than the mere observation and (intended?) deduction that he suffered so much in life on earth that he deserved a painless afterlife. It must be said, although perhaps obvious, that this story is a parable and not a recounting of an historical event. Still, it was meant to teach an authoritative moral lesson. It is questionable if it has the value of supporting dogmatic theology about the nature of life after death in all cases. But it does present an unmistakable picture of a wicked person (although he is never called evil, just described a filthy rich and uncaring) who is in a conscious state and in a place of pain and punishment after death, called Hades. Most versions leave this word as a proper noun because it typically symbolizes the realm of the grave or death. It is the word that translates *sheol* in the Greek OT so, at least traditionally, it meant "death" or "afterlife." This rich man has entered this realm and also is suffering from intense heat (but the *gehenna* of fire is not mentioned). If this is hell as traditionally understood, then this is the only verse in the NT using *hades* that gives a clear presentation of punishment in fire after death; but it is a parable, not a doctrinal dictation. The textual evidence for the traditional hell in the Gospels is slim at best, and possibly non-existent. See NIV (1984), CEV (1995), NRSV (1989), NASB (1988), ASV (1901), ETNT (1984), 553, and Vaughan, *New Testament*, 298.

Hell in the Acts of the Apostles

"Hell" is used in KJB Acts twice but in the same context: 2:27, 31, where Peter cites Psalm 16:10 (although this is part of Acts 2:25–28, where he quotes Psalm 16:8–11). *The Living Bible* keeps "hell," but most modern English versions have "Hades" or "D/death" or "world of the dead" or "grave."[49]

Hell in the Church Epistles

KJB has "hell" in two verses in the Epistles: James 3:6 and 2 Peter 2:4. NIV uses "hell" as well, as does NRSV and NASB. In the former verse, the word rendered "hell" is *Gehenna,* and in the latter, it is *tartaroö* (see pp. 185, 192). All eight versions consulted in the ETNT use "hell" in James 3. Of these, only the *Jerusalem Bible* avoids "hell" for "underworld" in 2 Peter 2:4. Weymouth chose to use a transliteration and proper name "Tartarus."[50]

---

49. See KJB (1611+); ETNT, 842–43; and Vaughan, *New* Testament, 441. That verse 10 is not about hell is evident from Peter's interpretation (Acts 2:29–35) in which he explains that the psalmist foresaw the resurrection of Christ. God did not leave him in the grave to rot (ὅτι οὔτε ἐγκατελείφθη εἰς ᾅδην οὔτε ἡ σάρξ αὐτοῦ εἶδεν διαφθοράν). The word used for "grave" is ᾅδην (*Hades*), which typically (in the LXX and elsewhere) translates OT *sheol* ("realm of death") as it does in Psalm 16:10, where "pit" is the word rendered "decay." This is a typical parallel term for *sheol* in the OT, also meaning "grave." In Psalm 16 David trusts that God will not allow him to die (go to the grave and rot). Peter sees this as a type of the Messiah to come, who would not stay in the ground. KJB made the mistake of thinking *sheol* speaks of hell, whereas it only points to the afterlife (regardless of one's eternal fate). Modern English versions use "grave" or *Hades* (which merely transliterates the Greek word and fails to translate it, except as a proper name for the underworld).

50. In James 3:6 the issue is the source of verbal abuse, so has nothing to do with a possible eternal place of torment. At best, the verse can establish there is a "hell" but says nothing about its human inhabitants (only Satan and his demons, implied) past, present, or future. In 2 Peter 2:4 Peter reflects on God sending sinful "angels" ("messengers") to a place called Tartarus, a gloomy dungeon where these disobedient spirits await future judgment. Again, this says nothing determinative about *gehenna* or *hades* as a place of eternal torment for unbelievers, even if it is for rebellious heavenly messengers. See KJB (1611+); NIV (1984); NRSV (1989); NASB (1988); ETNT, 1670–71, 1719 (1974); and Vaughan, *New Testament,* 1166. *The Jerusalem Bible* cited is dated 1968, and Weymouth's is entitled *The New Testament in Modern Speech.*

Hell in John's Revelation

"Hell" appears four times in three verses in KJB Revelation (once uppercase): Revelation 1:18; 6:8 ("Hell"); 20:13-14. Neither NIV, NRSV, nor NASB use "H/hell" in any of these verses. Rather, they translate the expression τοῦ θανάτου καὶ τοῦ ᾅδου as "D/death and H/hades." KJB uses uppercase ("Hell") in 6:8 because there the phrase is a proper name. But Phillips went with "death" and "grave." The JB has "Plague, and Hades."[51]

Summary and Conclusion

"Hell" is shared by KJB NT and several modern English versions (e.g. NIV and NRSV) only in thirteen verses: Matthew 5:22, 29-30; 10:28; 18:9; 23:15, 33; Mark 9:43-47; Luke 12:5; James 3:6; and 2 Peter 2:4. All of these use *gehenna* (picturing the Hinnom Valley where rubbish was burned in Jerusalem), except the last, which uses *tartaroö*. But here the place some name as "hell" is described as a place of darkness where sinful *angels* were cast and bound in chains to await judgment. The passage in James is about the influence of *gehenna* on evil speech, so not directly applicable to the question of a place of eternal punishment. All the other passages are found in the Synoptic Gospels, where Jesus is always the one mentioning *gehenna* and of which the verses in Mark and Luke are parallels of episodes in Matthew. And in Matthew, two of these texts are the same (5:29-30 and 18:9, both about the need to cut off any body part that causes you to sin, in order to avoid the "fire of hell" in the latter which is simply "hell" in the former). In James 3:6 the Greek word for the "fire" that *geheena* uses is different than the "fire" the describes the tongue itself. Regardless, this leaves us with the six remaining and different verses in five passages in Matthew as the key NT bases for defining "hell," since these have *gehenna* translated as "hell" in both older and newer English versions. "Hell" has been avoided one

---

51. In Revelation 20:14 "death and *hades*" are cast into the lake of fire, which traditionally is thought to represent hell, so if Hades is Hell, then Hell is cast into hell. In 20:13 the "sea" is parallel with "death and *hades*." Both give up their dead, so the latter seems to represent the dead in the ground, and the expression may be a hendiadys (buried corpses). In Revelation 1:18 the speaker (the one like a human; 1:13; the Alpha and Omega, 1:17) holds the keys of "death and *hades*," so it is the God-Man, the Christ, that unlocks the underworld and releases the resurrected humanity. If *hades* means "Hell," then one would expect the verse to say "I hold the keys to Heaven and Hell," and could expect *gehenna* to be used instead. See KJB (1611+); NIV (1984, 2011); NRSV (1989); NASB (1988); ETNT, 1811 (1984; Phillips *Modern English* is the 1972 revised edition).

way or another by more recent Bibles, where now only KJB or NKJV (or similar traditional versions) have "hell." Of these five passages in Matthew only three of them speak of *gehenna* as a place per se: 5:29–30, 10:28, and 23:33. When these three are studied closely they raise questions about the traditional view of hell. In Matthew 5:29–30 Jesus explains a better way to "enter life" or live on this earth. A contrast is made between having either a body part or the whole body thrown into *gehenna*. It appears he is using the place for burning garbage outside the city as an illustration of where the offensive body part would be destined. Then again, he is clearly speaking figuratively because an eye cannot cause someone to sin. This comes from the person's own inner character or state of mind, and interestingly, Jesus speaks of fearing the one who can destroy both body and "soul" or mind in *gehenna* in Matthew 10:28. If this is taken literally as the traditional "hell," then traditionalists will have to admit that this text strongly suggests annihilation more than endless torture. Finally, in Matthew 23:33 Jesus asks Jewish religious leaders who are hypocritical how they can escape being condemned to *gehenna*. If they are on their way to hell you would think he would tell them how to escape. Still, it makes most sense if he is reminding them of their own theology of afterlife punishment in line with what they have developed since OT times and through the teachings leading up to NT times (as reflected in apocryphal and other extra-biblical texts). He could just as easily in this context be warning them of being rejected like the garbage thrown into the Hinnom Valley for burning. That Jesus here has in mind exactly what the church later exposited and exhibited as our traditional hell is not a foregone conclusion.

Possibly, the current conservative views on hell in the English-speaking world are informed by Christian medieval art and literature, in addition to Bible versions since Wycliffe's and Tyndale's translations, and especially by the 1611 KJB, which depended on the Latin Vulgate. Most likely the words of the NT were chosen to speak to a society that had been conditioned in its thinking by pre-NT writings and teachings, which developed during the interim time between the close of the OT canon and the teachings of Jesus. Apparently, "Hell" is never an appropriate rendering for *sheol* in the OT, which is translated by *hades* in the LXX. And this has been recognized by the disappearance of "hell" from modern English version of the OT. "Hell," however, does still appear in the NT English versions only slightly less than in the KJB or NKJV. This raises the question if those passages where KJB and modern translations agree are unquestioned instances of teachings about "hell" as an eternal and literal fire of torture for all throughout human history who die without having faith in YHWH or the Messiah. If so, it still has to be demonstrated conclusively that the terms used are best translated in those contexts by the current evangelical understanding of the English word "hell," or what we mean by "Hell" (upper-case) has to be revised and refined to some degree and discerned only on the basis of the most relevant passages.

Bibliography

Aglen, Rev. Archdeacon. *The Book of Psalms, vol. 2. Psalms LI–CV*. Edited by Charles John Ellicott. Grand Rapids: Zondervan, 1960.
Ahroni, Reuben. "The Unity of Psalm 23." *Hebrew Annual Review* 6 (1982) 21–34.
Albright, William F. "The High Place in Ancient Palestine." Volume du Congrès: Strasbourg. In *VTSupp. 4*, 242–58. Leiden: Brill, 1957.
Alden, Robert L. *Psalms of Devotion, v. 1. Psalms 1–50*. Chicago: Moody, 1974.
Alexander, J. A. *The Prophecies of Isaiah*. 1953. Reprint, Grand Rapids: Zondervan, 1976.
———. *The Psalms Translated and Explained*. 1873. Reprint, Grand Rapids: Baker Book House, 1977.
Alter, Robert. *The Art of Biblical Poetry*. 1985. Reprint, New York: Basic Books, 1987.
Amos, Clare. *The Book of Genesis*. Peterborough: Epworth, 2004.
Archaeological Study Bible. New International Version. Grand Rapids: Zondervan, 2005.
Auffret, Pierre. "Essai sur la structure littéraire du Psaume 23." *Estudios Bíblicos* 43 (1985) 557–88.
Avalos, Hector. Review of "Essai sur la structure littéraire du Psaume 23," by Pierre Auffret. *Old Testament Abstracts* 9 (October 1986) 288.
Baltzer, Klaus. *Deutero-Jesaja*. Gütersloh: Gütersloher Verlagshaus, 1999.
Barr, James. *The Semantics of Biblical Language*. 1961. Reprint, Eugene, OR: Wipf & Stock, 2004.
Bartelt, Andrew H. *The Book Around Immanuel: Style and Structure in Isaiah 2–12*. Biblical and Judaic Studies 4. Winona Lake, IN: Eisenbrauns, 1996.
Bazak, Jacob. "Structural Geometric Patterns in Biblical Poetry." *Poetics Today* 6 (1985) 475–502.
Bazaq, Y. "Psalm 23 ('The Lord is My Shepherd')—As a Patterned Poem." *Beth Mikra* 26 (1981) 370–77.
Bell, Rob. *Love Wins: A Book About Heaven, Hell, and the Fate of Every Person Who Ever Lived*. San Francisco: HarperOne, 2011.
Bennett, Patrick R. *Comparative Semitic Linguistics: A Manual*. Winona Lake, IN: Eisenbrauns, 1998.
Berlin, Adele. *The Dynamics of Biblical Parallelism*. Grand Rapids: Eerdmans, 2008.
———. "Grammatical Aspects of Biblical Parallelism." *Hebrew Union College Annual* 50 (1979) 17–43.
———. "Parallelism." In *The Anchor Bible Dictionary V*, edited by David Noel Freedman, 155–60. New York: Doubleday, 1992.

———. "Parallel Word Pairs: A Linguistic Explanation." *Ugarit-Forschungen* 15 (1983) 7–16.
Blenkinsopp, Joseph. *Isaiah 1–39*. The Anchor Bible 19. New York: Doubleday, 2000.
———. *Isaiah 40–55*. The Anchor Bible 19A. New York: Doubleday, 2002.
Bliese, Loren F. "Structurally Marked Peak in Psalms 1–24." *Translation and Textlinguistics* 4 (1990) 265–321.
Boadt, Lawrence. "The A:B:B:A Chiasm of Identical Roots in Ezekiel." *Vetus Testamentum* 25 (October 1975) 693–99.
Boda, Mark J. "Chiasmus in Ubiquity: Symmetrical Mirages in Nehemiah 9." *Journal for the Study of the Old Testament* 21 (1996) 55–70.
Bonhoeffer, Dietrich. *Creation and Fall: A Theological Interpretation of Genesis 1–3*. Translated by John C. Fletcher. London: SCM, 1959.
Botterweck, G. Johannes, Helmer Ringgren, and Heinz-Josef Fabry, eds. *The Theological Dictionary of the Old Testament*, v. 11., ʿzz-pānim. Grand Rapids: Eerdmans, 2001.
Briggs, C. A. and E. G. Briggs. *The Book of Psalms*, V. 1, 1–50. 1907; 1952. Reprint, Edinburgh: T. & T. Clark, 2000.
———. *A Critical and Exegetical Commentary on the Book of Psalms*, v. 2, 51–150. 1907. Reprint, Edinburgh: T. & T. Clark, 2000.
Bronner, Leila Leah. *Journey to Heaven*. New York: Urim, 2011.
Brooks, Claire Vonk. "Psalm 51." *Interpretation* 49 (1995) 62–66.
Buber, Martin. *I and Thou (Ich und Du)*. Translated by Walter Kaufmann. 1923. Reprint, New York: Charles Scribner's Sons, 1970.
———. *I and Thou (Ich und Du)*. Translated by R. Gregor Smith. 2nd ed. 1923. Reprint, New York: Simon & Schuster, 1958.
Calvin, John. *Calvin's Commentaries, vol. 5: Commentary upon the Book of Psalms*. Translated by J. Anderson. 1846. Reprint, Grand Rapids: Baker, 1979.
Catholic University of America. *Fathers of the Church: A New Translation*. New York: Cima Pub. Co., 1947.
Charles, R. H., translator. "Fragments of a Zadokite Work." In *The Apocrypha and Pseudepigrapha of the Old Testament in Englis*h, vol. 2: *Pseudepigrapha*, edited by R. H. Charles, 799–834. Oxford: Clarendon Press, 1913. http://www. pseudepigrapha. com/pseudepigrapha/zadokite.html.
Charlesworth, James H., ed. *The Old Testament Pseudepigrapha*. Vol.1, *Apocalyptic Literature and Testaments*. London: Doubleday & Co., 1983.
———. *The Old Testament Pseudepigrapha*. Vol. 2. London: Doubleday & Co, 1985.
Chicago Assyrian Dictionary (2005). XII: 50–55.
Childs, Brevard S. *Isaiah*. OTL. Louisville: Westminster John Knox, 2001.
———. *Myth and Reality in the Old Testament*. 2nd ed. London: SCM, 1962.
Clarke, Arthur G. *Analytical Studies in the Psalms*. 3rd ed. 1976. Reprint, Grand Rapids: Kregel, 1979.
Clines, David J. A., gen. ed. *The Dictionary of Classical Hebrew*. 6 vols. Sheffield: Sheffield University Press, 1993–2007.
———. "The Parallelism of Greater Precision." In *Directions in Biblical Hebrew Poetry*, edited by Elaine R. Follis, 77–100. JSOT Supplement Series 40. Sheffield: JSOT, 1987.
———. "The Significance of the 'Sons of God' Episode (Gen. 6.1–4) in the Context of the 'Primaeval [sic] History' (Gen. 1–11)." *Journal for the Study of the Old Testament* 13 (1979) 9.

———. "The Significance of the 'Sons of God' Episode (Genesis 6:1-4) in the Context of the 'Primaeval [sic] History' (Genesis 1-11). In *On the Way to Postmodern: Old Testament Essays, 1967-1998*, edited by David J. A. Clines, 339-43. JSOT Supplement Series. Sheffield: Sheffield Academic Press, 1998.
Cohen, A. *The Psalms*. Soncino Books of the Bible. London: Soncino, 1945.
Cohen, Ernest B. "The Tower of Babel Revisited." *Reconstructionist* (January 1972) 25-29.
Collins, C. John. *Genesis 1-4*. Phillipsburg, NJ: P&R, 2006.
Collins, M. F. Review of "Structural Geometric Patterns in Biblical Poetry," by Jacob Bazak. *Old Testament Abstracts* 9 (June 1986) 185-86.
The Compact Edition of the Oxford English Dictionary. Vol. 1, A-O. Oxford: Oxford University Press, 1971.
Cooper, Alan M. *Biblical Poetics: A Linguistic Approach*. New Haven: Yale University Press, 1977.
Corpus Christianorum. Series Latina. Turnhout: Brepols, 1953.
Craigie, Peter C. *Psalms 1-50*. Word Biblical Commentary 19. Edited by John D. W. Watts. Waco, TX: Word Books, 1983.
Croatto, J. Severino. "A Reading of the Story of the Tower of Babel from a Perspective of Non-Identity." In *Teaching the Bible: The Discourses and Politics of Biblical Pedagogy*, edited by Fernando F. Segovia and Mary Ann Tolbert, 203-23. Maryknoll, NY: Orbis Books, 1998.
Crumpacker, M. M. "Formal Analysis and the Psalms." *Journal of the Evangelical Theological Society* 24 (March 1981) 11-21.
Culler, Jonathan. *Structuralist Poetics: Structuralism, Linguistics, and the Study of Literature*. Ithaca, NY: Cornell University Press, 1975.
Curtis, Byron. "'Private Spirits' in the *Westminster Confession of Faith* ¶1.10 and in Catholic-Protestant Debate [1588-1652]." *Westminster Theological Journal* 58 (Fall 1996) 257-66.
Dahood, Mitchell. *Psalms II: 51-100*. Edited by W. F. Albright and D. N. Freedman. The Anchor Bible 17. Garden City, NY: Doubleday, 1968.
Dalglish, Edward R. *Psalm Fifty-One*. Leiden: Brill, 1962.
Day, John. "The Sons of God and Daughters of Men and the Giants: Disputed Points in the Interpretation of Genesis 6:1-4." *Hebrew Bible and Ancient Israel* 1 (Dec 2012) 427-47.
Delitzsch, Franz. *Commentar Über Die Genesis*. Vierte gänzlich umgearbeitete Ausgabe. Leipzig: Dörffling und Franke, 1872.
———. *A New Commentary on Genesis*. Edinburgh: T. & T. Clark, 1899.
———. *Biblical Commentary on the Psalms*. Vol. 2. Foreign Biblical Library. Translated by Francis Bacon. 1908. Reprint, Grand Rapids: Eerdmans, 1949.
———. *Isaiah*. Translated by James Martin. 2 vols. in one. 1884. Reprint, Grand Rapids: Eerdmans, 1973.
Delley, Mary K. Review of *A Not-So-Bad Derridean Approach to Psalm 23*, by David Paul McCarthy. *Old Testament Abstracts* 14 (June 1991) 184-85.
De Moor, J. C. "Narrative Poetry in Canaan." *Ugarit-Forschungen* 20 (1988) 149-71.
De Moor, J. C., and W. G. E. Watson, eds. *Verse in Ancient Near Eastern Prose*. Neukirchen-Vluyn: Neukirchener Verlag, 1993.
Dempsey, Deirdre A. Review of "Structurally Marked Peak in Psalms 1-24," by Loren F. Bliese. *Old Testament Abstracts* 15 (October 1992) 396-97.

DeWitt, Dale S. "The Historical Background of Genesis 11:1–9: Babel or Ur?" *Journal of the Evangelical Theological Society* 22 (1979) 15–26.

Dickson, David. *A Commentary on the Psalms*. 2 vols. in one. London: The Banner of Truth, 1653.

Die Bibel oder die ganze Heilige Schrift des Alten und Neuen Testaments: Nach der deutschen Übersetzung Martin Luthers. Philadelphia: The National Bible, 1967.

Driver, S. R. *Introduction to the Literature of the Old Testament*. The International Theological Library. Edinburgh: T. & T. Clark, 1892.

Eaton, John. *Kingship and the Psalms*. SBT 32. London: SCM, 1976

———. "Problems of Translation Psalm 23:3f, [sic]." *Bible Translator* 16 (1965) 171–76.

Eight Translation New Testament. Wheaton, IL: Tyndale House, 1984.

Elliger, K., and W. Rudolph, eds. *Biblia Hebraica Stuttgartensia*. Stuttgart: Deutsche Bibelstiftung, 1977.

———. *Biblia Hebraica Stuttgartensia* Tagged. Fünfte, verbesserte Auflage. Edited by Adrian Schenker. Stuttgart: Deutsche Bibelgesellschaft, 1997. Accordance version 1.7. J. Alan Groves Center for Advanced Biblical Research, 1991–2010.

Ellul, Jacques. *The Meaning of the City*. 1951. Reprint, Great Britain: Paternoster, 1997.

Fokkelman, J. P. *Narrative Art in* Genesis. Assen: Van Gorcum, 1975.

———. *Reading Biblical Poetry: An Introductory Guide*. Philadelphia: Westminster, 2001.

Fredericks, Daniel C. "Chiasm and Parallel Structure in Qoheleth 5:9—6:9." *Journal of Biblical Literature* 108 (1989) 17–35.

Fredricks, Gary. "Rethinking the Role of the Holy Spirit in the Lives of Old Testament Believers." *Trinity Journal* 9 (Spring 1988) 81–104.

Freedman, David Noel. "What the Ass and the Ox Know—But the Scholars Don't." *Bible Review* 1 (Spring 1985) 42–43.

Galli, Mark. "Heaven, Hell, and Rob Bell: Putting the Pastor in Context." *News* (blog), *Christianity Today*, March 2, 2011, https://www.christianitytoday.com/ct/2011/marchweb-only/rob-bell-universalism.html.

———. "Q&A: Francis Chan on Rob Bell and Hell." *Reviews* (blog), *Christianity Today*, July 5, 2011, https://www.christianitytoday.com/ct/2011/julyweb-only/francis-chan-hell.html.

Gaster, T. H. "The Abode of the Dead." In *The Interpreter's Dictionary of the Bible*, edited by G. A. Buttrick et al., vol. I, 787–88. New York: Abingdon, 1962.

Gerstenberger, Erhard S. *Psalms, Part 1 with an Introduction to Cultic Poetry*. The Forms of Old Testament Literature 14. Grand Rapids: Eerdmans, 1988.

Gesenius, Wilhelm. *Gesenius' Hebrew-Chaldee Lexicon to the Old Testament*. Translated by Samuel P. Tregelles. Grand Rapids: Eerdmans, 1949.

Gilead, Chaim. "Psalm 23 in View of Biblical Realia." *Beth Mikra* 35 (1989–90) 341–47.

Goldingay, John. *Psalms 90–150*. Grand Rapids: Baker Academic, 2008.

Gordon, Cyrus H. "Ebla as Background for the Old Testament." In *Congress Volume: Jerusalem, 1986*, by John Adney Emerton, 293–97. VTSupp. 40. Leiden: Brill, 1988.

Gosling, F. A. "An Unresolved Problem of Old Testament Theology." *Expository Times* 106 (October–September 1995) 234–37.

Gray, G. B. *A Critical and Exegetical Commentary on the Book of Isaiah: Introduction and Commentary on I-XXVII*. Edited by S. R. Driver, et. al. International Critical Commentary. Edinburgh: T. & T. Clark, 1969; 1912.

Grayson, A. K. "Akkadian Prophecies." *Journal of Cuneiform Studies* 18 (1964) 7–30.

Greenspan, Frederick E. Review of "Psalm 23 ('The Lord is My Shepherd')," by Y. Bazaq. *Old Testament Abstracts* 5 (June 1982) 161.

———. Review of "Psalm 23 in View of Biblical Realia," by Chaim Gilead. *Old Testament Abstracts* 14 (June 1991) 184.

Gressmann, Hugo, ed. *Altorientalische Texte zum Alten Testament*. Berlin: De Gruyter, 2011.

Groves, J. Alan. "Chiasm as a Structuring Device in Old Testament Narrative." PhD diss., Westminster Theological Seminary, 1983.

Guillaume, Alfred. "A Contribution to Hebrew Lexicography." *Bulletin of the School of Oriental and African Studies* XVI (1954) 10.

Halligan, John M. Review of "Psalm 101: Royal Confession and Divine Oracle," by John S. Kselman. *Old Testament Abstracts* 9 (June 1986) 187.

———. Review of "Setting and Rhetoric in Psalm 23," by Mark S. Smith. *Old Testament Abstracts* 12 (February 1989) 67.

Hallo, W. W. "Akkadian Apocalypses." *Israel Exploration Journal* 16 (1966) 231–42.

Hamilton, Victor P. *The Book of Genesis Chapters 1–17*. NICOT. Grand Rapids: Eerdmans, 1990.

Harland, P. J. "Vertical or Horizontal: The Sin of Babel." *Vetus Testamentum* XLVIII (1998) 515–33.

Harris, R. Laird. "She^{ɔ}ol." In *Theological Wordbook of the Old Testament*, vol. II, edited by R. Laird Harris, Gleason L. Archer, and Bruce K. Waltke, 892–93. Chicago: Moody Press, 1980.

Harris, R. Laird, Gleason L. Archer, and Bruce K. Waltke, eds. *Theological Wordbook of the Old Testament*. Chicago: Moody, 2003.

Hartley, John E. *Genesis*. NIBC 1. Peabody, MA: Hendrickson, 2000.

Hendry, George S. *The Holy Spirit in Christian Theology*. London: SCM Press, 1965.

Hiebert, Theodore. "The Tower of Babel and the Origin of the World's Cultures." *Journal of Biblical Literature* 126 (2007) 29–58.

———. "The Tower of Babel: Babble or Blueprint? Calvin, Cultural Diversity, and the Interpretation of Genesis 11:1–9." In *Reformed Theology: Identity and Ecumenicity II: Biblical Interpretation in the Reformed Tradition*, edited by Wallace M. Alston, Jr. and Michael Welker, 127–45. Grand Rapids: Eerdmans, 2007.

Hilbrands, Walter. *Zehn Thesen zum biblischen Schöpfungsbericht (Gen 1,1—2,3) aus exegetischer Sicht*. Jahrbuch für Evangelikale Theologie 18. Wuppertal: Brockhaus, 2004.

Hurowitz, Victor. *I Have Built You an Exalted House*. JSOT Supp. 115. Sheffield: Sheffield Academic, 2009.

Jarvis, Peter G. "Expounding the Parables: V. The Tower-builders and the King Going to War (Luke 14:25–33)." *Expository Times* 77 (January 1966) 196–98.

Jerome, Adam. "Ethiopian Enoch." *1 Enoch (Ethiopic Apocalypse of Enoch)* (blog), *Pseudepigrapha, Apocrypha and Sacred Writings*, 2002, http://www.pseudepigrapha.com/pseudepigrapha/1enoch_all.html.

———. "Book of Enoch." *1 Enoch Composit (inc. Charles, Lawrence & others)* (blog), *Pseudepigrapha, Apocrypha and Sacred Writings*, 1995, http://www.pseudepigrapha.com/pseudepigrapha/1enoch_all.html.

Johnson, James J. S. "Genesis Is History, Not Poetry: Exposing Hidden Assumptions about What Hebrew Poetry Is and Is Not." *Acts & Facts* 40 (May 2011) 8–9. http://www.icr.org/article/6090.

Josephus, Flavius. *Antiquities IV: Jewish Antiquities, Books I–IV.* Loeb Classical Library. Translated by H. St. J. Thackeray. Cambridge: Harvard University Press, 1967.
Joüon, Paul. *A Grammar of Biblical Hebrew / 2. Part Three: Syntax.* Translated and revised by T. Muraoka. Subsida biblica 14,2. Rome: Editice Pontificio Instituto Biblico, 1991.
Joüon, Paul, and T. Muraoka. *A Grammar of Biblical Hebrew.* Two volumes in one. Revised English edition. Subsidia Biblica 27. Rome: Pontifical Biblical Institute, 2006.
Kaiser, Otto. *Isaiah 1–12.* OTL. 2nd ed. Translated by John Bowden. Philadelphia: Westminster, 1983.
Kaiser, Walter C. "Psalm 72: An Historical and Messianic Current Example of Antiochene Hermeneutical *Theoria*." *Journal of the Evangelical Theological Society* 52 (June 2009) 257–70.
Kautzsch, E., ed. *Gesenius' Hebrew Grammar.* 2nd ed. Revised by A. E. Cowley. 1910. Reprint, Oxford: Clarendon, 1974.
Keller, Phillip. *A Shepherd Looks at Psalm 23.* Grand Rapids: Zondervan, 1970.
Kidner, Derek. *Psalms 1–72.* Downers Grove, IL.: InterVarsity, 1973.
Kirkpatrick, A. F. *The Book of Psalms.* 1st ed. 1902. Reprint, Grand Rapids: Baker, 1982.
Koehler, Ludwig. "Psalm 23." *Zeitschrift für die alttestamentliche Wissenschaft* 68 (1956) 227–34.
Koehler, Ludwig, and Walter Baumgartner, eds. *Lexicon in Veteris Testamenti Libros.* Leiden: Brill, 1958.
———. *The Hebrew and Aramaic Lexicon of the Old Testament.* Translated and edited under the supervision of M. E. J. Richardson. Accordance Bible Version 3.0. Leiden: Brill, 2000.
———. *The Hebrew and Aramaic Lexicon of the Old Testament.* 5 vols. Translated under M. E. J. Richardson et al. Leiden: Brill, 1994–2000.
Krašovec, Jože. *Antithetic Structure in Biblical Hebrew Poetry.* Supplements to *Vetus Testamentum* 35. Leiden: Brill, 1984.
Kselman, John S. "Psalm 101: Royal Confession and Divine Oracle." *Journal for the Study of the Old Testament* 33 (1985) 45–62.
Kugel, James L. *The Idea of Biblical Poetry: Parallelism and Its History.* New Haven: Yale University Press, 1981.
———. "The Tower of Babel." In *Traditions of the Bible: A Guide to the Bible as It Was at the Start of the Common Era*, 228–42. Cambridge: Harvard University Press, 1998.
Lambert, W. G., and A. R. Millard, eds. *Atrahasis: The Babylonian Story of the Flood.* Winona Lake, IN: Eisenbrauns, 1999.
Lamsa, George M., trans. *Holy Bible: from the Ancient Eastern Text.* 1933. Reprint, A. J. Holman, 1967.
Landy, Francis. "Poetics and Parallelism: Some Comments on James Kugel's, *The Idea of Biblical Poetry*." *Journal for the Study of the Old Testament* 28 (1984) 61–87.
Leupold, H. C. *Exposition of the Psalms.* 1959. Reprint, Grand Rapids: Baker, 1969.
Lewis, Rev. George, trans. *St. Basil the Great on the Holy Spirit.* Christian Classics Series IV. London: Religious Tract Society, n.d.
Loretz, O. "Wortbericht-Vorlage und Tatbericht-Interpretation im Schöpfungsbericht Gn 1,1—2,4a." *Ugarit-Forschungen* 11 (1977) 279–87.
Louth, Andrew, ed. *Ancient Christian Commentary on Scripture: Old Testament I: Genesis 1–11.* Downers Grove, IL: InterVarsity, 2001.
Lowth, Robert. *De Sacra Poesi Hebraeorum Praelectiones Academicae.* 1753. Reprint, Oxford: Clarendon, 1810.

———. *Lectures on the Sacred Poetry of the Hebrews.* 1787. Translated by G. Gregory. 2 vols. Reprint, New York: Garland, 1971.
Lundbom, Jack R. "Psalm 23: Song of Passage." *Interpretation* 40 (1986) 6–16.
Luther, Martin. *Die Heilige Schrift.* Philadelphia: The National Bible, 1967.
Luzatto, Samuel David. *The Book of Genesis: A Commentary by ShaDaL.* Translated by Daniel A. Klein. Stiff Wraps edition. Lanham, MD: Jason Aronson, 1998.
Macrae, Allan A. "With the Rich in His Death." *Moody Monthly* 77 (September 1976) 70.
Maddux, Roy Clark. *The Psalms in Outline.* Grand Rapids: Baker, 1965.
Marlowe, W. Creighton. "David's I-Thou Discourse: Verbal Chiastic Patterns in Psalm 23." *Scandinavian Journal of the Old Testament* 25 (2011) 105–15.
———. "Gen 6:1–4 as a Chiasm." *Scandinavian Journal of the Old Testament: An International Journal of Nordic Theology* 30 (2016) 129–44.
———. "'Hell' as a Translation of שאול in the Hebrew Bible: De*hell*enizing the KJV and NKJV." *Asbury Theological Journal* 57 (Fall 2002) 5–24.
———. "'Hell' in English Bible Translations since the 1611 King James Bible," In *The King James Bible (1611–2011) Prehistory and Afterlife,* edited by Tibor Fabiny and Sara Toth, 157–78. Karoli Gaspar Reformatus Egyetem. Budapest: L'Harmattan Kiado, 2016.
———. "No Fear! Psalm 23 as a Careful, Conceptual Chiasm." *Asbury Theological Journal* 58 (Spring 2003) 65–80.
———. "Patterns, Parallels, and Poetics in Genesis 1." *The Journal of Inductive Biblical Studies* 3 (2016) 6–27.
———. "The Sin of Shinar (Genesis 11:4)." *European Journal of Theology* 20 (2011) 29–39.
———. "A Spirit Chiasm in Isa 11:2–3a." *Scandinavian Journal of the Old Testament* 28 (2014) 44–57.
———. "'Spirit of Your Holiness' (רוח קדשך) in Psalm 51:13." *Trinity Journal* 19 (Spring 1998) 29–49.
———. "The Wicked Wealthy in Isa 53:9." *The Asbury Journal* 64 (Fall 2009) 68–81.
Masterman, W. E. G. "Valley of Hinnom." In the *International Standard Bible Encyclopedia.* Electronic Edition STEP Files, QuickVerse, 1998.
Mathews, Kenneth A. *Genesis 1—11:26.* Vol. 1a. The New American Commentary. Nashville: B&H, 1996.
Mazor, Yair. "Psalm 23: The Lord is My Shepherd—Or is He My Host?" *Zeitshcrift für die alttestamentliche Wissenschaft* 100 (1988) 416–20.
McCarthy, David Paul. "A Not-So-Bad Derridean Approach to Psalm 23." *Proceedings, Eastern Great Lakes and Midwest Biblical Societies* 8 (1988) 177–92.
Meacham, Jon. "Pastor Rob Bell: What if Hell Doesn't Exist!" *Time,* April 14, 2011, http://content.time.com/time/magazine/article/0,9171,2065289,00.html.
Merrill, A. L. "Psalm XXIII and the Jerusalem Tradition." *Vetus Testamentum* 15 (1965) 354–60.
Millard, A. R. "A New Babylonian 'Genesis' Story (Epic of Atrahasis)." *Tyndale Bulletin* 18 (1967) 3–18.
Miller, Charles H. Review of "The Structure of Psalm 23," by Charles O'Connor. *Old Testament Abstracts* 9 (June 1986) 185.
Milton, John. *Paradise Lost.* Penguin Classics. London: Penguin Books, 2003.
Mitchell, David C. "'God Will Redeem My Soul from Sheol': The Psalms of the Sons of Korah." *Journal for the Study of the Old Testament* 30 (2006) 365–84.

Mittmann, Siegfried. "Aufbau und Einheit des Danklieds Psalm 23." *Zeitschrift für Theologie und Kirche* 77 (1980) 1–23.

Morfill, W. R., translator. "The Book of the Secrets of Enoch." *2 Enoch (Slavonic Book of the Secrets of Enoch)* (blog), Pseudepigrapha, Apocrypha and Sacred Writings, 2002, http://www.pseudepigrapha.com/pseudepigrapha/enochs2.htm.

Motyer, J. Alec. *The Prophecy of Isaiah: An Introduction and Commentary*. Downers Grove, IL: IVP Academic, 1993.

Muraoka, T. *A Greek-English Lexicon of the* Septuagint. Louvain: Peeters, 2009.

Nobel, H. *Gods gedachten tellen: Numerieke structuuranalyse en de elf gedachten Gods in Genesis—2Koningen*. Groningen, NL: Rijksuniversiteit, 1993.

North, Christopher. R. *The Second Isaiah*. Oxford: Clarendon, 1964.

———. *The Suffering Servant in Deutero-Isaiah*. 2nd ed. Oxford: Oxford University Press, 1956.

Nyberg, H. S. "Smärtornas man. En studie till Jes. 52, 13–53, 12." *Svensk Exegetisk Årsbok* 7 (1942) 5–82.

O'Connell, Robert H. *Concentricity and Continuity. The Literary Structure of Isaiah*. Sheffield: Sheffield Academic, 1994.

O'Connor, Charles. "The Structure of Psalm 23." *Louvain Studies* 10 (1985) 206–30.

O'Connor, M. *Hebrew Verse Structure*. Winona Lake, IN: Eisenbrauns, 1997.

Oesterley, W. O. E. *The Psalms: Translated with Text-Critical and Exegetical Notes*. London: SPCK, 1953.

Orr, James. "Hell." In the *International Standard Bible Encyclopedia*, n.p. Electronic Edition, STEP Files, QuickVerse, 1998.

Oswalt, John N. *The Book of Isaiah: Chapters 1–39*. Edited by R. K. Harrison. NICOT. Grand Rapids: Eerdmans, 1986.

———. *The Book of Isaiah: Chapters 40–66*. Edited by R. K. Harrison and R. L. Hubbard, Jr. NICOT. Grand Rapids: Eerdmans, 1998.

Oxford English Dictionary. Oxford: Oxford University Press, 2019.

Parrot, André. *The Tower of Babel*. Studies in Biblical Archaeology 2. New York: The Philosophical Library, 1955.

Pearl, Chiam, ed. *Rashi: Commentaries on the Pentateuch*. New York: Norton, 1970.

Pelikan, Jaroslav, ed. *Luther's Works, Vol. 2: Lectures on Genesis Chapters 6–14*. St. Louis: Concordia, 1960.

———. *Luther's Works*. Translated by J. Pelikan. Vol. 12. St. Louis: Concordia, 1955.

Perowne, J. J. Stewart. *The Book of Psalms*. 4th ed. 1878. Reprint, Grand Rapids: Zondervan, 1976.

Peterson, Eugene H. *The Message*. Colorado Springs: NavPress, 1995.

Pezhumkattil, Abraham. "The Spirit as the Power of God in the Old Testament." *Bible Bhashyam* 19 (1993) 283–99.

Pirson, Ron. *Belichting van het Bijbelboek Genesis*. Leuven, BE: Vlaamse Bijbelstichting, 2005.

Pitard, Wayne. Review of "Psalm XXIII: Some Regulative Linguistic Evidence," by N. A. van Uchelen. *Old Testament Abstracts* 13 (June 1990) 170–71.

Plumer, W. S. *Studies in the Book of Psalms*. 1867. Reprint, Edinburgh: The Banner of Truth Trust, 1978.

Polak, Frank H. "Poetic Style and Parallelism in the Creation Account (Genesis 1.1—2.3)." In *Creation in Jewish and Christian Tradition*, edited by Henning Graf Reventlow and Yair Hoffman, 2–31. Sheffield: Sheffield Academic, 2002.

Pseudo-Dionysius Areopagita. *Pseudo-Dionysius: The Complete Works.* Translated by Colm Luibheid et al. Mahwah, NJ: Paulist, 1987.

Rad, Gerhard von. *Genesis.* Translated by John H. Marks. 1961. Reprint, Philadelphia: Westminster, 1972.

Redditt, Paul L. Review of "Pastures New: The 23rd Psalm Revisited," by Bernard P. Robinson. *Old Testament Abstracts* 22 (October 1999) 461–62.

Reimer, Steve. "The Tower of Babel: An Archaeologically Informed Reinterpretation." *Direction* 25 (Fall 1996) 64–72.

Robinson, Bernard P. "Pastures New: The 23rd Psalm Revisited." *Scripture Bulletin* 29 (1999) 2–10.

Robinson, Robert B. "The Poetry of Creation." Unpublished paper presented at the Biblical Criticism and Literary Criticism Section, SBL Boston, November 23, 2008.

Sacon, K. K. "A Methodological Remark on Exegesis and Preaching of Psalm 113." *Nihon no Shingaku* 25 (1986) 26–42.

Sapp, David A. "The LXX, 1QIsa, and MT Versions of Isaiah 53." In *Jesus and the Suffering Servant,* edited by William H. Bellinger, Jr. and William R. Farmer, 197–216. Harrisburg, PA: Trinity International, 1998.

Sarfati, Jonathan. "Theologian: Genesis means what it says!" *Creation* 32 (July 2010) 16–19. http://creation.com/robert-mccabe-old-testament-scholar-genesis.

Schökel, Luis A. *A Manual of Hebrew Poetics.* Translated by A. Graffy. 1988. Reprint, Rome: Pontifical Biblical Institute, 2001.

Schoors, Anton. *Jesaja II.* De Boeken van het Oude Testament Deel IX. Roermond: J. J. Roman & Zonen, 1973.

Segert, Stanislav. *A Basic Grammar of the Ugaritic Language: With Selected Texts & Glossary.* Berkeley: University of California Press, 1984.

———. "A Short Vocabulary of Ugaritic," n.p. Accessed September 21, 2015. http://ancientroad publications.com/Studies/AncientLanguage/Ugaritic.pdf.

Silva, Moisés. *Biblical Words and Their Meaning: An Introduction to Lexical Semantics.* Revised ed. Grand Rapids: Zondervan, 1995.

Skelton, John. "Why Come Ye Not to Court?" *The Works of John Skelton* (blog), *The Ex-Classics Web Site,* accessed January 20, 2019, https://www. exclassics.com/skelton/skelo65.htm, https://www.exclassics.com/skelton/skelo66.htm.

Skinner, John. *Genesis.* 2nd edition. ICC. Edinburgh: T. & T. Clark, 1930.

Smith, Mark S. "Setting and Rhetoric in Psalm 23." *Journal for the Study of the Old Testament* 13 (1988) 61–66.

Smith, Ralph L. *Old Testament Theology: Its History, Method, and Message.* Nashville: Baptist Sunday School Board, 1993.

Soden, Wolfram von. *Akkadisches Handwörterbuch.* Wiesbaden: Harrassowitz, 1959.

Soggin, J. Alberto. *Das Buch Genesis: Kommentar.* Darmstadt: Wissenschaftliche Buchgesellschaft, 1997.

Speiser, E. A. *Genesis.* The Anchor Bible. Garden City, NY: Doubleday, 1964.

Spero, Shubert. "Sons of God, Daughters of Men?" *Jewish Bible Quarterly* 40 (2012) 15–18.

St. Basil the Great. *On the Holy Spirit.* Translated by Rev. George Lewis. London: Religious Tract Society, n.d.

Stenger, Werner. "Strukturale 'relecture' von Ps 23." In *Freude an der Weisung des Herrn, Beiträge zur Theologie der Psalmen,* edited by Ernst Haag and Frank-Lothar Hossfeld, 441–55. Stuttgart: Katholisches Bibelwerk, 1986.

Stipp, Hermann-Josef. "Anfang und Ende: Once More on the Syntax of Gen 1:1." *Zeitschrift für Althebräistik* 17 (2004–2007) 188–96.
Stott, John, and David L. Edwards. *Essentials: A Liberal-Evangelical Dialogue*. London: Hodder & Stoughton, 1988.
———. *Evangelical Essentials*. 1988. Reprint, Downers Grove, IL: InterVarsity, 1989.
Sweeney, Marvin A. *Isaiah 1–39*. Edited by Rolf P. Knierim and Gene M. Tucker. FOTL XVI. Grand Rapids: Eerdmans, 1996.
Taylor, Kenneth N. *The Living Bible*. Carol Stream, IL: Tyndale House, 1971.
Thackery, H. St. J., trans. *Selections from Josephus*. London: SPCK, 1919.
Thierry, G. J. "Remarks on Various Passages in the Psalms." *Oud Testamentische Studien* 13 (1963) 97.
Thomas, D. Winton. "A Consideration of Is 53 in the Light of Recent Textual and Philological Study." *Ephemerides Theologicae Lovanienses* 44 (1968) 79–86.
Torrey, C. C. *The Second Isaiah: A New Interpretation*. Edinburgh: T. & T. Clark, 1928.
Torrey, R. A. "The Holy Spirit and You, On or In?" *Christian Life* 44 (April 1983) 32–39.
Uehlinger, Christoph. *Weltreich und „eine Rede": Eine neue Deutung der sogennaten Turmbauerzahlung (Gen 11, 1–9)*. Göttingen: Vandenhoeck & Ruprecht, 1990.
Urbrock, William J. Review of "The Unity of Psalm 23," by Reuben Ahroni. *Old Testament Abstracts* 11 (June 1988) 165–66.
VanGemeren, Willem A., gen. ed. *New International Dictionary of Old Testament Theology and Exegesis*. Grand Rapids: Zondervan, 1996.
———. "Psalms." In *The Expositor's Bible Commentary*, edited by Frank. E. Gaebelein et al., 214–17. Grand Rapids: Zondervan, 1991.
———. "The Sons of God in Genesis 6:1–4 (An Example of Evangelical Demythologization?)." *Westminster Theological Journal* 43 (September 1981) 320–348.
Van Uchelen, N. A. "Psalm XXIII: Some Regulative Linguistic Evidence." *Old Testament Studies* 25 (1989) 156–62.
Vaughan, Curtis, ed. *The New Testament from 26 Translations*. Grand Rapids: Zondervan, 1967.
Vincent, Jean Marcel. "Recherches exégétiques sur le Psaume xxiii." *Vetus Testamentum* 28 (1978) 442–54.
Vogt, Ernest. "The 'Place in Life' of Ps. 23." *Biblia* 34 (1953) 195–211.
Waltke, Bruce K. "The Creation Account in Genesis 1:1–3, Part III: The Initial Chaos Theory and the Precreation Chaos Theory." *Bibliotheca Sacra* 132 (July 1975) 216–28.
———. "The First Seven Days: What is the Creation Account Trying to Tell Us?" *Christianity Today* 222 (August 1988) 46.
Walton, John H. *Ancient Near Eastern Thought and the Old Testament*. Nottingham, UK: Apollos, 2007.
———. *Genesis 1 as Ancient Cosmology*. Winona Lake, IN: Eisenbrauns, 2011.
———. *The Lost World of Genesis One: Ancient Cosmology and the Origins Debate*. Kindle Edition. Downers Grove, IL: IVP Academic, 2009.
———. "The Mesopotamian Background of the Tower of Babel and Its Implications." *Bulletin for Biblical Research* 5 (1995) 155–75.
Walton, John H., and D. Brent Sandy. *The Lost World of Scripture*. Downers Grove, IL: IVP Academic, 2013.

Warmington, E. H., ed. *Josephus IV, Jewish Antiquities Books I-IV*. 1930. Translated by H. St. J. Thackeray. Loeb Classical Library, 242. Cambridge: Harvard University Press, 1967.
Watson, W. G. *Classical Hebrew Poetry: A Guide to Its Techniques*. Sheffield: JSOT, 1984.
———. *Classical Hebrew Poetry: A Guide to Its Techniques*. 2nd ed. JSOT Supplement Series. Sheffield: Sheffield Academic, 1986.
Watts, Isaac. *The Poetic Interpretation of the Psalms*. St. Louis: Miracle Press, 1974.
Watts, John D. W. *Isaiah 1-33*. WBC 24, edited by David A. Hubbard et al. Waco, TX: Word Books, 1985.
———. *Isaiah 34-66*. Word Biblical Commentary 25. Waco, TX: Word Books, 1987.
Weiser, Artur. *The Psalms*. OTL. Philadelphia: Westminster, 1959.
Wendland, Ernst R. *Analyzing the Psalms*. Dallas: Summer Institute of Linguistics, 1998.
Wenham, Gordon J. 1987. *Genesis 1-15*. Word Biblical Commentary. UK edition. Dallas/Waco, TX: Word Books, 1991.
Westermann, Claus. *Das Buch Jesaja 40-66*. Göttingen: Bandenhoed & Ruprecht, 1966.
———. *Genesis*. BKAT 1.1. Neukirchen, DE: Neukirchener, 1976.
———. *Genesis I: Een praktische bijbelverklaring, Tekst en Toelichting*. Kampen, NL: J. J. Kok, 1986.
———. *Genesis 1-11*. Neukirchen, DE: Neukirchen-Vluyn, 1974.
———. *The Living Psalms* [*Ausgewählte Psalmen* 1984]. Translated by J. R. Porter. Grand Rapids: Eerdmans, 1989.
Whately, William. *Prototypes or, the Primarie Precedent Presidents of the Booke of Genesis*. London: Edvvard Langham Bookeseller, 1640.
Whybray, R. N. *Isaiah 40-66*. The New Century Bible. London: Marshall, Morgan & Scott, 1975.
Whitekettle, Richard. "Leviticus 15:18 Reconsidered: Chiasm, Spatial Structure and the Body." *Journal for the Study of the Old Testament* 16 (1991) 31-45.
Wildberger, Hans. *Isaiah 1-12: A [Continental] Commentary*. Translated by Thomas H. Trapp. Minneapolis: Fortress, 1991.
Willems, Kurt. "Evolving Evangelicalism (part 4): Genesis 1 is MORE than poetry." *Progressive Christian* (blog), *The Pangea Blog by Kurt Willems*, May 11, 2012, https://www.patheos.com/blogs/thepangeablog/2012/05/11/evolving-evangelicalism-part-4/.
Willis, Timothy M. "A Fresh Look at Psalm xxiii 3a." *Vetus Testamentum* 37 (1987) 104-6.
Wood, Leon J. *The Holy Spirit in the Old Testament*. Grand Rapids: Zondervan, 1976.
Wright, John W. Review of "Psalm 23: The Lord is My Shepherd—Or is He My Host?," by Yair Mazor. *Old Testament Abstracts* 14 (June 1991) 184.
Yerkes, J. "'*Glauben und Genuss*': Hegel, Luther, and the Holy Spirit." *Christian Scholar's Review* 12 (March 1983) 237-43.
Young, E. J. *The Book of Isaiah, vol. 3: Chapters XL-LXVI*. NICOT. Grand Rapids: Eerdmans, 1972.
Youngblood, Ronald. *The Book of Genesis: An Introductory Commentary*. 2nd ed. Eugene, OR: Wipf & Stock, 2000.
Zimmerman, J. E. *Dictionary of Classical Mythology*. New York: Bantam Books, 1964.
Zogbo, Lynell, and Ernst R. Wendland. *Hebrew Poetry in the Bible: A Guide for Understanding and for Translating*. Helps for Translators. New York: United Bible Societies, 2000.

Subject Index

Angel(s), 23 n.2, 33–34 n. 16, , 37, 37 n. 23, 54, 182, 185 n.34, 191 n. 50, 192
ANE, xxvii, 14 n. 35, 39 n. 27
Antithetic(al), 5 n. 10, 74 n. 51, 135 n. 5, 138, 139 n. 17, 142, 142 n. 24, 146, 157 n. 9, 164, 179, 200

Bi-colon/cola, 6 n. 14, 15, 15 n. 36, 16, 18, 64, 64 n. 13, 66, 73, 74, 75, 76, 77, 87, 87 n. 11, 88, 108, 122, 123, 124, 127, 129 n. 17, 131, 135, 135 n. 5, 136 n. 8, 138 n. 15, 140, 142, 143, 144, 147, 155, 157 n. 9, 160, 164,

Chiasm(us), Chiastic, ix, 4 n. 10, 7, 8, 8 n. 18, 11, 14, 15, 15 n. 36, 16, 19, 24, 28, 30, 31 n. 13, 32, 33, 34 n. 16, 35, 37, 38, 39, 40, 55 n. 28, 61, 62, 63, 64, 65, 66, 68 n. 32, 69, 70, 71, 72, 74, 75, 76, 77, 78, 79, 80, 80 nn. 1, 2, 81, 82, 83 n. 9, 84, 85, 86, 87, 88, 89, 91, 92, 93, 108, 119, 119 n. 1, 120, 123, 125, 126, 129, 130, 132, 168, 196, 198, 199, 201, 205
Climax, 13, 28, 37, 39, 39 n. 27, 40, 55 n. 28, 62, 78, 79, 83, 86, 87, 93, 127, 130, 132
Creation (ברא), 3, 4, 4 nn. 7, 9, 5, 6, 6 n. 13, 7, 8, 9, 9 n. 22, 10, 10 nn. 24–26, 11, 11 n. 29, 12, 12 n. 30, 13, 13 n. 32, 14, 14 n. 35, 15, 17, 17 nn. 38–39, 19, 19 n. 40, 20, 21, 22, 25, 25 n. 7, 29 n. 12, 39 n. 27, 43 n. 8, 54, 76, 108, 115, 128, 165, 196, 202, 203, 204

Evil, xvii, 26, 43, 43 n. 8, 49, 54 n. 25, 70 n. 44, 82, 82 n. 7, 85 n. 10, 86, 88, 102 n. 29, 112 n. 55, 122 n. 10, 134 n. 3, 135, 139, 140, 140 n. 19, 162, 179, 181, 182, 190 n. 48, 192
Evil-doers, 134, 140 n. 19
Exegesis, xv, xvi, xvii, xxvi, xxvii, 9 n. 22, 66, 95, 96, 98, 98 n. 8, 102 n. 33, 124, 125, 137, 139 n. 17, 152, 176, 178, 203, 204

Fulcrum, 11, 15, 29, 31, 37, 40, 45, 62, 77, 78, 85, 120, 127

Genitive (case), 6 n. 14, 104, 105, 106, 132

Hell, vii, x, 149, 151, 151 nn. 1, 2, 152, 152 nn. 3, 4, 153, 153 n. 5, 154, 154 n. 7, 156, 157, 160, 161, 162, 163, 164, 165, 166, 167, 168, 169, 170, 171, 172, 173, 174, 175, 175 nn. 1, 3, 176, 176 n. 9, 177, 177 nn. 10, 11, 178, 178 n. 13, 178–69 n. 16, 179, 180, 181, 182, 182 nn. 22, 23, 183, 183 nn. 25, 27, 184, 185, 186, 186 nn. 36, 37, 187, 187 nn. 40, 41, 42, 188, 189, 189 n. 45, 190, 190 nn. 47, 48, 191, 191 nn.

SUBJECT INDEX

49, 50, 192, 192 n. 51, 193, 194, 195, 198, 201, 202

LXX (Septuagint), xiii, 5 n. 11, 31, 36 n. 21, 50 n. 22, 53, 55, 96, 97, 97 n. 7, 99 n. 9, 109 n. 45, 113, 121, 122 n. 10, 123, 123 n. 11, 127, 131, 137 n. 13, 138, 138 n. 16, 142 n. 23, 144 n. 32, 146, 146 n. 38, 152, 152 n. 3, 159, 160, 173, 177, 177 n. 11, 178, 191 n. 49, 193, 202, 203

Messiah, 122, 124 n. 15, 141 n. 23, 146, 191 n. 49, 194

Nephilim, 33, 34 n. 17, 35, 36 n. 20, 38

Parallelism, 3, 4, 4 nn. 7, 8, 4–5 n. 10, 6, 16, 16 n. 37, 17 n. 38, 19, 74, 74 n. 51, 75, 76, 77, 87, 103, 108, 122, 135 n. 5, 136, 138, 139 n. 17, 142, 143, 144, 145, 146, 156, 157, 157 n. 9, 158, 159, 160, 162, 164, 171, 172, 195, 196, 200, 202

Poetry, 3, 4, 4 nn. 7, 8, 9, 4–5 n. 10, 9, 16, 16 n. 37, 63, 64, 74 n. 50, 76, 85, 135 n. 5, 138 n. 16, 139, 139 n. 17, 140 n. 18, 143, 157 n. 9, 159, 195, 196, 197, 198, 199, 200, 201, 203, 205

Righteous/(Un)righteous, xvii, 24, 25 nn. 6, 7, 26 n. 8, 75, 81–82 n. 6, 86, 110, 133, 137, 139, 142, 143 n. 27, 147, 161–62 n. 11, 167, 168, 179, 181, 187, 187 n. 42

Satan(ic)/Lucifer, 23 n. 2, 50 n. 22, 82 n. 7, 85 n. 10, 166, 166 n. 15, 183, 191 n. 50

Serpent(s), 27, 27 n. 9, 165, 182

Sons of G/god/s, 11 n. 29, 23 n. 2, 24, 26 n. 8, 28, 29, 29 n. 12, 30, 32, 33–34 n. 16, 34 n. 17, 35 n. 19, 38 n. 24, 39, 196, 197, 203, 204

S/spirit(ual)/ spirituality, xxvi, 6 n. 14, 7, 7 n. 17, 8, 17 n. 39, 25, 25 n. 6, 30, 37, 38, 38 nn. 24–25, 39 n. 27, 43 n. 8, 50, 61, 65, 71, 78, 81 n. 6, 85, 86, 88, 90, 91, 93, 95, 95 n. 1, 96, 97, 97 nn. 5–6, 98, 99, 98–99 n. 9, 100, 101, 101 nn. 24, 27, 102, 102 nn. 28–30, 32–33, 102–103 n. 33, 103, 103. n. 34, 104, 104 n. 36, 105, 105 n. 40, 106, 107, 107 n. 42, 108, 109, 109 nn. 45–46, 110, 110 n. 50, 111, 111 n. 53, 112, 112 n. 55, 113–115, 119, 119 n. 1, 120, 121, 121 n. 8, 122, 122 n. 10, 123, 123 n. 12, 124, 125, 126, 127, 128, 129, 130 n. 18, 131, 132, 133, 145, 154, 154 n. 7, 158, 166, 167, 181, 187 n. 38, 191 n. 50, 197, 198, 199, 200, 201, 202, 203, 204, 205

S/spirit of God/gods (רוח אלוהים), 6 n. 14, 96, 97, 98, 102, 102 n. 32, 103, 105, 107, 109 n. 45, 115, 125, 126, 131

S/spirit of [your] holiness (ורוח קדשך), ix, 95 n. 1, 96, 97, 100, 101, 103 n. 33, 104, 105, 108, 110, 111 n. 53, 114, 121, 12 n. 8, 124, 132, 201

Static (parallel), 74 n. 51, 75, 84, 87, 108, 135 n. 5, 143, 157, 157 n. 9

Synonymous, 52, 64, 74 n. 51, 75, 76, 77, 87, 87 n. 11, 107, 108, 109, 135, 135 n. 5, 136, 136 n. 8, 138, 139 n. 17, 140, 140 n. 18, 141, 142, 143, 144, 145, 146, 155, 156, 157, 157 n. 9, 159, 160, 164, 165, 167, 168, 169

Synthetic(al), 5 n. 10, 64 n. 13, 74, 74 n. 51, 75, 76, 108, 110, 135 n. 5, 138, 143, 146, 155, 157 n. 9, 159, 162, 164

Tri-colon/cola, 14, 15, 15 n. 36, 18, 64 n. 13, 73, 74, 75, 88, 124, 124 n. 13, 135 n. 5

Ugaritic, 34, 34 n. 17, 35, 35–36 n. 20, 141 n. 21, 165 n. 14, 203

SUBJECT INDEX

Vulgate (Jerome), x, xxiii, 5 n. 11, 47 n. 18, 97, 99, 109 n. 45, 113, 123, 137 n. 13, 138 n. 16, 144 n. 32, 146 n. 38, 152, 152 n. 3, 159, 160, 166, 173, 177, 177 n. 11, 179, 180, 180 n. 17, 181 n. 18, 193, 199

Wicked(ness), ix, 24, 25 n. 6, 26, 26 n. 8, 27, 52, 82 n. 7, 85 n. 10, 133, 134, 134 n. 1, 135, 136, 136 n. 8, 137, 138, 138 n. 16, 139, 139 n. 17, 140, 141 n. 20, 142, 143, 143 n. 27, 145, 146, 147, 152, 154, 155, 161–62 n. 11, 166, 167, 168, 172, 175, 176, 179, 182, 183, 185, 186–87 n. 38, 190, 190 n. 48, 201

Wisdom, 103, 106, 120, 122, 122 n. 10, 123, 124, 126, 127, 128, 129, 130, 131, 132, 145, 157, 158, 161, 161 n. 11, 178 n. 14, 179

Selected Author Index

Clines, David J. A., 5 n. 10, 11 n. 29, 29 n. 12, 38 n. 25, 39 n. 27, 135 n. 5, 143 n. 28, 144 n. 34, 196, 197

Dahood, Mitchell, 99, 99 nn. 12, 16, 103, 103 n. 34, 104, 104 n. 35, 114, 197

Delitzsch, Franz, 24 n. 5, 114, 134 n. 3, 139 n. 17, 141 n. 20, 197

Gunkel, Hermann, 124 n. 15

Kaiser, Walter C., 124, 124 n. 15, 125, 200

Muraoka, T., 9 nn. 20, 21, 44 n. 11, 200, 202

Rad, G. von, 3, 3 n. 5, 24 n. 5, 42, 42 n. 5, 203

Waltke, Bruce K., 11 n. 29, 16–17 n. 38, 24 n. 5, 199, 204

Westermann, Claus, 5 n. 11, 24 n. 5, 29 n. 12, 42 n. 7, 99, 99 n. 13, 111, 111 nn. 52–54, 114, 134 n. 3, 137 n. 13, 205

Scripture Index

OLD TESTAMENT

Genesis
1—2	10 n. 26, 14 n. 35
1:1—2:4a	5 n. 11
1	3–21, 4 nn. 7, 5 n. 10, 7 n. 17, 9, 9 nn. 22–23, 11 n. 29, 15, 16, 19, 20, 21, 22, 54, 54 n. 27, 128
1:1–2	5, 6 n. 15, 16 n. 38, 27 n. 9
1:20, 24, 26	7 n. 17, 54 n. 27
2	17 n. 39, 36 n. 20, 38 n. 25
2:7	7 n. 17
2:24, 25	27 n. 9
3	165
3:1	27 n. 29, 165
3:5, 20, 22	27 n. 9
4:1–8	27 n. 9, 50
4:2, 14, 20, 21	27 n. 9, 50
5–6	27
5	25, 25 n. 6, 26 n. 8
5:31–32	27 n. 11
6	xvi, 23–40, 23 n. 2, 24 n. 5, 26 n. 8, 182
6:1–4	28–39, 182, 182 n. 23
6:3, 4, 9, 21	27, 27 n. 9, 102
9	41, 48–49
10	37 n. 22; 43 n. 8, 44, 51 nn. 23–24
11	xvi, 11 n. 29, 29, 41–57, 55 n. 28, 137 n. 13
11:4	43, 46 n. 15, 47 n. 16
12	4 n. 7, 5 n. 10
16:5	144 n. 34
32:22	177 n. 12
37:35	177 n. 12
45:27	102 n. 28

Exodus
23:1	144 n. 34
25:23	69 n. 40
30:15	143 nn. 27, 29

Numbers
5:14	102 n. 28
11:16–26	125
14:17	112 n. 55
16:3–35	155, 177 n. 12
27:16	102 n. 28

Deuteronomy
2:30	102 n. 28
19:16	144 n. 34
32:22	152 n. 4, 172, 173, 177 n. 12

Judges
2:17	25 n. 6
5:15	177 n. 12

SCRIPTURE INDEX

Ruth
3:10	143 nn. 27, 29

1 Samuel
1:16	102 n. 28
16:13–14	100, 112 n, 55

2 Samuel
11:1—12:15	106 n. 41
12:1–4	142 n. 26, 143 n. 29
22:6	173, 177 n. 12

1 Kings
5:7	69 n. 40

2 Kings
3:15	112 n. 55
13:23	104

Ezra
1:1	102 n. 28

Job
2:9—3:1	145 n. 36
2:8	177 n. 12
7:9	177 n. 12
7:11	102 n. 28
10:7	142 n. 25
11:8	173, 177 n. 12
14:13	177 n. 12
16:17	142 n. 25
17:13, 16	177 n. 12
19:7	144 n. 34
21:27	144 n. 34
21:32, 33	159, 177 n. 12
26:6	173, 177 n. 12
27:13, 15, 19	141 n. 22, 142 n. 26, 143 nn. 27–29
28:28	112 n. 10
31:24	142 n. 26
34:6	142 n. 25
38:36	127

Psalms
3	67 n. 29
6:5	156, 177 n. 12
9:17	154–55, 172, 173, 177 n. 12
13	67 n. 29
16:8–11	173, 177 n. 12, 191, 191 n. 49
18:5	173, 177 n. 12
19:9	122 n. 10, 126, 128
23	61–94, 65 nn. 22–23, 66 nn. 25-26, 80 nn. 2–3
25	64
27:12	144 n, 34
30:3	177 n. 12
31:17	177 n. 12
32:2	102 n. 28
34	64
35:11	144 n. 34
37; 37:16	64, 143 n. 27
45:12	143 n. 29
49:2, 3, 5	127, 142 n. 26, 143 nn. 27, 29
49:14, 15	159, 177 n. 12
51	95–115, 101 n. 25, 102 n. 33, 121, 132
51:12–14/10–12	102, 102 n. 28, 103, 104
52:9	142 n. 26
55	155, 156 n. 8
55:15	155, 172, 173, 177 n. 12
69:9	133
72	124 n. 15
86:13	173, 178 n. 12
88:3	178 n. 12
88:11	159
89:48	178 n. 12
94:17	178 n. 12
101	65 n. 16
102:10	104
111:10	127
112:3	143 n. 26
113–116	65, 66 n. 28
115:17	178 n. 12
116:3	173, 178 n. 12
139:8	156–57, 172, 173, 178 n. 12

SCRIPTURE INDEX

141		156	
141:7		178 n. 12	
143:10		104, 112 n. 55	
145		64	

Proverbs

1:2, 7	127
1:12	178 n. 12
2:2-6	122 n. 10, 127
2:18	178 n. 12
3:13, 19	127
4:5	127
4:24	145 n. 36
5:1-6	157
5:5	157-58, 172, 173, 178 n. 12
7:4	127
7:27	172
6:12	145 n. 36
7:27	158, 173, 178 n. 12
8:14	131 n. 20
8:33-36	156
8:36	144 n. 34
9:1-5, 10-18	156
9:18	158, 172, 173, 178 n. 12
10:15	143 n. 29
10:27	112 n. 10
11:28	142 n. 26
13:3	145 n. 36
14:20	143 n. 29
15:11	159, 172, 173, 178 n. 12
15:24	160-62, 172, 174, 178 n. 12
16:6	122 n. 10
16:18	102 n. 28
17:27	145 n. 36
18:7	145 n. 36
18:11, 23	142 n. 26, 143 n. 29
22:2, 4, 7, 16	142 n. 26, 143 nn. 26-27, 29
23:14	162-64, 172, 174, 178 n. 12
26:4-5	161 n. 11
27:20	159-160, 172, 174, 178 n. 12
28:6, 11	142 n. 26, 143 nn. 27, 29
30:16	178 n. 12

Ecclesiastes

4:8	142 n. 26
5:2, 6	145 n. 36
5:11, 12	143 nn. 27, 29
6:11	145 n. 36
7:8	102 n. 28
9:17	145 n. 36
10:6, 12-13, 20	143 nn. 27, 29, 145 n. 36
12:10	145 n. 36

Song of Solomon

8:6	178 n. 12

Isaiah

5:14	174, 178 n. 12
6:9	127
6:13	141 n. 22
7:11	178 n. 12
9:6, 7	130, 130 n. 19, 133
10:3	143
11	119-133, 124 n. 15
14:3-20	166-67, 178 n. 12, 183
14:9	172, 174, 176, 178 n. 12
14:15	174, 176, 178 n. 12
16	128
21:15	69 n. 40
25:6	143
28:15, 18	174, 178 n. 12
28:29	128
30:15, 23	128, 143
30:33	178 n. 12
33:6, 13	128, 143
38:10, 18	178 n. 12
40:14, 19	127
41:28	128
45:3	143
53/53:9	134-147, 141 nn. 22-23, 143 n. 28
57:9	174, 178 n. 12
57:15	102 n. 28

60:5, 11 — 143
61:6 — 143
63:10–11 — 102, 102 n. 28, 104, 105
66:12 — 143
66:22–24 — 186 n. 37

Jeremiah
7:32 — 183
9:23 — 143 nn. 27, 29
19:6 — 183
51:46 — 144 n. 34

Ezekiel
18:31 — 102 n. 28
28 — 183
31:1 — 172
31:15–17 — 151 n. 2, 151 n. 3, 169–70, 172, 174, 177 nn. 10–11, 178 n. 12
32:21, 27 — 170, 172, 174, 178 n. 12
40:39 — 69 n. 40
43:7 — 141 n, 22

Hosea
13:14 — 178 n. 12

Amos
4:1 — 142 n. 26
9:2, 3 — 164–65, 172, 174, 178 n. 12

Jonah
Jonah — 4 n. 8
2:2 — 174, 178 n. 12
2:3, 5–6 — 164

Micah
6:12 — 142 n. 26, 143 n. 29, 144 n. 34

Habakkuk
2:5 — 167–68, 172, 174, 178 n. 12

Haggai
2:5 — 100

Malachi
2:15–16 — 102 n. 28

APOCRYPHA

Sirach, Wisdom of
16:13 — 178 n. 14
17:14 — 179, 180
21:10 — 178 n. 14
51:5–6 — 180

Tobit
13:2 — 178 n. 14, 179

Daniel
3:66 — 178 n. 14

NEW TESTAMENT

Matthew
5:15 — 176 n. 7
5:22, 29–30 — 176 nn. 4, 5, 183 nn. 27–29, 184, 184 nn. 30–32, 185, 186, 186 nn. 34, 36, 192, 193
6:7 — 145 n. 37
7:13 — 184 n. 32
10:28 — 176 nn. 4, 5, 183 nn. 27–29, 184, 184 nn. 30–32, 185, 186, 192, 193
11:23 — 176 nn. 4, 6, 183 n. 27, 184 nn. 31–32, 188, 189
11:24 — 189 n. 45
12:34, 37 — 145 n. 37

SCRIPTURE INDEX

16:18	176 nn. 4, 6, 183 n. 27, 188, 190
18:9	176 nn. 4, 5, 183 nn. 27–29, 184, 184 nn. 30–32, 185, 186 n. 36, 192
19:23–24	143 n. 26
23:15, 33	176 nn. 4, 5, 183 nn. 27–29, 184, 184 nn. 30–32, 185, 187, 187 n. 42, 192, 193
25:41. 46	182, 185
27:12–14	145
27:57–61	138 n. 14

Mark

4:21	176 n. 7
9:43, 45, 47	176 nn. 4, 5, 183 nn. 27–29, 184, 184 nn. 30–32, 185, 186, 186 n. 36, 192
11:33	176 n. 7
15:42–47	138 n. 14

Luke

5:17	112 n. 55
6:24	143 n. 26
8:31	176 n. 8, 189
10:15	176 nn. 4, 6, 183 n. 27, 184 nn. 31–32, 188, 189
12:5	176 nn. 4, 5, 183 nn. 27–29, 184, 184 nn. 30–32, 185, 186, 192
12:11	186 n. 38
16:19–25	143 n. 26, 176, 176 nn. 4, 6, 183 nn. 27–29, 184 n. 31, 188, 189, 190
23:50–56	138 n. 14

John

2:13–17	133
19:38–42	138 n. 14

Acts

2:14–21	112 n. 55
2:24, 25–35	176 nn. 4, 6, 8, 189, 191, 191 n. 49
8:20	184 nn. 31–32

Romans

8:2–6	190 n. 47
10:7	176 n. 8, 189
12:11	133

1 Corinthians

10:18	176, 176 n. 7
15:26, 54–56	176, 176 n. 7, 189, 190 n. 47

Galatians

1:8–9	184 n. 32

Philippians

3:5	176, 176 n. 7
3:19	184 nn. 31–32

2 Thessalonians

2:3	184 n. 32

1 Timothy

6:17	143 n. 26

Hebrews

2:14	190 n. 47
8:10	176, 176 n. 7

James

1:9–11	143 n. 26
2:5–7	143 n. 26
3:6	176 nn. 4, 5, 184 nn. 31–32, 185, 191, 191 n. 50, 192
5:1–6	143 n. 26

1 Peter

2:21–24	138 n. 15, 145, 146

2 Peter

2:4	176 nn. 4, 5, 182, 184 nn. 31–32, 185, 191, 191 n. 50

Jude

1:6	182
1:13	184 n. 31

Revelation

1:13, 17	192 n. 51
1:18	176 nn. 4, 6, 182, 189, 192
2:14	176 n. 7
6:8	176 nn. 4, 6, 189, 192
7:4	176 n. 7
20:13–14	176 nn. 4, 6, 189, 192, 192 n. 51

DEAD SEA SCROLLS

1QIsaa	141 n 21

Damascus Document

8:12–13; 16:7, 12	182

RABBINIC

Genesis Rabbah	43, 44 n. 9

www.ingramcontent.com/pod-product-compliance
Lightning Source LLC
Chambersburg PA
CBHW071939240426
43669CB00048B/2333